3⟋

CLARENDON MEDIEVAL AND TUDOR SERIES

General Editor

J. A. W. BENNETT

CLARENDON MEDIEVAL AND TUDOR SERIES

Already Published

HENRY HOWARD, EARL OF SURREY
Reproduced by gracious permission of Her Majesty the Queen

HENRY HOWARD
EARL OF SURREY

Poems

Appreciations by

THOMAS WARTON · G. F. NOTT

C. S. LEWIS · MAURICE EVANS

With an Introduction, Notes
and Glossary by

EMRYS JONES

OXFORD
AT THE CLARENDON PRESS
1964

Oxford University Press, Amen House, London E.C. 4

GLASGOW   NEW YORK   TORONTO   MELBOURNE   WELLINGTON
BOMBAY   CALCUTTA   MADRAS   KARACHI   LAHORE   DACCA
CAPE TOWN   SALISBURY   NAIROBI   IBADAN   ACCRA
KUALA LUMPUR   HONG KONG

PRINTED IN GREAT BRITAIN

PREFACE

I ACKNOWLEDGE with pleasure the help and criticism given by Dr. J. A. W. Bennett, the general editor of this series, and by Mr. I. R. Browning. Mr. C. G. Hardie, the late Mr. J. B. Leishman and Mr. J. Norton-Smith kindly helped me on particular points. Copyright material is reprinted by permission of the late Professor C. S. Lewis and the Clarendon Press, and Mr. Maurice Evans and the Hutchinson Publishing Group.

Holbein's drawing of Henry Howard, Earl of Surrey, is reproduced by gracious permission of Her Majesty The Queen. The designation 'Thomas' on the drawing has been shown to be erroneous.

7/31/73 Carnegie 3.00

CONTENTS

CONTENTS

CONTENTS

CONTENTS

INTRODUCTION

IN his *History of English Poetry* (1781) Thomas Warton pronounced Surrey 'the first English classical poet'. For him the observation did not need justifying, it was self-evidently true; but today it may perplex. Literary history is attended with many difficulties: it is rarely possible to say of a writer that he is doing something quite new and that he is ushering in a new school. The sixteenth century presents a confused scene—especially to the historian eager to distinguish 'medieval' and 'Renaissance' elements in literary compositions. We are accustomed to regarding the late seventeenth and eighteenth centuries as the age of neo-classicism; the term is not usually extended to the sixteenth. Nevertheless, the poetry of Henry Howard, Earl of Surrey, has qualities that led Warton to salute him in the way he did : as a forerunner of Milton, Dryden, and Pope. The justice of Warton's remark may be appreciated when Surrey's work is considered in its historical setting.

Surrey's life fell entirely within the reign of Henry VIII. It was the prime age of northern humanism. Erasmus, Colet, and others had propounded new educational ideals, and their work could not fail to affect literature. It was an age of great teachers and of great faith in the power of teaching. Old methods were denounced, new ones confidently adopted. One innovation is of special importance for the new poetry of the early and middle Tudor period. It concerned the teaching of Latin. The method of teaching Latin that prevailed in the later Middle Ages was not strictly philological. It neglected the study of historical usage and was coloured by metaphysical habits of thought. The change in approach to Latin originated in Italy. Humanists, led by Lorenzo Valla (1415–65), directed attention to the study of idiom as it was exemplified in the best writers of antiquity. Valla's great manual of 'correct' latinity, *Elegantiae Linguae Latinae*, was printed in 1471. Not abstract rules but the usage of the best authors was his concern : 'Ego pro lege accipio quidquid magnis

auctoribus placuit.'[1] The 'elegance' in composition that he ad-
mired in classical authors and that he held up for imitation was
a new kind of artistry in the choice and disposition of words.

Erasmus epitomised the *Elegantiae* in 1484 when he was
eighteen, and frequently recommended Valla's work to friends.
The spirit of Valla, and of his disciple Erasmus, can be recognized
in Colet's contribution to Lily's *Grammar* (1527), written for the
school that he had founded at St. Paul's and that was eventually
to admit John Milton :

Of these viii partes of speche in ordre well construed, be made reasons
and sentences, and longe oracyons. But how and in wat maner, and with
what construccyon of wordes, and all the varietees, and diuersitees, and
chaunges in latyn speche (whiche be innumerable), if ony man wyl know,
and by that knowlege attayne to vnderstande latyn bokes, and to speke
and to wryte the clene latyn, Let hym aboue all besyly lerne and rede
good latyn authours of chosen poetes and oratours, and note wysely how
they wrote, and spake, and study alway to folowe them, desyryng none
other rules but their examples. For in the begynnynge men spake not
latyn, by cause suche rules were made, but contrari wyse, bycause men
spake suche latyn, Vpon that folowed the rules were made. That is to
saye, latyn speche was before the rules, not the rules before the latyn
speche.

The ideal of 'elegance' informs the educational writings of Roger
Ascham. On the first page of his *Scholemaster* (1570) he borrows
a motto from Cicero's *Brutus*: 'right choice of wordes, saith
Caesar, is the foundation of eloquence'.

This insistence of the Latinists on the right choice of words and
on the imitation of the classics influenced writing in the verna-
culars. Medieval poets had been acquainted with some of the
works of classical antiquity, but they had neglected their formal
qualities. Chaucer's versions of Virgil and Ovid, for example, do
not seek to reproduce the stylistic qualities of the originals. But
with the new stimulus from the humanists writers sought to
imitate the construction of words and the varieties and diversities of

---

[1] Quoted by W. H. Woodward, *Desiderius Erasmus concerning the Aim and
Method of Education* (1904), p. 104. See also Foster Watson, *Vives on Education*
(1913); Beatrice White (ed.), *The Vulgaria of John Stanbridge and the Vulgaria of
Robert Whittinton* (1932); T. W. Baldwin, *Shakspere's Small Latine & Lesse Greeke*
(1944); and William Nelson (ed.), *A Fifteenth Century School Book* (1956).

Latin speech. They cultivated the niceties of diction and syntax, and emulated the formal characteristics of the classical genres. The sixteenth century witnessed the revival of epic, satire, pastoral, elegy, and epigram, and of tragedy and comedy. In this way was English classicism, or neo-classicism, inaugurated.

Surrey, as Warton attests, was the first English poet who conspicuously responded to the new teaching. From the nature of his metrical effects, we may guess that his response to it was firm and intimately felt. Surrey's most characteristic verse moves to an assured and regular rhythm which will be familiar to those whose ears are already attuned to Augustan measures. This movement may be termed neo-Latin. It echoes, in thin strains, the rich orchestration of Virgil and Horace. It shares that Roman concern with quantity and number which was carried to its farthest elaboration in English poetry by Milton, Pope, and Johnson. As we should expect, it is in Surrey's translations of Virgil that this pronounced regular movement can be most easily observed. When examined in its full poetic context, it reveals itself as part of an intricate balancing system, composed of varied yet predictably recurring patterns. It encourages in the reader a sense of mass and momentum. Here, for example, is Aeneas consenting to narrate the fall of Troy:

> And loe, moist night now from the welkin falles,
> And sterres declining counsel us to rest.
> But sins so great is thy delight to here
> Of our mishaps, and Troyes last decay,
> Though to record the same my minde abhorres
> And plaint eschues, yet thus wil I begyn.

Such writing was new in Surrey's time. A brief account of it will illustrate the topics already touched on : neo-classical imitation; interest in syntax; the revival of the classical genres; and 'elegance'. It may also suggest a helpful approach to those poems of Surrey's —the sonnets and the poems in stanzas—which most readers have considered his best. These poems have usually been read in isolation from the Virgilian translations which, in studies of Surrey, have hitherto been relegated to a secondary position so that they have been discussed in the light of the poems rather than the poems in the light of the translations. There is some point in reversing the customary order. For it is easier to make sense of the title bestowed on Surrey by Warton if we suppose his reading of the Latin poets rather than the Italian to have been the main formative influence in his literary development. According to this view, Petrarch yields precedence to Virgil.

Surrey's translations of Books Two and Four of the *Aeneid* are the earliest blank-verse poems in English. They show how, by imitation, a poet may invent something new. For it was by composing unrhyming verse after a Virgilian pattern that Surrey introduced this notable metre to English poetry. At the same time he made free use of Gavin Douglas's rhyming version of the *Aeneid*. He thus has two sources, one Latin and one English (or Scottish). His dependence on both poets facilitates an inquiry into the structural principles of his 'heroic verse without rhyme' (in Milton's phrase) and indeed of blank verse generally. Surrey was guided by a single working rule: fidelity to the syntactical and rhetorical forms of Virgil. His aim was to reproduce, as closely as was consistent with the idiom of an uninflected language, the disposition of sense-masses and the figures of speech of the Latin. In many cases he tried to follow Virgil's word-order. The result is at times uncomfortably compressed, and violence is sometimes done to English idiom. But at best he achieves a rounded sonority of utterance, not limited to a single blaring note,[1] but sensitively modulated.

A close and extensive comparison between Surrey, Virgil, and Douglas would be necessary to establish the critical nature of Surrey's reading of Douglas and his own positive stylistic aims.[2] Such an investigation would prove that Surrey's translations amount to much more than a mere recasting of Douglas into unrhyming verse. The elements taken over from Douglas are absorbed into a new poetic system whose habits of movement, laws of harmony, verbal colouring, and vocal pitch are alien to Douglas's practice. So different is this system that phrases and even whole lines taken from Douglas with little or no alteration assume a different value. They become integral elements in a new poem.

[1] Although Surrey's greatest poetic contemporary, Ariosto, refers to 'la tuba di Virgilio' (*Orlando Furioso*, xxxiv. 25); quoted by Dryden, *Dedication of the Aeneis*.
[2] See pp. 134 ff. for a detailed comparison of short passages of Surrey, Virgil, and Douglas.

This is because the structural unit in Surrey's unrhyming verse is not the line, as some critics have stated, but the phrase or the clause. Once rhyme is abandoned, the poet is obliged to focus attention on the minuter shapes within the line: the forms assumed by sentences, clauses, and phrases. Surrey was fortunate to have as a model a poet so magnificently inventive in syntactical forms as Virgil, but it shows critical perception on his part to have seen that fidelity to those forms was essential if his blank verse was to be aesthetically interesting and delightful. Blank verse of its very nature may easily become relaxed and nerveless.

Nevertheless, the translations are disconcertingly uneven in quality. Some passages have a dignity and expressiveness remarkable in a difficult metre used for the first time. In others the syntax is huddled and the rhythm lifeless. Surrey tends to be more successful in speeches that are oratorical in cast than in passages of elaborate description or narrative. In Book Two he is unsuccessful in the description of Laocoon and his sons crushed by the serpents, and far from his best in the middle parts of the Book which deal with the fighting that precedes the death of Priam. In Book Four he fails in the descriptions of Dido's hunt, of Fame, of the Massylian priestess and of the magical rites performed by Dido before her death. He is defeated by most of the similes. On the other hand, the best-sustained parts of Book Two are those towards the beginning and towards the end, which are rich in speeches. Indeed, the last forty lines of the Book, which include the apparition and speech of Creusa, are probably the best blank verse Surrey wrote (they are unusually independent of Douglas). In Book Four the writing is less sustained over long passages, but the poetic quality improves in the speeches, although there are exceptions. A line-by-line comparison of Surrey and Virgil suggests that there is a simple set of conditions which will afford a general explanation for these lapses in quality. Surrey is at his best in those passages of Virgil which are clearly organized into bold syntactical and rhetorical patterns. This is only to be expected, because such patterns lend themselves to reproduction or imitation even in a language which, like English, is uninflected. Therefore figures of repetition (in all their variety) are especially to be welcomed by a translator using Surrey's method since they can be transposed into English without great modification and used as formal principles: they are both faithful to the original and invaluable as structural elements in the new poem.[1] It is for this reason that Surrey tends to be better at speeches than at close description or narrative. Speeches in epic are usually impassioned, for epic situations naturally prompt outcries of exhortation, prayer, reproach, entreaty, invective, and lament. Dido's ten speeches alone show an impressive range of emotion and tone. Impassioned utterance tends to formality, it slips easily into bold figures of speech and emphatic iteration. Consequently, the strong rhetorical cast of the speeches in Virgil and their comparatively loose texture ease the translator's task. But whether it is a speech or not, if a passage is exuberantly shaped, it will give the translator his opportunity. Conversely, passages in Virgil which are emotionally subdued and which do not resort to vividly expressive word-ordering offer less. This is particularly apparent in the case of the similes. If the verbal texture of the speeches is comparatively loose, in the similes it is exceptionally close-knit. There is no room for figures of repetition or developed rhetorical schemes. It is in the similes that the inflexional expressiveness of the Latin language fully comes into its own : the *nuances* inhering in the use of the oblique cases, for instance, quite defy translation into English. These observations go some way towards explaining Surrey's almost regular failure in these parts of the poem. They also apply to those other places which defeat Surrey such as the death of Laocoon and Dido's hunt. Failure to solve the syntactical problem is always recorded in lifeless rhythms, whereas confident and sensitive rhythms owe their existence to strong syntactical foundations.

What clearly emerges from a study of these translations is the importance in them of the strictly aesthetic element in the arrangements of words: the importance assumed by the phrasal shapes and patterns. Many of these features were already in Douglas; but in him they solicit less attention, partly because there are also other, more Chaucerian, features present, and partly because Douglas writes in couplets. Rhyme, and especially

---

[1] e.g. compare with the Latin Surrey's ii. 178–205, 864–84, 1030–50; iv. 96–108 (which is not a speech), 341–56, 477–509, 545–76, 900–10.

couplet rhyming, is so insistent a feature that it may weaken the reader's sensitivity to subtler and more irregular modes of organization. (This seems true of Douglas at least; Pope is a different matter.)[1] The result is that Douglas's reader is more free to concentrate on the narrative, while in Surrey, it has to be allowed, there is an increase in the element of pure verbality: words, phrases, and sentences occupy more attention, they themselves become aesthetic objects. The reader senses a continual striving after balance, parallelism, antithesis, symmetry, and pleasurable asymmetry. Even while his attention is given to the narrative, he is aware of the continual sympathetic enactment of the words so that, compared with his predecessors', Surrey's verse seems to enjoy a more intimate relation between matter and manner. Such writing can be said to possess 'verbal beauty' in a way foreign to Chaucer, Lydgate, and Wyatt. But inevitably this classic, formal charm entails a loss of ordinary vitality. There is no room for Douglas's generous bustle in Surrey's carefully ordered medium. Nevertheless, Surrey has made a literary choice of some historical importance, and (as the admirers of Douglas too seldom admit) there is gain as well as loss. The gain is largely a matter of verbal sensitivity: it put at the disposal of English poets new expressive resources. The new poetic syntax enlarged the poet's mimetic power; for, as so often happens in the arts, by restricting himself to a narrow range of variously repetitive elements, the artist has increased his power of minute adjustment and hence of mimetic expression.

The verbal beauty which has been mentioned appears most strikingly in single lines when Surrey is kindled by something he has seen in Virgil. An elusive aura adheres to them, yet when examined they show that same sensitivity to linguistic forms and that enthusiasm for aesthetic discrimination which have been already remarked. Such lines are

> Thinfortunate Andromache alone (ii. 589)
> As for my grave, I wey the losse but light (ii. 849)
> Me here the gods great mother holdes. (ii. 1048)

---

[1] See Dryden on Waller's reformation of rhyme, in *Epistle prefixed to The Rival Ladies* (1664); and W. K. Wimsatt, Jr.'s essay 'One Relation of Rhyme to Reason' in *The Verbal Icon* (1954).

The first line gains, like the others, from its context, but in itself it stands out for its mysterious musical quality. This is partly a matter of sensitive syllabic distribution (4, 4, 2) and of vowel arrangement. But the disyllabic 'alone', thrown into prominence by its two tetrasyllabic companions, really is alone, and the line slows down with an effect as of poignant silence. The second line owes its odd distinction to a kind of subdued wit. It reads as if there were an antithesis between 'grave' and 'light'. Whether consciously or not, Surrey seems to be making a play on 'grave'—there is nothing corresponding in Virgil's 'facilis iactura sepulchri'—but the suspicion of wit is quite in keeping with the calm hopelessness of the old Anchises. The third line is arresting in context, and of course gains from its position in Creusa's magnificent speech. It is close in form to Virgil ('sed me magna deum genetrix his detinet oris', ii. 788), and startlingly anticipates Tennyson, whose Tithonus ('Me only cruel immortality / Consumes') is remembering this same Virgilian line.

Other lines prove that their author had a gift for intelligent simplification. They would have pleased Ascham, who desired 'proprietie in wordes, simplicitie in sentences, plainnesse and light':

> Whoso thou art, learn to forget the Grekes (ii. 186)
> Pelias lamed by Ulissez hand (ii. 562)

Such lines succeed through forceful or witty statement. Others use the more elusive resources of poetry: the happy collocation of words and sounds which may liberate the imagination :

> Offring to speak, amid her voice, she whistes (iv. 96)
> Alone she mournes within her palace voide (iv. 103)
> This she to none, not to her sister told (iv. 602)
> And oft the owle with rufull song complaind (iv. 609)

In others Surrey achieves a large heroic diction which commands a dramatic urgency:

> Ye everlasting lampes, I testifye,
> Whoes powr divine may not be violate (ii. 193–4)
> Rue on this realme, whoes ruine is at hande (iv. 410)
> To Italie passe on by helpe of windes,
> And through the floods go searche thy kingdom new (iv. 499–500)

Her comly brest thrise or foure times she smote
With her own hand, and tore her golden tresse (iv. 785–6)

In the last two examples Surrey has adapted the chiastic habit of
Latin verse, although in neither case is the source itself chiastic.
Their diagonal arrangement—together with, in the last example,
syntactical *enjambement* (highly characteristic of Virgil)—makes
possible a buoyancy of movement which anticipates the Augustan
heroic couplet. On such occasions as these Surrey is seen to be
learning a poetic manner, with its own range of rhythmical and
musical effects, which may be used on other occasions in original
poems.

One other, smaller, matter shows how Surrey alerts his reader
to the niceties of linguistic form. This is the choice of English
equivalents for the Latin genitive—a problem in which Surrey
shows interest. The Latin genitive can be rendered in English in
two ways: either by the uninflected construction with *of*, or by
the inflected form with final *s*. (The use of the genitival apostrophe
is later than both Surrey and Tottel.) What Surrey does, in an
unsystematic yet quite perceptible way, is to use both forms so
as to exploit the value of alternation or variation between them.
They are repeatedly played against each other, and elicit from the
reader a discriminating sharpness of response. It often happens
that two genitive phrases occur in the same line, and are rendered
in contrasting ways:

Upsprang the crye of men and trompettes blast[1] (ii. 399)
In Priams ayd and rescue of his town (ii. 439)

Sometimes they occur in succeeding lines, when both genitive
forms are set against each other, as in

Parcase yow wold ask what was Priams fate.
When of his taken town he saw the chance,
And the gates of his palace beaten down . . . (ii. 654–6)

Here the inflected form in l. 654 is followed by two genitives
with *of*, the first of which is in inverted order; the effect is chiastic.
This frequently happens: if two genitives with *of* occur in suc-
cessive lines, one of them is inverted: e.g. the conclusion to Book

[1] Taken over from Douglas; see note.

Two (ll. 1066–7): 'th'entries of the gates beset', 'Of help there was no hope'.[1] Sometimes a more complex pattern is discernible, and two of the various meanings of the word *of* are discriminated:

> Here were we first ybatred with the dartes
> Of our own feers, from the hye temples top;
> Wherby of us grete slaughter did ensue (ii. 523–5)

Here the words 'with the dartes / Of our own feers, from the hye temples top' have a kind of syntactical density which convincingly renders the involved Latin phrase with its pairs of genitives and ablatives: 'ex alto delubri culmine telis / nostrorum' (ii. 410–11). However, the usual effect of this attention given to the genitive is to set going a free pattern of looseness and compression, and to bestow on the form in –*s* ('Cassandra, Priams daughter dere', 'in all Troies overthrow', 'like Orestes Agamemnons son') something of the Latin's convoluted elegance.

It is safe to say that the translations of Virgil played an important part in Surrey's literary development. They are also important in their own right: some of his best writing is to be found in them. It seems likely that they were comparatively early,[2] although the possibility remains that Surrey revised and improved them. Whether chronologically earlier or not, they can be seen as logically prior, so to speak, to the Petrarchan sonnets. These amatory poems have come to seem insipid and excessively smooth, and it is true that they are not distinguished by much feeling. However, they have some interest, not as love poems but (to use the term in no very disparaging sense) as performances in elocution.[3] C. S. Baldwin has said (he is discussing the gradual reception of Tuscan as the literary language of Italy): 'Used by scholars who also wrote Latin, Italian naturally learned from Cicero and Vergil more logical and rhythmical sentence habits, more adroit shaping of verse. Thus the best result of humanism, perhaps, was the one least sought by the humanists, the refinement of the vernacular.'[4] This suggests why in the first place Wyatt

[1] For this use of the genitive in other poems, cf. Nos. 1. 11 and 43. 1.
[2] See notes to 4. 13, 7. 5, and 28. 30, 31.
[3] Ezra Pound said of Petrarch: 'An excellent author for an Italian law student seeking to improve his "delivery" ' (*The Spirit of Romance*, p. 166).
[4] *Renaissance Literary Theory and Practice* (1939), p. 30.

and Surrey should have turned to Petrarch—although, it is true, they put him to very different uses. Petrarch was, perhaps more than anyone else, the original instigator of the neo-classical movement. His vernacular poems were closely modelled, in diction and clausal structure, on the Roman poets (particularly Virgil and Horace); and accordingly, it was Petrarch rather than Dante whom Bembo recommended for imitation to those who, like himself, were seeking to establish Tuscan as the standard Italian dialect.[1] To Surrey, Petrarch must have seemed in many ways the modern Virgil, a master of sweet, sonorous, and strong speech. And it was not only as a love-poet that he figured : on occasion he could write powerfully in a mood of civic indignation and protest.[2] It should not be overlooked that such strong declamatory sonnets as 'The great Macedon' and 'Th'Assyryans king' are, like Surrey's amatory sonnets, Petrarchan in manner (although not, like them, with definite Petrarchan sources).[3] 'Th'Assyryans king' is one of Surrey's most successful poems. In its nice adjustment of tones (directness for the first quatrain, obliquity for the second, and a reversion to direct aggressiveness for the sestet), it shows his phrasing at its most elegant.

Surrey's more personal poems need little introduction. They are direct and natural in feeling, and have suffered little from the passage of time. They are happily uncomplicated by conventional machinery, and in this, perhaps, they show the good effect of Christian humanist teaching. At its best such teaching exhaled a kindly Erasmian spirit: it encouraged realism in matters of feeling and respect for domestic affections and the institution of the family. This group includes the two poems written in the person of Lady Surrey, the lines on the ages of man, the sonnet commemorating the death of Thomas Clere, and the stanzaic poem on Windsor. The last mentioned speaks across four centuries directly and intimately. It uses the stanza of Gray's *Elegy*,[4] and

[1] *Prose della Volgar Lingua* (first printed 1525, written *c.* 1510–19).
[2] See, for example, his fine *canzone* 'Italia mia'.
[3] J. W. Lever discusses the sonnets in *The Elizabethan Love Sonnet* (1956). See also F. T. Prince's essay 'The Sonnet from Wyatt to Shakespeare' in *Elizabethan Poetry* (Stratford upon Avon Studies 2, 1960).
[4] 'Nor should it be forgotten, that at the same time that Surrey gave us the form of an Elegy, he fixed the measure which was the properest, and best suited to it. . . . Experience has proved that the solemnity of the Heroic Quatrain adds

has something of Gray's essentially unaffected naturalness. It is worth remark that a poem of this date treating nostalgically of past joys should make not a single mention of fortune's inconstancy. But Surrey is on the whole free from the tired medieval paraphernalia of tragedy and from the heavy didacticism which depresses mid-Tudor poetry. Unlike most poems which bewail lost happiness, this one wisely spends most of its time re-creating the happiness instead of dwelling on the loss. It makes its strongest impression as a record of adolescent friendship:

> On fominge horse, with swordes and frendlye hertes.

The epitaph on Wyatt is arguably Surrey's best poem. It is not possible here to examine the nature of Surrey's poetic debt to Wyatt; what is clear is the esteem which this remarkable man and poet aroused in his younger contemporary.[1] The contemplation of Wyatt's character drew from Surrey a terse, almost senatorial, gravity of statement which is not matched elsewhere in his writing. (At the same time, formal considerations played their part: epitaph required terseness.) Surrey's praise of Wyatt's poetry is confined to the *Penitential Psalms*. His own Biblical paraphrases, clearly prompted by Wyatt's example, deserve to be read. Without them we miss the tragic side of a man whose life was judicially cut short before he was thirty. The Ecclesiastes poems have good lines, but the last three of the Psalms are written from a deeper level of the spirit. Indeed, a recent critic[2] is of the opinion that in Psalm lxxxviii (along with the epitaph on Wyatt) Surrey is at his best as a poet. Certainly the feelings of the man are engaged to a painfully intense degree; one is awed by their uncompromising sincerity and drawn to sympathize with a human being awaiting death. These Psalms are valuable as human documents. But their impact, unlike that of the poems of Ralegh written in a similar situation, seems to be not primarily literary; they offer less to the reader whose main interest is poetry.

dignity to complaint; and is mournful without being querulous' (G. F. Nott). For an earlier use of this stanza, see Wyatt's 'Hevyn and erth and all that here me plain' (ed. Muir, No. 73); its rhythm is irregular and quite different in effect.

[1] Surrey was fourteen years younger than Wyatt.

[2] H. A. Mason, *Humanism and Poetry in the Early Tudor Period* (1959), p. 247.

Surrey wrote a number of poems in poulter's measure. This form (alternating lines of twelve and fourteen syllables) has met with a great deal of critical abuse. 'The very draff and scum of contemporary English poetry, the lumbering Poulter's Measure' is how C. S. Lewis refers to it. A little may be said in its defence. It is, though crude, a musical metre. And although it encourages a jigging or prancing movement, it does not entirely resist modification, as Lewis himself has shown (p. xxxiii below). Moreover, if we want to understand how it was that the efflorescence of late Elizabethan lyrical poetry came about, we ought to be prepared to give these ungainly poems a sympathetic reading. Surrey's poems in this metre are by no means contemptible. Most of them have some successful details.

The bulk of Surrey's important work was translation or adaptation. His powers of invention and of forming independent structures were small. The best and longest of his original poems, the epitaph on Wyatt and the stanzas on Windsor, both make use of simple accumulative schemes; and in those places in the sonnets where he deserts Petrarch[1] he usually exposes his incapacity. His important inventions were in metre, in syntax, and in diction. One of his achievements was to help to slow down the movement of English poetry. He made a stand against the vague and diffuse style that prevailed in his time. He combated the prolix and inert management of literary formulas, and to a great extent dropped the worn-out diction inherited from the 15th-century love lyric (which even Wyatt had retained) with its plethora of abstract nouns of love and service (*comfort, disdainfulness, doubleness, enterprise, intent, pain, price, proof, steadfastness*) and of fortune (*case, chance, change, hap, lot*). Attention is now focused on the newly forged phrase, not dissipated by strings of formulas. G. F. Nott's remarks on these matters are just (see p. xxx below), except that he exaggerates Surrey's originality by quite failing to acknowledge his debt to the educational effort of the humanists, which was directed to precisely these ends: *verborum delectus origo est eloquentiae*. Surrey's best original poems are those of a man who has studied Latin poetry in the neo-classical way. His attitude to individual words and phrases is that of a close admirer

[1] As in the second part of No. 7.

of Virgil and Horace. This accounts for his interest in expressive cadence—

> Calme is the sea, the waves worke lesse and lesse

(which derives via Petrarch from Virgil[1])—as well as in those devices, like *hyperbaton* (i.e. disturbed word-order), which contrive to give English something of the interwoven density of Latin.

If we are primarily concerned with intrinsic poetic worth and only secondarily with the study of origins, then Surrey's place in the history of English poetry will be a minor one. Although he created a distinct literary personality, a severe criticism will find his achievement small in scale and flawed. The poems which can be enjoyed as wholes are few, but surprisingly numerous are good single lines and short passages which prove that Surrey was a poet of real talent.

Within the sixteenth century his importance is clear. But the traditional pairing of Surrey with Wyatt has not been helpful to an understanding of either of them. For all Surrey's admiration for Wyatt, they are poets of different kinds. He is better paired with Sackville, author of the Induction and the Complaint of the Duke of Buckingham in *The Mirror for Magistrates* and co-author of *Gorboduc*, the first English tragedy and the first English play in blank verse. In both of them Sackville's debt to Surrey in phrasing (not to speak of the metre of *Gorboduc*) is evident. Indeed, Sackville wrote what is probably the earliest extant tribute to Surrey as a poet:[2]

> not surrea he that hiest sittes in chair
> of glistering fame for ay to live and raighn
> not his proud ryme that thunders in the aier
> nor al the plaintes wherin he wrote his pain
> when he lay fetterd in the fyry chain
> of cruell love.

---

[1] 'silvaeque et saeva quierant / aequora' (*Aeneid* iv. 523–4). Cf. Surrey's version, No. 42. 704.

[2] From the 'additional stanzas' of Sackville's *Complaint of Henrie Duke of Buckingham*, ed. Marguerite Hearsey (1936). These unfinished lines are transcribed from MS. 364 of St. John's College, Cambridge.

But Surrey is best seen in the company of his own contemporaries, the humanist teachers of the middle decades of the century: Sir Thomas Elyot, Sir John Cheke, and Roger Ascham. He could not, of course, compare with them as a scholar, but the general direction of his work is most easily understood in terms of what they laboured to accomplish. If Professor Hughey is right, the poem[1] by Sir John Cheke on an unnamed contemporary poet was occasioned by Surrey's death. Its lack of literary merit should not obscure the fitness of the gesture. The pioneer classical scholar salutes 'the first English classical poet'.

[1] No. 282 in the *Arundel Harington Manuscript of Tudor Poetry*, edited by Ruth Hughey (1960). It is in unrhyming hexameters.

BIOGRAPHICAL AND TEXTUAL NOTE

FOR biographies of Surrey, see Edmond Bapst, *Deux Gentilshommes-poètes de la Cour d'Henry VIII* (1891) and Edwin Casady, *Henry Howard, Earl of Surrey* (1938); a recent interpretation appears in Hester W. Chapman's *Two Tudor Portraits* (1960). The main facts of Surrey's life are as follows. Henry Howard was born early in 1517, the elder son of Thomas Howard, Earl of Surrey. Thomas Howard became the third Duke of Norfolk in 1524, whereupon Henry was given the courtesy title of Earl of Surrey. (The notion, often repeated, that Surrey's tutor was a distinguished scholar called John Clerk has recently been undermined.)[1] In 1530 Surrey joined the Duke of Richmond, the natural son of Henry VIII, at Windsor; they enjoyed an intimate friendship, and in 1532 accompanied Henry VIII to France, where they remained a year travelling with the French Court. (The Court of Francis I was at this time dominated by Italian fashions; Surrey may have met the Florentine poet Luigi Alamanni, who had written several poems in unrhyming verse.) Also in 1532 Surrey married Lady Frances Vere, daughter of the Earl of Oxford; he began to live with her in 1535. In 1536 he witnessed the trial of Anne Boleyn; and later served under his father against the Pilgrimage of Grace. Both Surrey and Norfolk were alleged to be in sympathy with the rebels, and in 1537, within the precincts of the Court, Surrey struck Sir Edward Seymour (then Viscount Beauchamp) who had repeated this charge; Surrey was imprisoned at Windsor. In 1539 he was put in charge of the anti-invasion defences of Norfolk. In 1540 he distinguished himself at a tournament in honour of the new queen, Anne of Cleves. In 1541 he was made Knight of the Garter. In 1542 he attended the execution of his cousin, Catherine Howard; was imprisoned for sixteen days for challenging a

[1] Sergio Baldi, 'The Secretary of the Duke of Norfolk and the first Italian Grammar in England', in *Studies in English Language and Literature* presented to Karl Brunner (1957).

courtier; and later joined his father in the campaign against Scotland. In 1543 he was imprisoned again for riotous behaviour in the streets of London (eating flesh in Lent and breaking windows); later in the year he served, with the Emperor Charles V, at the siege of Landrecy. Early in 1544 he began to build a magnificent house, in the Italian classical style, at Mount Surrey near Norwich. (It was reputed to be the earliest of English classical buildings; no traces of it remain.) In 1545 he served at the siege of Montreuil as Marshall of the Field, and was wounded. In 1545 he was put in charge of Boulogne with the title 'Lieutenant General of the King on Sea and Land'; later in the year he was reprimanded for exposing himself to unnecessary danger. In January 1546 he lost a skirmish at St. Étienne; in March he was recalled to England. In December he was arrested on several charges of treason; on 19 January 1547 he was beheaded. He left two sons and three daughters. His elder son, Thomas, became fourth Duke of Norfolk in 1554; in 1572 he was beheaded for plotting with Mary Queen of Scots against Elizabeth.

There are complete editions of the poems by G. F. Nott (1815) and F. M. Padelford (1920; 1928). 'Songes and Sonettes' (1557) or 'Tottel's Miscellany' has been edited by H. E. Rollins (1928, 1929), *The Arundel Harington Manuscript of Tudor Poetry*—which contains eighteen poems by Surrey—by Ruth Hughey (1960), and the Day-Owen print of the version of *Aeneid* iv by H. Hartman (1933). The bulk of Surrey's verse is included in Gerald Bullett's *Silver Poets of the Sixteenth Century* (Everyman's Library, 1947); it omits Book 4 of the *Aeneid* and the Biblical paraphrases.

This edition contains almost the whole of Surrey's verse: omitted are five short lyrics of small merit, one poem in poulter's measure of 76 lines ('Eache beste can chuse his feere'), and the paraphrase of the fifth chapter of Ecclesiastes. Where possible, sixteenth-century manuscripts have been used (except in the case of the version of *Aeneid* iv; see introductory note to No. 41); none of them is holograph, but they are likely to be closer to what Surrey wrote than the versions in Tottel's edition, which in some cases have been 'improved'. (See F. M. Padelford, 'The MS. Poems of . . . Surrey', *Anglia*, xxix (1906); also J. M.

Berdan, *Early Tudor Poetry* (1920).) The manuscripts used are in the British Museum. MS. Egerton 2711 is the source of No. 31 in this edition; MS. Add. 36529 is the source of Nos. 3, 4, 5, 6, 9, 11, 13, 14, 26, 27, 29, 30, 32, 33, 36, 37, 40, 43, 44, 45, 46, 48, 49, and 50; and MS. Add. 28635 is the source of Nos. 22, 24, 25, and 47. Tottel's 'Songes and Sonettes' is the source of Nos. 1, 2, 7, 8, 10, 12, 15, 16, 17, 18, 19, 20, 21, 23, 28, 34, 38, and 39. Tottel's 'Certain Bokes of Virgiles Aenaeis turned into English metre . . .' is the source of Nos. 41 and 42, and Camden's *Remaines of a Greater Work concerning Britaine*, 1605 of No. 35.

The prints and manuscripts have been closely followed, but *u* and *v*, and *i* and *j* have been given their modern values. The original capitalization has often been retained if it seemed to be used for emphasis. The punctuation is editorial.

The following abbreviations have been used in the Notes: *C.T.* (*Canterbury Tales*); *J.E.G.P.* (*Journal of English and Germanic Philology*); *M.L.N.* (*Modern Language Notes*); *M.L.R.* (*Modern Language Review*); *O.E.D.* (*Oxford English Dictionary*); *P.M.L.A.* (*Publications of the Modern Language Association of America*); *T.L.S.* (*Times Literary Supplement*).

CRITICAL COMMENT

THOMAS WARTON

IN the sonnets of Surrey we are surprised to find nothing of that metaphysical cast which marks the Italian poets, his supposed masters, especially Petrarch. Surrey's sentiments are for the most part natural and unaffected: arising from his own feelings, and dictated by the present circumstances. His poetry is alike un-embarrassed by learned allusions or elaborate conceits. If our author copies Petrarch, it is Petrarch's better manner: when he descends from his Platonic abstractions, his refinements of passion, his exaggerated compliments, and his play upon opposite senti-ments, into a track of tenderness, simplicity, and nature. . . . [He quotes No. 27] In the poet's situation, nothing can be more natural and striking than the reflection with which he opens his complaint. There is also much beauty in the abruptness of his exordial exclamation. The superb palace, where he had passed the most pleasing days of his youth with the son of a king, was now converted into a tedious and solitary prison! This unexpected vicissitude of fortune awakens a new and interesting train of thought. The comparison of his past and present circum-stances recalls their juvenile sports and amusements; which were more to be regretted, as young Richmond was now dead. Having described some of these with great elegance, he recurs to his first idea by a beautiful apostrophe. He appeals to the place of his confinement, once the source of his highest pleasures: 'O place of bliss, renewer of my woes! And where is now my noble friend, my companion in these delights, who was once your inhabitant! Echo alone either pities or answers my question, and returns a hollow plaintive sound!' He closes his complaint with an affecting and pathetic sentiment, much in the style of Petrarch. 'To banish the miseries of my present distress, I am forced on the wretched expedient of remembering a greater!' This is the consolation of a warm fancy. It is the philosophy of poetry.

Some of the following stanzas, on a lover who presumed to

compare his lady with the divine Geraldine, have almost the ease and gallantry of Waller. The leading compliment, which has been used by later writers, is in the spirit of an Italian fiction. It is very ingenious, and handled with a high degree of elegance: [He quotes No. 12]. . . .

The versification of these stanzas is correct, the language polished, and the modulation musical. The following stanza, of another ode, will hardly be believed to have been produced in the reign of Henry the Eighth: [He quotes No. 20. 7–10]. . . .

Surrey, for his justness of thought, correctness of style, and purity of expression, may justly be pronounced the first English classical poet. He unquestionably is the first polite writer of love-verses in our language. It must, however, be allowed, that there is a striking native beauty in some of our love-verses written much earlier than Surrey's. But in the most savage ages and countries rude nature has taught elegance to the lover.

(*History of English Poetry* (1781), section xxxviii)

G. F. NOTT

Such were the leading defects in our poetic style and diction, when Surrey began to write. All those defects he reformed. He first rejected the use of those 'aureate and mellifluate' terms, which he found disfiguring our language with a sort of prescriptive tyranny, and restricted himself to the use of those words alone which were approved by common use, and were natural to the language.

He next introduced a studied mode of involution in his periods, which gives dignity to what is so expressed, and a certain remoteness from common life, essential to the higher branches of poetic composition.

And lastly, he discountenanced altogether the French mode of laying an unnatural stress upon final syllables; he followed the obvious and common pronunciation of our language; carefully avoiding all double terminations, and using only those words for rhyme which were noble and harmonious, and such as the ear might dwell upon with pleasure. . . .

The only remaining point to be considered is, what Surrey did towards establishing a correct system of Rhyming. It has been shewn that much was to be done in this particular. What Surrey did, was as follows: he pointed out the propriety of excluding all double rhymes: he taught us to avoid all rhymes constructed unnaturally on the French mode of accentuation, and laid it down as a principle that those words alone should be selected for rhymes, in heroic and elegant composition, which were elegant and sonorous; for without these the numbers themselves could be neither harmonious nor dignified. Surrey chose, in preference to all other, those words which were disyllables, and formed in themselves a perfect iambic foot, as the following, *return, restore, refuse, desire, remove, delight,* &c. and when he rhymed on mono-syllables, they were full and sonorous, and were always preceded by a short syllable. From this rule it is remarkable that Surrey seldom departed. The effect was that his versification became dignified as well as musical. The charm of his poetry is never interrupted by the sudden occurrence of familiar sounds, which while they offend the ear, excite unpleasing ideas in the mind.

We come now to consider what were the improvements of a general nature made by Surrey in our poetry. They may be reduced to the following heads.

I. He exhibited correct models of composition, in all the branches of poetry which he attempted;

II. He reformed that rude and diffusive mode of writing which was common to all our poets who preceded him;

III. He shewed what could be done by proper embellishment, without which thoughts, noble and dignified in themselves, are lowered and debased; and,

IV. He taught succeeding writers how to imitate the Classics and the best authors of other languages without pedantry; so adapting the passages borrowed to the genius of the English language, as to give them an air of originality; a point of parti-cular nicety in taste and judgment. . . .

Of Surrey's compression, contrasted with the diffusive mode of writing used by all the authors who preceded him, a more striking instance cannot well be found than that which occurs in the opening to his sonnet on Sir Thomas Wyatt's death. [He quotes No. 29. 1–4.] The compression of thought in the last line is exquisite. It comprehends the whole of the following quatrain of Petrarch. [He quotes the Petrarchan source, given in the Notes.]

The circumstance that next deserves to be noticed in Surrey's style, is the gradation of it. This was a refinement of taste which originated entirely with himself. He had three distinct styles, the heroic, the amatory, and the popular, or ballad style. To each of these styles, moreover, he appropriated its peculiar verse and form of stanza. To the heroic style he appropriated the decasyllabic verse of ten syllables, and with it he used the elegiac stanza, the sonnet system, and the terza rima. To the amatory style, he appropriated the octosyllabic verse, using it either in continued couplets, or in stanzas of four, six, or nine lines; and to the popular style, the Alexandrine verse of twelve syllables with alternate lines of fourteen syllables, rhyming in couplets.

That what I have here advanced may not be thought a fanciful refinement on my part, I will adduce a few specimens of Surrey's variation of style, in these different forms of composition.

In a piece written in the ballad measure, Surrey thus describes the disquietude of the lover's mind when absent from his mistress. [He quotes No. 17. 5–10.] The same thought is thus expressed in heroic verse. [No. 11. 21–25.] Now, there is no other difference in these passages than what arises from difference of style.

[Nott goes on to compare 17. 21–22 with 11. 47–50, and 24. 17–20 with 23. 29–35.]

(From *The Works of Henry Howard, Earl of Surrey and of Sir Thomas Wyatt the Elder*, edited by G. F. Nott, 1815.)

C. S. LEWIS

His Petrarchan pieces are by no means his best; yet even in them it is easy to see why the Elizabethans preferred him to Wyatt. He was more accomplished, more useful. For the sonnet he often adopted that modified form less greedy of rhymes, which Shakespeare perfected, and availed himself of its greater ease to make sonnets which, if never very moving, are smooth and elegant and work up to a tolerable climax. Sometimes he produced equally good results with a more exacting rhyme scheme; as in 'The Soote Season' and his sonnet on sleep. His lyrics nearly all have the completeness, the shape, which Wyatt sometimes lacked. But the truth is that his love poetry is usually best when it is least about love. He takes every opportunity of bringing in external nature, or narrative, as if to take a holiday from the erotic treadmill. Oddly enough, the only two poems in which we are really moved by the theme of love are both put into the mouth of a woman; and of these women one certainly is, and the other may be, a wife in love with her husband. The better of the two is the lyric 'O happie dames' (freely adapted from an Italian original) which contains the best stanza he ever wrote. The other, in poulter's ('Good Ladies'), nearly triumphs over that jigging metre. . . .

. . . the real interest of the [Biblical] paraphrases is metrical: not chiefly because in Psalm lv Surrey attempts the unrhymed alexandrine (nothing was to come of that till the *Testament of Beauty*) but because he is now trying to reform the poulter's measure.

The vices of that metre are two. The medial break in the alexandrine, though it may do well enough in French, quickly becomes intolerable in a language with such a tyrannous stress-accent as ours: the line struts. The fourteener has a much pleasanter movement, but a totally different one; the line dances a jig. Hence in a couplet made of two such yoke-fellows we seem to be labouring up a steep hill in bottom gear for the first line, and then running down the other side of the hill, out of control, for the second. In his *Paraphrases* (chiefly in the Ecclesiastes) Surrey is, I think, attempting to remedy this by restraining the run-away tendency of the fourteener. He does this sometimes by putting in another pause as strong as that at the eighth syllable, and thus cutting his line in three—

The World is false, man he is fraile, and all his pleasures payne

sometimes by inversions of stress in the neighbourhood of the pause—

Then aged Kings, wedded to will, that worke without advice—

sometimes by trisyllabic feet—

And carrey the roodde that skorgeth them that glorey in their gold.

With the alexandrine he takes fewer liberties, but those which he allows himself yield impressive lines, as

  I, Salamon, Dauids sonne, King of Jerusalem,

or

  We that live on the earth draw towards our decay.

Even if the process had been carried further it would hardly have made poulter's a good measure, but it might have made more of the fourteener than Chapman ever did, and shows the continually growing and exploring artistry of Surrey.

(English Literature in the Sixteenth Century, 1954.)

MAURICE EVANS

  He banished the aureate and the alliterative once and for all, and he established a standard of clear, controlled language which was what the century needed above all things. Read any aureate love-lyric of the XVth century, and then turn to the clarity and precision of Surrey's six-line stanza: [He quotes No. 1]. I have quoted the whole of this lyric because its excellence lies not in individual lines but in the cumulative effect. In the whole thirty lines there are only three sentences, yet the poem unfolds itself with a clear and ordered logic. It has a form entirely appropriate to its content, and, while never pretending to more feeling than the occasion deserves, it treats a conventional theme with dignity and sincerity. It is a new form of art, urbane, controlled and self-conscious; and it embodies the qualities which the new poets, exploring their medium, most needed to cultivate. It has a classical restraint and clarity which the more exuberant taste of the Elizabethans tended to ignore and which does not really appear again until Ben Jonson came on the scene.

(English Poetry in the Sixteenth Century, 1955.)

AMATORY POEMS

I

When ragyng love with extreme payne
Most cruelly distrains my hart;
When that my teares, as floudes of rayne,
Beare witnes of my wofull smart;
When sighes have wasted so my breath   5
That I lye at the poynte of death:

I call to minde the navye greate
That the Grekes brought to Troye towne,
And how the boysteous windes did beate
Their shyps, and rente their sayles adowne,   10
Till Agamemnons daughters bloode
Appeasde the goddes that them withstode.

And how that in those ten yeres warre
Full manye a bloudye dede was done,
And manye a lord, that came full farre,
There caught his bane, alas, to sone,   15
And many a good knight overronne,
Before the Grekes had Helene wonne.

Then thinke I thus: sithe suche repayre,
So longe time warre of valiant men,   20
Was all to winne a ladye fayre,
Shall I not learne to suffer then,
And thinke my life well spent to be
Servyng a worthier wight than she?

Therfore I never will repent,   25
But paynes contented stil endure:
For like as when, rough winter spent,
The pleasant spring straight draweth in ure,
So after ragyng stormes of care
Joyful at length may be my fare.   30

2

The soote season, that bud and blome furth bringes,
With grene hath clad the hill and eke the vale;
The nightingale with fethers new she singes;
The turtle to her make hath tolde her tale.
Somer is come, for every spray nowe springes;   5
The hart hath hong his olde hed on the pale;
The buck in brake his winter cote he flinges;
The fishes flote with newe repaired scale;
The adder all her sloughe awaye she slinges;
The swift swalow pursueth the flyes smale;   10
The busy bee her honye now she minges;
Winter is worne that was the flowers bale.
  And thus I see among these pleasant thinges
  Eche care decayes, and yet my sorow springes.

3

Set me wheras the sonne dothe perche the grene,
Or whear his beames may not dissolve the ise;
In temprat heat wheare he is felt and sene;
With prowde people, in presence sad and wyse;
Set me in base, or yet in highe degree,   5
In the long night, or in the shortyst day,
In clere weather, or whear mysts thikest be,
In loste yowthe, or when my heares be grey;
Set me in earthe, in heaven, or yet in hell,
In hill, in dale, or in the fowming floode;   10

Thrawle, or at large, alive whersoo I dwell,
Sike, or in healthe, in yll fame or in good:
   Yours will I be, and with that onely thought
   Comfort my self when that my hape is nowght.

4

Love that doth raine and live within my thought,
And buylt his seat within my captyve brest,
Clad in the armes wherin with me he fowght
Oft in my face he doth his banner rest.
But she that tawght me love and suffre paine,   5
My doubtfull hope and eke my hote desire
With shamfast looke to shadoo and refrayne,
Her smyling grace convertyth streight to yre.
And cowarde love than to the hert apace
Taketh his flight where he doth lorke and playne   10
His purpose lost, and dare not show his face.
For my lordes gylt thus fawtless byde I payine;
   Yet from my lorde shall not my foote remove.
   Sweet is the death that taketh end by love.

5

In Cypres springes, wheras dame Venus dwelt,
A well so hote that who so tastes the same,
Were he of stone, as thawed yse shuld melt,
And kindled fynde his brest with secret flame;
Whose moist poison dissolved hath my hate.   5
This creping fier my cold lymms so oprest
That in the hart that harbred fredom late
Endles dispaire long thraldom hath imprest.
One eke so cold in froson snow is found,
Whose chilling venume of repugnaunt kind   10
The fervent heat doth quenche of Cupides wound,
And with the spote of change infects the mynd;
   Whereof my deer hath tasted to my payne.
   My service thus is growne into disdayne.

3

6

I never saw youe, madam, laye aparte
Your cornet black in colde nor yet in heate
Sythe first ye knew of my desire so greate
Which other fances chased cleane from my harte.
Whiles to my self I did the thought reserve   5
That so unware did wounde my wofull brest
Pytie I saw within your hart dyd rest;
But since ye knew I did youe love and serve
Your golden treese was clad alway in blacke,
Your smilyng lokes were hid thus evermore,   10
All that withdrawne that I did crave so sore.
So doth this cornet governe me alacke,
 In sommere sonne, in winter breath of frost,
 Of your faire eies whereby the light is lost.

7

Alas, so all thinges nowe doe holde their peace,
Heaven and earth disturbed in nothing;
The beastes, the ayer, the birdes their song doe cease;
The nightes chare the starres aboute dothe bring.
Calme is the sea, the waves worke lesse and lesse;   5
So am not I, whom love alas doth wring,
Bringing before my face the great encrease
Of my desires, whereat I wepe and syng
In joye and wo as in a doutfull ease.
For my swete thoughtes sometyme doe pleasure bring,   10
But by and by the cause of my disease
Geves me a pang that inwardly dothe sting,
 When that I thinke what griefe it is againe
 To live and lacke the thing should ridde my paine.

8

The golden gift that Nature did thee geve
To fasten frendes and fede them at thy wyll

With fourme and favour, taught me to beleve
How thou art made to shew her greatest skill.
Whose hidden vertues are not so unknowen,   5
But lively domes might gather at the first
Where beauty so her perfect seede hath sowen,
Of other graces folow nedes there must.
Now certesse, Ladie, sins all this is true,
That from above thy giftes are thus elect,   10
Do not deface them than wyth fansies newe,
Nor chaunge of mindes let not thy minde infect;
   But mercy him thy frende that doth thee serve,
   Who seekes alway thine honour to preserve.

9

From Tuscan cam my ladies worthi race;
Faire Florence was sometime her auncient seate;
The westorne ile, whose pleasaunt showre doth face
Wylde Chambares cliffes, did geve her lyvely heate.
Fostred she was with mylke of Irishe brest;   5
Her syer an erle, hir dame of princes bloud;
From tender yeres in Britaine she doth rest,
With a kinges child, where she tastes gostly foode.
Honsdon did furst present her to myn eyen:
Bryght ys her hew, and Geraldine she hight;   10
Hampton me tawght to wishe her furst for myne,
And Windsor, alas, doth chase me from her sight.
   Bewty of kind, her vertues from above;
   Happy ys he that may obtaine her love.

10

The fansy which that I have served long,
That hath alway bene enmy to myne ease,
Semed of late to rue upon my wrong
And bad me flye the cause of my misease.

And I forthwith dyd prease out of the throng,   5
That thought by flight my painfull hart to please
Som other way, till I saw faith more strong.
And to my self I sayd: 'Alas, those dayes
In vayn were spent, to runne the race so long.'
And with that thought I met my guyde, that playn   10
Out of the way wherin I wandred wrong
Brought me amiddes the hylles in base Bullayn;
    Where I am now, as restlesse to remayn,
    Against my will, full pleased with my payn.

II

The sonne hath twyse brought forthe the tender grene,
    And cladd the yerthe in livelye lustynes;
    Ones have the wyndes the trees dispoyled clene,
And now agayne begynnes their cruelnes,
    Sins I have hidd under my brest the harme   5
    That never shall recover helthfulnes.
The wynters hurt recovers with the warme;
    The perched grene restored is with shade:
    What warmth, alas, may sarve for to disarme
The froosyn hart that my inflame hath made?   10
    What colde agayne is hable to restore
    My freshe grene yeres that wither thus and faade?
Alas, I see nothinge to hurt so sore
    But tyme somtyme reduceth a retourne;
    Yet tyme my harme increseth more and more,   15
And semes to have my cure allwayes in skorne.
    Straunge kynd of death, in lief that I doo trye:
    At hand to melt, farr of in flame to bourne;
And like as time list to my cure aply,
    So doth eche place my comfort cleane refuse.   20
    Eche thing alive that sees the heaven with eye
With cloke of night maye cover and excuse
    Him self from travaile of the dayes unrest,
    Save I, alas, against all others use,
That then sturre upp the torment of my brest   25

To curse eche starr as cawser of my faat.
And when the sonne hath eke the darke represt
And brought the daie, it doth nothing abaat
    The travaile of my endles smart and payne.
    For then, as one that hath the light in haat,   30
I wishe for night, more covertlye to playne
    And me withdrawe from everie haunted place,
    Lest in my chere my chaunce should pere to playne;
And with my mynd I measure paas by paas
    To seke that place where I my self hadd lost,   35
    That daye that I was tangled in that laase,
In seming slacke that knytteth ever most;
    But never yet the trayvaile of my thought
    Of better state could catche a cawse to bost.
For yf I fynde somtyme that I have sought,   40
    Those starres by whome I trusted of the port,
    My sayles do fall, and I advaunce right nought,
As anchord fast; my sprites do all resort
    To stand atgaas, and sinke in more and more
    The deadlye harme which she doth take in sport.   45
Loo, yf I seke, how I do fynd my sore!
    And yf I flye, I carrey with me still
    The venymd shaft which dothe his force restore
By hast of flight. And I maye playne my fill
    Unto my self, oneles this carefull song   50
    Prynt in your hert some percell of my will.
For I, alas, in sylence all to long
    Of myne old hurt yet fele the wound but grene.
    Rue on my lief, or elles your crewell wrong
Shall well appeare, and by my deth be sene.   55

12

    Geve place, ye lovers, here before
    That spent your bostes and bragges in vain:
    My ladies beawtie passeth more
    The best of yours, I dare well sayen,

Than doth the sonne the candle light   5
Or brightest day the darkest night.

And thereto hath a trothe as just
As had Penelope the fayre:
For what she saith, ye may it trust
As it by writing sealed were.   10
And vertues hath she many moe
Than I with pen have skill to showe.

I coulde rehearse, if that I wolde,
The whole effect of Natures plaint,
When she had lost the perfit mold,   15
The like to whom she could not paint;
With wringing handes howe she dyd cry,
And what she said, I know it, I.

I knowe she swore with ragyng mind,
Her kingdom onely set apart,   20
There was no losse, by lawe of kind,
That could have gone so nere her hart.
And this was chiefly all her payne:
She coulde not make the lyke agayne.

Sith Nature thus gave her the prayse   25
To be the chiefest worke she wrought,
In faith, me thinke some better waies
On your behalfe might well be sought,
Then to compare, as ye have done,
To matche the candle with the sonne.

13

Suche waiwarde waies hath love that moste parte in discorde;
Our willes do stand wherby our hartes but seldom dooth accorde.
  Disceyte is his delight, and to begyle and mocke
The symple hertes which he doth stryke with froward dyvers
    stroke.

He cawseth hertes to rage with golden burninge darte,   5
And doth alaye with ledden cold agayne the tothers harte.
  Hot gleames of burning fyre and easye sparkes of flame
In balaunce of unegall weight he pondereth by ame.
  From easye fourde, where I might wade and passe full well,
He me withdrawes, and doth me drive into the darke diep well; 10
  And me withholdes where I am cald and offerd place,
And wooll that still my mortall foo I do beseche of grace.
  He lettes me to pursue a conquest well nere woon,
To follow where my paynes were spilt or that my sute begune.
  Lo, by these rules I know how sone a hart can turne   15
From warr to peace, from trewce to stryf, and so again returne.
  I know how to convert my will in others lust;
Of litle stuff unto my self to weyve a webb of trust;
  And how to hide my harme with soft dissembled chere,
When in my face the paynted thoughtes wolde owtwardlye
    appere.   20
  I know how that the blood forsakes the faas for dredd,
And how by shame it staynes agayne the cheke with flaming
    redd.
  I know under the grene the serpent how he lurckes;
The hamer of the restles forge I know eke how yt workes.
  I know, and can be roote, the tale that I wold tell,   25
But ofte the wordes come forth a wrye of hym that loveth well.
  I know in heat and cold the lover how he shakes,
In singinge how he can complayne, in sleaping how he wakes,
  To languishe without ache, sickles for to consume,
A thousand thinges for to devyse resolving all hys fume.   30
  And thoughe he lyke to see his ladies face full sore,
Such pleasure as delightes his eye doth not his health restore.
  I know to seke the tracke of my desyred foo,
And feare to fynd that I do seke; but chefelye this I know,
  That lovers must transforme into the thing beloved,   35
And live (alas, who colde beleve?) with spryte from lief removed.
  I know in hartye sighes and lawghters of the splene
At ones to chaunge my state, my will, and eke my colour clene.
  I know how to disceyve myself withouten helpp,
And how the lyon chastysed is by beating of the whelpp.   40

9

In standing nere my fyer, I know how that I frese;
Farr of, to burn; in both to wast, and so my lief to lese.
  I know how love doth rage uppon the yeldon mynd,
How small a nett may take and mashe a harte of gentle kynd;
    With seldome tasted swete, to season heaps of gall,   45
Revyved with a glyns of grace olde sorowes to let fall.
  The hidden traynes I know, and secret snares of love;
How sone a loke may prynt a thought that never will remove.
  That slipper state I know, those sodayne tournes from welthe,
That doubtfull hope, that certayne woo, and sure dispaire of
    helthe.   50

14

Yf he that erst the fourme so livelye drewe
Of Venus faas, tryumpht in paynteres arte;
Thy father then what glorye shall ensue,
By whose pencell a goddesse made thow arte!
Touchid with flame, that figure made some rewe,   5
And with her love surprysed manye a hart.
  There lackt yet that should cure their hoot desyer:
  Thow canst enflame and quenche the kyndled fyre.

15

When sommer toke in hand the winter to assail
With force of might and vertue gret his stormy blasts to quail,
  And when he clothed faire the earth about with grene,
And every tree new garmented, that pleasure was to sene,
  Mine hart gan new revive, and changed blood dyd stur   5
Me to withdraw my winter woe, that kept within the dore.
  'Abrode', quod my desire, 'assay to set thy fote,
Where thou shalt finde the savour swete, for sprong is every rote.
  And to thy health, if thou were sick in any case,   9
Nothing more good than in the spring the aire to fele a space.
  There shalt thou here and se all kindes of birdes ywrought,
Well tune their voice with warble smal, as Nature hath them
    tought.'

Thus pricked me my lust the sluggish house to leave,
And for my health I thought it best suche counsail to receave.
So on a morow furth, unwist of any wight,   15
I went to prove how well it would my heavy burden light.
And when I felt the aire so pleasant round about,
Lorde, to my self how glad I was that I had gotten out!
There might I see how Ver had every blossom hent,
And eke the new betrothed birdes ycoupled how they went. 20
And in their songes me thought they thanked Nature much
That by her lycence all that yere to love, their happe was such,
Right as they could devise to chose them feres throughout.
With much rejoysing to their Lord thus flew they all about.
Which when I gan resolve, and in my head conceave,   25
What pleasant life, what heapes of joy, these litle birdes receave,
And sawe in what estate I wery man was brought,
By want of that they had at will, and I reject at nought;
Lorde, how I gan in wrath unwisely me demeane!
I curssed Love, and him defied; I thought to turne the streame. 30
But whan I well behelde he had me under awe,
I asked mercie for my fault, that so transgrest his law.
'Thou blinded god', quod I, 'forgeve me this offense.
Unwittingly I went about to malice thy pretense.'
Wherewith he gave a beck, and thus me thought he swore: 35
'Thy sorow ought suffice to purge thy faulte, if it were more.'
The vertue of which sounde mine hart did so revive
That I me thought was made as hole as any man alive.
But here ye may perceive mine errour all and some,
For that I thought that so it was; yet was it still undone: 40
And all that was no more but mine empressed mynde,
That fayne woulde have some good relefe of Cupide wel assinde.
I turned home forthwith, and might perceive it well
That he agreved was right sore with me for my rebell.
My harmes have ever since increased more and more,   45
And I remaine, without his help, undone for ever more.
A miror let me be unto ye lovers all:
Strive not with love; for if ye do, it will ye thus befall.

In winters just returne, when Boreas gan his raigne,
And every tree unclothed fast, as Nature taught them plaine;
  In misty morning darke, as sheepe are then in holde,
I hyed me fast, it sat me on, my sheepe for to unfolde.
  And as it is a thing that lovers have by fittes,   5
Under a palm I heard one crye as he had lost hys wyttes.
  Whose voice did ring so shrill in uttering of his plaint,
That I amazed was to hear how love could hym attaint.
  'Ah wretched man', quod he, 'come death, and ridde thys wo;
A just reward, a happy end, if it may chaunce thee so.   10
  Thy pleasures past have wrought thy wo withoute redresse;
If thou hadst never felt no joy, thy smart had bene the lesse.'
  And retchlesse of his life, he gan both sighe and grone:
A rufull thing me thought it was, to hear him make such mone.
  'Thou cursed pen,' said he, 'wo worth the bird thee bare;   15
The man, the knife, and all that made thee, wo be to their share.
  Wo worth the time and place where I could so endite,
And wo be it yet once agayne, the pen that so can write.
  Unhappy hand, it had ben happy time for me
If when to write thou learned first, unjoynted hadst thou be.'   20
  Thus cursed he himself, and every other wight,
Save her alone whom love him bound to serve both day and
    night.
  Which when I heard, and saw how he himselfe fordid,
Against the ground, with bloudy strokes, himself even there to rid,
  Had ben my heart of flint, it must have melted tho;   25
For in my life I never saw a man so full of wo.
  With teares, for his redresse, I rashly to him ran,
And in my arms I caught him fast, and thus I spake hym than:
  'What wofull wight art thou, that in such heavy case   29
Tormentes thy selfe with such despite, here in this desert place?'
  Wherewith, as all agast, fulfild wyth ire and dred,
He cast on me a staring loke, with colour pale and ded.
  'Nay what art thou', quod he, 'that in this heavy plight,
Doest finde me here, most wofull wretch, that life hath in
    despight?'

'I am', quoth I, 'but poore, and simple in degre;   35
A shepardes charge I have in hand, unworthy though I be.'
    With that he gave a sighe, as though the skye should fall,
And lowd (alas) he shryked oft, and 'Shepard', gan he call;
    'Come, hie the fast at ones, and print it in thy hart;   39
So thou shalt know, and I shall tell the, giltlesse how I smart.'
    His backe against the tree, sore febled all with faint,
With weary sprite hee stretcht him up, and thus hee told his
    plaint.
    'Ones in my hart', quoth he, 'it chanced me to love
Such one, in whom hath Nature wrought, her cunning for to
    prove.
    And sure I can not say but many yeres were spent   45
With such good will so recompenst, as both we were content.
    Whereto then I me bound, and she likewise also,
The sonne should runne his course awry ere we this faith forgo.
    Who joyed then but I who had this worldes blisse?   49
Who might compare a life to mine, that never thought on this?
    But dwelling in thys truth, amid my greatest joy,
Is me befallen a greater losse than Priam had of Troy.
    She is reversed clene, and beareth me in hand
That my desertes have given her cause to break thys faithful
    band;
    And for my just excuse availeth no defense.   55
Now knowest thou all; I can no more. But shepard, hye the
    hense,
    And give him leave to die that may no lenger live.
Whose record, lo, I claim to have, my death, I doe forgive.
    And eke, when I am gone, be bolde to speake it plain:
Thou hast seen dye the truest man that ever love did pain.'   60
    Wherewith he turned him round, and gasping oft for breath,
Into his armes a tree he raught, and sayd, 'Welcome my death;
    Welcome a thousand fold, now dearer unto me
Than should, without her love to live, an emperour to be.'
    Thus, in this wofull state, he yelded up the ghost;   65
And little knoweth his lady what a lover she hath lost.
    Whose death when I beheld, no marvail was it, right
For pitie though my heart did blede, to see so piteous sight.

My blood from heat to colde oft changed wonders sore;
A thousand troubles there I found I never knew before.   70
    Twene dread and dolour so my sprites were brought in feare,
That long it was ere I could call to minde what I did there.
    But as eche thing hath end, so had these paynes of mine:
The furies past, and I my wits restord by length of time.
    Then, as I could devise, to seke I thought it best   75
Where I might finde some worthy place for such a corse to rest.
    And in my mind it came, from thence not farre away,
Where Chreseids love, king Priams sonne, the worthy Troilus
    lay.
    By him I made his tomb, in token he was treew,
And as to him belonged well, I covered it with bleew.   80
    Whose soule, by Angels power, departed not so sone
But to the heavens, lo, it fled, for to receive his dome.

17

If care do cause men cry, why do not I complaine?
If eche man do bewaile his wo, why shew I not my paine?
    Since that amongest them all, I dare well say is none
So farre from weale, so full of wo, or hath more cause to mone.
    For all thynges having life sometime have quiet rest;   5
The bering asse, the drawing oxe, and every other beast.
    The peasant and the post, that serve at al assayes,
The shyp boy and the galley slave, have time to take their ease,
    Save I, alas, whom care of force doth so constraine
To waile the day and wake the night continually in paine;   10
    From pensiveness to plaint, from plaint to bitter teares,
From teares to painful plaint againe; and thus my life it wears.
    No thing under the sunne that I can here or se,
But moveth me for to bewaile my cruell destenie.
    For wher men do rejoyce, since that I can not so,   15
I take no pleasure in that place, it doubleth but my woe.
    And when I heare the sound of song or instrument,
Me thinke eache tune there dolefull is and helpes me to lament.
    And if I se some have their most desired sight,
'Alas', think I, 'eche man hath weal save I most wofull wight.'   20

Then as the striken dere withdrawes him selfe alone,
So do I seke some secrete place where I may make my mone.
There do my flowing eyes shew forth my melting hart,
So that the stremes of those two welles right well declare my smart.
And in those cares so colde I force my selfe a heate,   25
As sick men in their shaking fittes procure them self to sweate;
With thoughtes that for the time do much appease my paine.
But yet they cause a ferther fere and brede my woe agayne.
Me thinke within my thought I se right plaine appere
My hartes delight, my sorowes leche, mine earthly goddesse
  here,   30
With every sondry grace that I have sene her have;
Thus I within my wofull brest her picture paint and grave.
And in my thought I roll her bewties to and fro;
Her laughing chere, her lovely looke, my hart that perced so;
Her strangenes when I sued her servant for to be;   35
And what she sayd, and how she smiled, when that she pitied me.
Then comes a sodaine feare that riveth all my rest
Lest absence cause forgetfulness to sink within her brest.
For when I thinke how far this earth doth us devide,
Alas, me semes love throwes me down; I fele how that I slide. 40
But then I thinke againe, why should I thus mistrust
So swete a wight, so sad and wise, that is so true and just?
For loth she was to love, and wavering is she not.
The farther of, the more desirde; thus lovers tie their knot.
So in dispaire and hope plonged am I both up an doune,   45
As is the ship with wind and wave when Neptune list to froune.
But as the watry showers delaye the raging winde,
So doth good hope clene put away dispayre out of my minde,
And biddes me for to serve and suffer pacientlie;
For what wot I the after weale that fortune willes to me?   50
For those that care do knowe, and tasted have of trouble,
When passed is their woful paine, eche joy shall seme them
  double.
And bitter sendes she now, to make me tast the better
The plesant swete, when that it comes to make it seme the sweter.
And so determine I to serve untill my brethe.   55
Ye, rather dye a thousand times then once to false my feithe.

And if my feble corps through weight of wofull smart
Do fayle or faint, my will it is that still she kepe my hart.
    And when thys carcas here to earth shalbe refarde,
I do bequeth my weried ghost to serve her afterwarde.　60

18

To dearely had I bought my grene and youthfull yeres,
If in mine age I could not finde when craft for love apperes;
    And seldom though I come in court among the rest,
Yet can I judge in colours dim as depe as can the best.
    Where grefe tormentes the man that suffreth secret smart,　5
To breke it forth unto som frend it easeth well the hart.
    So standes it now with me for my beloved frend:
This case is thine for whom I fele such torment of my minde,
    And for thy sake I burne so in my secret brest
That till thou know my hole disseyse my hart can have no
    rest.　10
    I see how thine abuse hath wrested so thy wittes
That all it yeldes to thy desire, and folowes the by fittes.
    Where thou hast loved so long with hart and all thy power,
I se thee fed with fayned wordes, thy fredom to devour.
    I know, though she say nay and would it well withstand,　15
When in her grace thou held the most, she bare the but in hand.
    I see her pleasant chere in chiefest of thy suite:
When thou art gone I se him come, that gathers up the fruite.
    And eke in thy respect I se the base degre
Of him to whom she gave the hart that promised was to the.　20
    I se, what would you more? stode never man so sure
On womans word, but wisedome would mistrust it to endure.

19

O lothsome place, where I
Have sene and herd my dere,
When in my hert her eye
Hath made her thought appere

16

By glimsing with such grace   5
As fortune it ne would
That lasten any space
Betwene us lenger should.

As fortune did avance
To further my desire,   10
Even so hath fortunes chance
Throwen all ammiddes the myre.
And that I have deserved
With true and faithful hart,
Is to his handes reserved   15
That never felt the smart.

But happy is that man
That scaped hath the griefe
That love well teache him can,
By wanting his reliefe.   20
A scourge to quiet mindes
It is, who taketh hede,
A comon plage that bindes,
A travell without mede.

This gift it hath also,   25
Who so enjoies it most,
A thousand troubles grow
To vexe his weried ghost.
And last it may not long,
The truest thing of all,   30
And sure the greatest wrong
That is within this thrall.

But sins thou, desert place,
Canst give me no accompt
Of my desired grace   35
That I to have was wont,
Farewel, thou hast me tought
To thinke me not the furst
That love hath set aloft
And casten in the dust.   40

Syns fortunes wrath envieth the welth
Wherin I raygned, by the sight
Of that that fed mine eyes by stelth
With sower, swete, dreade and delight,
Let not my griefe move you to mone,   5
For I will wepe and wayle alone.

Spite drave me into Borias raigne,
Where hory frostes the frutes do bite,
When hilles were spred and every playne
With stormy winters mantle white.   10
And yet my deare, such was my heate,
When others frese then did I swete.

And now though on the sunne I drive,
Whose fervent flame all thinges decaies,
His beames in brightnesse may not strive   15
With light of your swete golden rayes,
Nor from my brest this heate remove
The frosen thoughtes graven by love.

Ne may the waves of the salt floode
Quenche that your beauty set on fire,   20
For though mine eyes forbere the fode
That did releve the hote desire,
Such as I was such will I be,
Your owne: what would ye more of me?

Wrapt in my carelesse cloke, as I walke to and fro,
I se how love can shew what force there reigneth in his bow;
   And how he shoteth eke, a hardy hart to wound;
And where he glanceth by agayne, that litle hurt is found.
   For seldom is it sene he woundeth hartes alike;   5
The tone may rage, when tothers love is often farre to seke.

All this I se, with more; and wonder thinketh me
Howe he can strike the one so sore, and leave the other fre.
　I se that wounded wight that suffreth all this wrong,
How he is fed with yeas and nayes, and liveth all to long.　10
　In silence though I kepe such secretes to my self,
Yet do I se how she somtime doth yeld a loke by stelth,
　As though it seemd, 'Ywys, I will not lose the so',
When in her hart so swete a thought did never truely go.
　Then say I thus: 'Alas, that man is farre from blisse　15
That doth receive for his relief none other gayn but this.
　And she that fedes him so, I fele and finde it plain,
Is but to glory in her power, that over such can reign.
　Nor are such graces spent but when she thinkes that he,
A weried man, is fully bent such fansies to let flie.　20
　Then to retain him stil, she wrasteth new her grace,
And smileth, lo, as though she would forthwith the man embrace.
　But when the proofe is made to try such lokes withall,
He findeth then the place all voyde, and fraighted full of gall.
　Lorde, what abuse is this! who can such women praise　25
That for their glory do devise to use such crafty wayes!
　I that among the rest do sit, and mark the row,
Fynde that in her is greater craft then is in twenty mo,
　Whose tender yeres, alas, with wyles so well are spedde:
What will she do when hory heares are powdred in her hedde!'

22

　Gyrtt in my giltlesse gowne, as I sytt heare and sowe,
I see that thinges are not in dead as to the owtward showe.
　And who so lyst to looke and note thinges somwhat neare,
Shall fynde, where playnesse seemes to haunte, nothing but craft
　　appeare.
　For with indifferent eyes my self can well discearne　5
How som to guyd a shyppe in stormes styckes not to take the
　　stearne;
　Whose skill and connynge tryed in calme to steare a bardge,
They wolde sone shaw, yow shold sone see, it weare to great a
　　chardge.

And some I see agayne sytt still and say but small
That can do ten tymes more than they that say they can do all.   10
Whose goodlye gyftes are suche, the more they understand,
The more they seeke to learne and know and take lesse chardge
    in hand.
And to declare more playne, the tyme flyttes not so fast
But I can beare right well in mynd the song now sung and past.
The auctour whearof cam, wrapt in a craftye cloke,   15
In will to force a flamyng fyre wheare he could rayse no smoke.
If powre and will had mett, as it appeareth playne,
The truth nor right had tane no place, their vertues had bene
    vayne.
So that you may perceave, and I may saflye see,
The innocent that giltlesse is condempned sholde have be.   20
Muche lyke untruth to this the storye doth declare,
Wheare th'elders layd to Susans chardge meete matter to com-
    pare.
They did her both accuse and eke condempne her to,
And yet no reason, right, nor truthe did lead them so to do.
And she thus judged to dye, toward her death went forthe   25
Fraughted with faith a pacient pace, taking her wrong in worthe.
But he that dothe defend all those that in hym trust,
Did raise a Childe for her defence to shyeld her from th'unjust.
And Danyell chosen was then of this wrong to weete
How, in what place, and eke with whome she did this cryme
    commytt.   30
He caused the Elders part the one from th'others sight,
And did examyne one by one and chardged them bothe say
    right.
'Undra a Mulberye trye it was', fyrst sayd the one;
The next namde a pomegranate trye, whereby the truth was
    knowne.
Than Susan was dischardged, and they condempned to dye,   35
As right requeares and they deserve, that framde so fowll a lye.
And he that her preserved, and lett them of their lust,
Hath me defendyd hetherto, and will do still I trust.

O happy dames, that may embrace
The frute of your delight,
Help to bewaile the wofull case
And eke the heavy plight
Of me, that wonted to rejoyce   5
The fortune of my pleasant choyce:
Good Ladies, help to fill my moorning voyce.

In ship, freight with rememberance
Of thoughtes and pleasures past,
He sailes that hath in governance   10
My life, while it wil last;
With scalding sighes, for lack of gale,
Furdering his hope, that is his sail
Toward me, the swete port of his avail.

Alas, how oft in dreames I se   15
Those eyes, that were my food,
Which somtime so delited me,
That yet they do me good;
Wherwith I wake with his returne
Whose absent flame did make me burne.   20
But when I find the lacke, Lord how I mourne!

When other lovers in armes acrosse
Rejoyce their chief delight,
Drowned in teares to mourne my losse
I stand the bitter night   25
In my window, where I may see
Before the windes how the cloudes flee.
Lo, what a mariner love hath made me!

And in grene waves when the salt flood
Doth rise by rage of wind,   30
A thousand fansies in that mood
Assayle my restlesse mind.

Alas, now drencheth my swete fo,
That with the spoyle of my hart did go,
And left me; but, alas, why did he so?   35

And when the seas waxe calme againe,
To chase fro me annoye,
My doubtfull hope doth cause me plaine:
So dreade cuts of my joye.
Thus is my wealth mingled with wo,   40
And of ech thought a dout doth growe,
Now he comes, will he come? alas, no, no!

24

Good ladies, you that have your pleasure in exyle,
Stepp in your foote, come take a place, and mourne with me
    awhyle;
And suche as by their lords do sett but lytle pryce,
Lett them sitt still, it skills them not what chaunce come on the
    dyce.
But you whome love hath bound, by order of desyre,   5
To love your lordes, whose good desertes none other wold
    requyre,
Come youe yet once agayne, and sett your foote by myne,
Whose wofull plight, and sorowes great, no tongue may well
    defyne.
My lord and love, alas, in whome consystes my wealth,
Hath fortune sent to passe the seas, in haserd of his health.   10
That I was wontt for to embrace, contentyd myndes,
Ys now amydd the foming floodds, at pleasure of the wyndes.
Theare God hym well preserve, and safelye me hym send;
Without whiche hope, my lyf, alas, weare shortlye at an ende.
Whose absence yet, although my hope doth tell me plaine   15
With short returne he comes anon, yet ceasith not my paine.
The fearefull dreames I have, oft tymes they greeve me so
That then I wake, and stand in dowbtt yf they be trew or no.
Somtyme the roring seas, me seemes, they grow so hye,
That my sweete lorde in daunger greate, alas, doth often lye. 20

22

Another tyme, the same doth tell me he is comme,
And playng wheare I shall hym fynd with T. his lytle sonne.
  So forthe I goe apace, to see that lyfsome sight,
And with a kysse me thinckes I say, 'Now well come home, my
    knight;
  Welcome, my sweete, alas, the staye of my welfare;   25
Thye presence bringeth forthe a truce betwixt me and my care'.
  Then lyvelye doth he looke, and saluith me agayne,
And saith, 'My deare, how is it now that you have all this payne?'
  Wheare with the heavie cares, that heapt are in my brest,   29
Breake forth, and me dischardgeth cleane of all my great unrest.
  Butt when I me awayke and fynde it but a dreame,
The angwyshe of my former woe beginneth more extreme,
  And me tourmentith so that unneth may I fynde
Some hydden wheare, to steale the gryfe of my unquyet mynd.
  Thus everye waye you see with absence how I burne,   35
And for my wound no cure there is but hope of some retourne,
  Save when I feele by sower, how sweete is felt the more,
It doth abate some of my paynes that I abode before;
  And then unto my self I saye, 'When that we two shall meete,
But lyttle tyme shall seeme this payne, that joye shall be so
    sweete'.   40
  Ye wyndes, I you convart, in chiefest of your rage,
That you my lord me safelye send, my sorowes to asswage;
  And that I may not long abyde in suche excesse,
Do your good will to cure a wight that lyveth in distresse.

ETHICAL AND ELEGIAC POEMS

25

  Laid in my quyett bedd, in study as I weare,
I saw within my troubled hed a heape of thoughtes appeare;
  And every thought did shew so lyvelye in myne eyes,
That now I sight, and then I smylde, as cawse of thought did
    ryse.

23

I saw the lytle boye, in thought how ofte that he 5
Did wishe of Godd to scape the rodd, a tall yong man to be;
The yong man eke that feeles his bones with paynes opprest,
How he wold be a riche olde man, to lyve and lye att rest;
The ryche olde man, that sees his end draw on so sore,
How he wolde be a boy agayne, to lyve so moche the more. 10
Wheare at full ofte I smylde, to see how all theise three,
From boy to man, from man to boy, wold chopp and chaunge
degree;
And musinge thus, I thincke the case is very straunge,
That man from wealth, to lyve in woe, doth ever seeke to
chaunge.
Thus thoughtfull as I laye, I saw my witheryd skynne, 15
How it doth shew my dynted jawes, the flesshe was worne so
thynne,
And eke my tothelesse chapps, the gates of my right way
That opes and shuttes as I do speake, do thus unto me say:
'Thie whyte and horishe heares, the messengers of age,
That shew lyke lynes of true belief that this lif doth asswage, 20
Bides the lay hand, and feele them hanging on thie chyn;
The whiche do wryte twoe ages past, the thurd now cumming in.
Hang upp therfore the bitt of thie yonge wanton tyme,
And thow that theare in beaten art, the happyest lif defyne'.
Wheare at I sight, and said, 'Farewell, my wonted joye; 25
Trusse upp thie pack, and trudge from me to every lytle boye,
And tell them thus from me, theire tyme moste happie is,
Yf, to their tyme, they reason had to know the truthe of this'.

26

When Windesor walles sustained my wearied arme,
My hand my chyn, to ease my restless hedd,
Ech pleasant plot revested green with warm,
The blossomed bowes with lustie veare yspred,
The flowred meades, the weddyd birds so late 5
Myne eyes discovered. Than did to mynd resort
The joily woes, the hateles shorte debate,
The rakhell life that longes to loves disporte.

Wherwith, alas, myne hevy charge of care
Heapt in my brest brake forth against my will,   10
And smoky sighes that over cast the ayer.
My vapored eyes such drery teares distill
    The tender spring to quicken wher thei fall,
    And I half bent to throwe me down withall.

27

So crewell prison howe could betyde, alas,
As prowde Wyndsour, where I in lust and joye
With a kinges soon my childishe yeres did passe,
In greater feast then Priams sonnes of Troye;

Where eche swete place retournes a tast full sowre.   5
The large grene courtes, where we wer wont to hove,
With eyes cast upp unto the maydens towre,
And easye syghes, such as folke drawe in love.

The statelye sales; the ladyes bright of hewe;
The daunces short, long tales of great delight,   10
With wordes and lookes that tygers could but rewe,
Where eche of us did plead the others right.

The palme playe, where, dispoyled for the game,
With dased eyes oft we by gleames of love
Have mist the ball and got sight of our dame   15
To bayte her eyes which kept the leddes above.

The graveld ground, with sleves tyed on the helme,
On fomynge horse, with swordes and frendlye hertes,
With chere as thoughe the one should overwhelme,
Where we have fought and chased oft with dartes.   20

With sylver dropps the meades yet spredd for rewthe,
In active games of nymblenesse and strengthe
Where we dyd strayne, trayled by swarmes of youthe,
Our tender lymes, that yet shott upp in lengthe.

The secret groves, which ofte we made resound   25
Of pleasaunt playnt and of our ladyes prayes,
Recording soft what grace eche one had found,
What hope of spede, what dred of long delayes.

The wyld forest, the clothed holtes with grene,
With raynes avald and swift ybrethed horse,   30
With crye of houndes and mery blastes bitwen,
Where we did chase the fearfull hart a force.

The voyd walles eke, that harbourd us eche night;
Wherwith, alas, revive within my brest
The swete accord, such slepes as yet delight,   35
The pleasaunt dreames, the quyet bedd of rest,

The secret thoughtes imparted with such trust,
The wanton talke, the dyvers chaung of playe,
The frendshipp sworne, eche promyse kept so just,
Wherwith we past the winter nightes awaye.   40

And with this thought the blood forsakes my face,
The teares berayne my cheke of dedlye hewe;
The which, as sone as sobbing sighes, alas,
Upsupped have, thus I my playnt renewe:

'O place of blisse, renewer of my woos,   45
Geve me accompt wher is my noble fere,
Whome in thy walles thou didest eche night enclose,
To other lief, but unto me most dere.'

Eache stone, alas, that dothe my sorowe rewe,
Retournes therto a hollowe sound of playnt.   50
Thus I alone, where all my fredome grew,
In pryson pyne with bondage and restraynt,

And with remembraunce of the greater greif,
To bannishe the lesse I fynde my chief releif.

W. resteth here, that quick could never rest;
Whose heavenly giftes encreased by disdayn
And vertue sank the deper in his brest:
Such profit he by envy could obtain.

A hed, where wisdom misteries did frame; 5
Whose hammers bet styll in that lively brayn
As on a stithe, where that some work of fame
Was dayly wrought to turne to Britaines gayn.

A visage stern and myld; where bothe did grow
Vice to contemne, in vertue to rejoyce; 10
Amid great stormes whom grace assured so
To lyve upright and smile at fortunes choyce.

A hand that taught what might be sayd in ryme;
That reft Chaucer the glory of his wit;
A mark the which, unparfited for time, 15
Some may approche, but never none shall hit.

A toung that served in forein realmes his king;
Whose courteous talke to vertue did enflame
Eche noble hart; a worthy guide to bring
Our English youth by travail unto fame. 20

An eye, whose judgement none affect could blinde,
Frendes to allure, and foes to reconcile;
Whose persing loke did represent a mynde
With vertue fraught, reposed, voyd of gyle.

A hart, where drede was never so imprest 25
To hyde the thought that might the trouth avance;
In neyther fortune loft nor yet represt,
To swell in wealth, or yeld unto mischance.

A valiant corps, where force and beawty met;
Happy, alas, to happy, but for foes; 30
Lived and ran the race that nature set;
Of manhodes shape, where she the molde did lose.

But to the heavens that simple soule is fled,
Which left with such as covet Christ to know
Witnesse of faith that never shall be ded;   35
Sent for our helth, but not received so.

Thus, for our gilte, this jewel have we lost.
The earth his bones, the heavens possesse his gost.

29

Dyvers thy death doo dyverslye bemone.
Some that in presence of that livelye hedd
Lurked, whose brestes envye with hate had sowne,
Yeld Cesars teres uppon Pompeius hedd.
Some that watched with the murdrers knyfe   5
With egre thurst to drynke thy guyltless blood,
Whose practyse brake by happye end of lyfe,
Weape envyous teares to here thy fame so good.
But I that knowe what harbourd in that hedd,
What vertues rare were tempred in that brest,   10
Honour the place that such a jewell bredd,
And kysse the ground where as thy coorse doth rest
    With vaporde eyes; from whence such streames avayle
    As Pyramus did on Thisbes brest bewayle.

30

In the rude age when science was not so rife,
If Jove in Crete and other where they taught
Artes to reverte to profyte of our lyfe
Wan after deathe to have their temples sought;
If vertue yet in no unthankfull tyme   5
Fayled of some to blast her endles fame:
A goodlie meane bothe to deter from cryme
And to her steppes our sequell to enflame;
In dayes of treuthe if Wyattes frendes then waile
(The only debte that ded of quycke may clayme)   10

That rare wit spent employde to our avayle
Where Christe is tought, deserve they monnis blame?
  His livelie face thy brest how did it freate
  Whose cynders yet with envye doo the eate!

31

The great Macedon that out of Perse chasyd
Darius, of whose huge power all Asy rang,
In the rich arke if Homers rymes he placyd,
Who fayned gestes of hethen prynces sang;
What holly grave, what wourthy sepulture   5
To Wyates Psalmes shulde Christians then purchase?
Wher he dothe paynte the lyvely faythe and pure,
The stedfast hope, the swete returne to grace
Of just Davyd by parfite penytence,
Where Rewlers may se in a myrrour clere   10
The bitter frewte of false concupiscense,
How Jewry bought Uryas deathe full dere.
  In Prynces hartes Goddes scourge yprinted depe
  Myght them awake out of their synfull slepe.

32

Th'Assyryans king, in peas with fowle desyre
And filthye luste that staynd his regall harte,
In warr that should sett pryncelye hertes afyre
Vanquyshd dyd yeld for want of martyall arte.
The dent of swordes from kysses semed straunge,   5
And harder then hys ladyes syde his targe;
From glotton feastes to sowldyers fare a chaunge,
His helmet far above a garlandes charge.
Who scace the name of manhode dyd retayne,
Drenched in slouthe and womanishe delight,   10
Feble of sprete, unpacyent of payne,
When he hadd lost his honor and hys right,
  Prowde tyme of welthe, in stormes appawld with drede,
  Murdred hym selfe to shew some manfull dede.

London, hast thow accused me
  Of breche of lawes, the roote of stryfe?
  Within whose brest did boyle to see,
So fervent hotte thy dissolute lief,
  That even the hate of synnes, that groo   5
  Within thy wicked walles so rife,
For to breake forthe did convert soo
  That terrour colde it not represse.
  The which, by wordes syns prechers knoo
What hope is left for to redresse,   10
  By unknowne meanes it liked me
  My hydden burden to expresse,
Wherby yt might appere to the
  That secret synn hath secret spight;
  From justice rodd no fault is free;   15
But that all such as wourke unright
  In most quyet are next ill rest.
  In secret sylence of the night
This made me, with a reckles brest,
  To wake thy sluggardes with my bowe: 20
  A fygure of the Lordes behest,
Whose scourge for synn the Screptures shew.
  That, as the fearfull thonder clapp
  By soddayne flame at hand we knowe,
Of peoble stones the sowndles rapp   25
  The dredfull plage might mak the see
  Of Goddes wrath, that doth the enwrapp;
That pryde might know, from conscyence free,
  How loftye workes may her defend;
  And envy fynd, as he hath sought,   30
  How other seke hym to offend;
  And wrath tast of eche crewell thought
  The just shapp hyer in the end;
  And ydell slouthe, that never wrought,
  To heven hys spirite lift may begyn;   35
  And gredye lucre lyve in drede

To see what haate ill gott goodes wynn;
The lechers, ye that luste do feed,
Perceve what secrecye is in synne;
And gluttons hartes for sorow blede,   40
Awaked when their faulte they fynd.
In lothsome vyce eche dronken wight
To styrr to Godd, this was my mynd.
Thy wyndowes had don me no spight;
But prowd people that drede no fall,   45
Clothed with falshed and unright
Bred in the closures of thy wall.
But wrested to wrathe in fervent zeale
Thow hast to strief my secret call.
Endured hartes no warning feale.   50
Oh shamles hore! is dred then gone
By suche thy foes as ment thy weale?
Oh membre of false Babylon!
The shopp of craft! the denne of ire!
Thy dredfull dome drawes fast uppon.   55
Thy martyres blood, by swoord and fyre,
In Heaven and earth for justice call.
The Lord shall here their just desyre;
The flame of wrath shall on the fall;
With famyne and pest lamentablie   60
Stricken shalbe thy lecheres all;
Thy prowd towers and turretes hye,
Enmyes to God, beat stone from stone;
Thyne idolles burnt, that wrought iniquitie;
When none thy ruyne shall bemone,   65
But render unto the right wise Lord,
That so hath judged Babylon,
Imortall praise with one accord.

My Ratclif, when thy rechlesse youth offendes,
Receve thy scourge by others chastisement;
For such callyng, when it workes none amendes,
Then plages are sent without advertisement.
    Yet Salomon sayd, the wronged shall recure;   5
    But Wiat said true, the skarre doth aye endure.

35

Norfolk sprang thee, Lambeth holds thee dead,
Clere of the County of Cleremont though hight;
Within the wombe of Ormondes race thou bread,
And sawest thy cosine crowned in thy sight.
Shelton for love, Surrey for Lord thou chase: 5
Ay me, while life did last that league was tender;
Tracing whose steps thou sawest Kelsall blaze,
Laundersey burnt, and battered Bullen render.
At Muttrell gates, hopeles of all recure,
Thine Earle halfe dead gave in thy hand his Will;   10
Which cause did thee this pining death procure,
Ere Sommers four times seaven thou couldest fulfill.
    Ah Clere, if love had booted, care, or cost,
    Heaven had not wonn, nor Earth so timely lost.

36

When recheles youthe in an unquiet brest,
Set on by wrath, revenge and crueltye,
After long warr pacyens had opprest,
And justice wrought by pryncelye equitie;
My Deny, then myne errour, depe imprest,   5
Began to worke dispaire of libertye,
    Had not David, the perfyt warriour, tought
    That of my fault thus pardon shold be sought.

The soudden stormes that heave me to and froo
Had welneare perced faith, my guyding saile,
For I, that on the noble voyage goo
To succhor treuthe and falshed to assaile,
Constrayned am to beare my sayles ful loo   5
And never could attayne some pleasaunt gale,
For unto such the prosperous winds doo bloo
As ronne from porte to porte to seke availe.
This bred dispayre, whereof such doubts did groo
That I gan faint, and all my courage faile.   10
 But now, my Blage, myne errour well I see:
 Such goodlye light King David giveth me.

The stormes are past, these cloudes are overblowne,
And humble chere great rygour hath represt;
For the defaute is set a paine foreknowne,
And pacience graft in a determed brest.
And in the hart where heapes of griefes were grown   5
The swete revenge hath planted mirth and rest;
No company so pleasant as myne owne.

   . . .

Thraldom at large hath made this prison fre;
Danger well past remembred workes delight.
Of lingring doutes such hope is sprong pardie,   10
That nought I finde displeasaunt in my sight
But when my glasse presented unto me
The curelesse wound that bledeth day and night.
To think, alas, such hap should graunted be
Unto a wretch that hath no hart to fight,   15
 To spill that blood that hath so oft bene shed
 For Britannes sake, alas, and now is ded.

39

Of thy lyfe, Thomas, this compasse well mark:
Not aye with full sayles the hye seas to beat,
Ne by coward dred, in shonning stormes dark,
On shalow shores thy keel in perill freat.
Who so gladly halseth the golden meane   5
Voyde of dangers advisdly hath his home:
Not with lothsom muck, as a den uncleane,
Nor palacelyke wherat disdayn may glome.
The lofty pyne the great winde often rives;
With violenter swey falne turrets stepe;   10
Lightninges assault the hye mountains and clives.
A hart well stayd, in overthwartes depe
Hopeth amendes; in swete doth feare the sowre.
God that sendeth withdrawth winter sharp.
Now ill, not aye thus. Once Phebus to lowre   15
With bow unbent shall cease, and frame to harp
His voyce. In straite estate appere thou stout;
And so wisely, when lucky gale of winde
All thy puft sailes shall fil, loke well about,
Take in a ryft. Hast is wast, profe doth finde.   20

40

Marshall, the thinges for to attayne
The happy life be thes, I finde:
The riches left, not got with payne;
The frutfull grownd; the quyet mynde;
The equall frend; no grudge nor stryf;   5
No charge of rule nor governance;
Without disease the helthfull life;
The howshold of contynuance;
The meane dyet, no delicate fare;
Wisdom joyned with simplicitye;   10
The night discharged of all care,

Where wyne may beare no soverainty;
The chast wife wyse, without debate;
Such sleapes as may begyle the night;
Contented with thyne owne estate,   15
Neyther wisshe death nor fear his might.

41

The Aeneid, Book Two

They whisted all, with fixed face attent,
When prince Aeneas from the royal seat
Thus gan to speak: "O quene, it is thy wil
I shold renew a woe can not be told,
How that the Grekes did spoile and overthrow   5
The Phrygian wealth and wailful realm of Troy,
Those ruthfull things that I my self beheld,
And wherof no small part fel to my share.
Which to expresse, who could refraine from teres?
What Myrmidon? or yet what Dolopes?   10
What stern Ulysses waged soldiar?
And loe, moist night now from the welkin falles,
And sterres declining counsel us to rest.
But sins so great is thy delight to here
Of our mishaps, and Troyes last decay,   15
Though to record the same my minde abhorres
And plaint eschues, yet thus wil I begyn.
    The Grekes chieftains, all irked with the war
Wherin they wasted had so many yeres
And oft repulst by fatal destinie,   20
A huge hors made, hye raised like a hill,
By the divine science of Minerva;
Of cloven firre compacted were his ribbs;
For their return a fained sacrifice,
The fame wherof so wandred it at point.   25
In the dark bulk they closde bodies of men
Chosen by lot, and did enstuff by stealth
The hollow womb with armed soldiars.

There stands in sight an isle hight Tenedon,
Rich and of fame while Priams kingdom stood: 30
Now but a bay, and rode unsure for ship.
Hether them secretly the Grekes withdrew,
Shrouding themselves under the desert shore.
And, wening we they had ben fled and gone,
And with that winde had fet the land of Grece,   35
Troye discharged her long continued dole.
The gates cast up, we issued out to play,
The Grekish camp desirous to behold,
The places void and the forsaken costes.
Here Pyrrhus band, there ferce Achilles pight,   40
Here rode their shippes, there did their battells joyne.
Astonnied some the scathefull gift beheld,
Behight by vow unto the chast Minerve,
All wondring at the hugenesse of the horse.
    And fyrst of all Timoetes gan advise   45
Wythin the walles to leade and drawe the same,
And place it eke amidde the palace court:
Whether of guile, or Troyes fate it would.
Capys, wyth some of judgement more discrete,
Wild it to drown, or underset with flame   50
The suspect present of the Grekes deceit,
Or bore and gage the hollowe caves uncouth.
So diverse ranne the giddy peoples minde.
    Loe, formest of a rout that followd him,
Kindled Laocoon hasted from the towre,   55
Crieng far of, 'O wreched citezens,
What so great kind of frensie freteth you?
Deme ye the Grekes our enemies to be gone?
Or any Grekish giftes can you suppose
Devoid of guile? Is so Ulysses known?   60
Either the Grekes ar in this timber hid,
Or this an engin is to anoy our walles,
To view our tours, and overwhelme our towne.
Here lurkes some craft. Good Troyans, geve no trust
Unto this horse, for what so ever it be,   65
I dred the Grekes, yea, when they offer gyftes.'

And with that word, with all his force a dart
He launced then into that croked wombe:
Which tremling stack, and shoke within the side,
Wherwith the caves gan hollowly resound.   70
And but for faites and for our blind forcast,
The Grekes devise and guile had he discried,
Troy yet had stand, and Priams toures so hie.
    Therwyth behold, wheras the Phrygian herdes
Brought to the king with clamour, all unknown   75
A yongman, bound his handes behinde his back,
Whoe willingly had yelden prisoner
To frame his guile and open Troyes gates
Unto the Grekes, with courage fully bent
And minde determed either of the twaine: 80
To worke his feat, or willing yeld to death.
Near him, to gaze, the Troyan youth gan flock,
And strave whoe most might at the captive scorne.
The Grekes deceit beholde, and by one profe
Imagine all the rest.   85
For in the preasse as he unarmed stood,
Wyth troubled chere, and Phrigian routes beset,
'Alas,' quod he, 'what earth nowe or what seas
May me receyve? Catif, what restes me nowe?
For whom in Grece doth no abode remayne.   90
The Troians eke offended seke to wreke
Their hainous wrath wyth shedyng of my bloud.'
With this regrete our hartes from rancor moved.
The brute appeasde, we askte him of his birth,
What newes he brought, what hope made hym to yeld. 95
    Then he, al dred removed, thus began:
'O king, I shall, what ever me betide,
Say but the truth: ne first will me denie
A Grecian borne, for though fortune hath made
Sinon a wretche, she can not make him false.   100
If ever came unto your eares the name,
Nobled by fame, of the sage Palamede,
Whom traitrously the Grekes condemd to dye,
Giltlesse, by wrongfull dome, for that he dyd

Dyssuade the warres; whose death they nowe lament;　105
Underneth him my father bare of wealth
Into his band yong and nere of his blood
In my prime yeres unto the war me sent.
While that by fate his state in stay did stand,
And when his realm did florish by advise,　110
Of glory then we bare som fame and brute.
But sins his death by false Ulyssez sleight
(I speak of things to all men wel beknown)
A drery life in doleful plaint I led,
Repining at my gyltlesse frends mischaunce.　115
Ne could I, fool, refrein my tong from thretes,
That if my chaunce were ever to return
Victor to Arge, to folowe my revenge.
With such sharp words procured I great hate.
Here sprang my harm. Ulysses ever sithe　120
With new found crimes began me to affray.
In common eares false rumors gan he sowe.
Weapons of wreke his gylty minde gan seke,
Ne rested ay till he by Calchas meane—
But whereunto these thanklesse tales in vaine　125
Do I reherse, and linger fourth the time,
In like estate if all the Grekes ye price?
It is enough ye here: rid me at ones.
Ulysses, Lord, how he wold this rejoise!
Yea, and either Atride would bye it dere.'　130
　　This kindled us more egre to enquire,
And to demand the cause, without suspect
Of so great mischef thereby to ensue,
Or of Grekes craft. He then with forged words
And quivering limes thus toke his tale again:　135
　　'The Grekes oft times entended their return
From Troye town, with long warrs all ytired,
For to dislodge: which would God they had done!
But oft the winter storms of raging seas,
And oft the boisteous winds did them to stay;　140
And chiefly when of clinched ribbes of firre
This hors was made, the storms rored in the aire.

38

Then we in dout to Phebus temple sent
Euripilus, to weet the prophesye.
From whens he brought these woful news again: 145
"With blood, O Grekes, and slaughter of a maid,
Ye pleasd the winds, when first ye came to Troy.
With blood likewise ye must seke your return.
A Grekish soule must offred be therfore."
   'But when this sound had pearst the peoples eares,   150
With sodein fere astonied were their mindes;
The chilling cold did overrunne their bones,
To whom that fate was shapte, whom Phebus wold.
Ulysses then amid the preasse bringes in
Calchas with noise, and wild him to discusse   155
The gods intent. Then some gan deme to me
The cruell wrek of him that framde the craft,
Foreseing secretly what wold ensue.
In silence then, yshrowding him from sight,
But dayes twise five he whisted, and refused   160
To death by speche to further any wight.
At last, as forced by false Ulyssez crye,
Of purpose he brake fourth, assigning me
To the altar; whereto they graunted all;
And that that erst eche one dred to himself   165
Returned all unto my wretched death.
And now at hand drew nere the woful day,
All things preparde wherwyth to offer me,
Salt, corne, fillets my temples for to bind.
I scapte the deth, I graunt, and brake the bands,   170
And lurked in a marrise all the nyght,
Among the ooze, while they did set their sailes;
If it be so that they in dede so dyd.
Now restes no hope my native land to see,
My children dere, nor long desired sire,   175
On whom parchaunce they shall wreke my escape:
Those harmlesse wights shal for my fault be slayn.
   'Then, by the gods, to whom al truth is known,
By fayth unfiled, if any any where
Wyth mortal folk remaines, I thee beseche,   180

39

O king, thereby rue on my travail great:
Pitie a wretch that giltlesse suffreth wrong.'
    Life to these teres, wyth pardon eke, we graunt.
And Priam first himself commaundes to lose
His gyves, his bands, and frendly to him sayd: 185
'Whoso thou art, learn to forget the Grekes.
Hencefourth be oures; and answere me with truth.
Wherto was wrought the masse of this huge hors?
Whoes the devise? and wherto should it tend?
What holly vow? or engin for the warres?'   190
    Then he, instruct with wiles and Grekish craft,
His loosed hands lift upward to the sterrs:
'Ye everlasting lampes, I testifye,
Whoes powr divine may not be violate,
Th'altar and swerd,' quod he, 'that I have scapt,   195
Ye sacred bandes I wore as yelden hoste,
Leful be it for me to breke mine othe
To Grekes; lefull to hate their nacion;
Lefull be it to sparcle in the ayre
Their secretes all, whatsoe they kepe in close: 200
For free am I from Grece and from their lawes.
So be it Troy, and saved by me from scathe
Kepe faith with me and stand to thy behest,
If I speake truth, and opening thinges of weight
For graunt of life requite thee large amendes.   205
    'The Grekes whole hope of undertaken war
In Pallas help consisted evermore.
But sith the time that wicked Diomede,
Ulysses eke, that forger of all guile,
Aventurde from the holly sacred fane   210
For to bereve dame Pallas fatall forme,
And slew the watches of the chefest toure,
And then away the holly statue stale,
That were so bold with handes embrued in blood
The virgin goddesse veiles for to defile: 215
Sith that, their hope gan faile, their hope to fall,
Their powr appeir, their goddesse grace withdraw.
Whych with no doutfull signes she did declare.

Scarce was the statue to our tentes ybroughte,
But she gan stare with sparcled eyes of flame;   220
Along her limes the salt sweat trickled downe;
Yea, thrise her selfe (a hideous thinge to tell)
In glaunces bright she glittered from the ground,
Holding in hand her targe and quivering spere.
Calchas by sea then bad us hast our flight,   225
Whoes engins might not break the walles of Troy,
Unlesse at Greece they wold renew their lottes,
Restore the god that they by sea had brought
In warped keles. To Arge sith they be come,
They pease their godds and war afresh prepare,   230
And crosse the seas unloked for eftsones
They wil return. This order Calchas set.
   'This figure made they for th'agreved god
In Pallas stede, to clense their hainous fault.
Which masse he willed to be reared hye   235
Towards the skies, and ribbed all with oke,
So that your gates ne wall might it receive;
Ne yet your people might defensed be
By the good zele of old devotion.
For if your hands did Pallas gift defile,   240
To Priams realm great mischef shold befall
(Which fate the gods first on him self return!).
But had your owne handes brought it in your town,
Asie should passe and carrie offred warr
In Grece, even to the walles of Pelops town,   245
And we and oures that destenie endure.'
   By such like wiles of Sinon the forsworne
His tale with us did purchace credit; some
Trapt by deceite, some forced by his teres,
Whom neither Diomede nor great Achille,   250
Nor ten yeres war, ne a thousand saile could daunt.
   Us caitifes then a far more dredful chaunce
Befell, that trobled our unarmed brestes.
Whiles Laocon, that chosen was by lot
Neptunus priest, did sacrifice a bull   255
Before the holy altar, sodenly

From Tenedon, behold, in circles great
By the calme seas come fletyng adders twaine
Which plied towardes the shore (I lothe to tell)
With rered brest lift up above the seas,   260
Whoes bloody crestes aloft the waves were seen.
The hinder parte swamme hidden in the flood;
Their grisly backes were linked manifold.
With sound of broken waves they gate the strand,
With gloing eyen, tainted with blood and fire;   265
Whoes waltring tongs did lick their hissing mouthes.
We fled away, our face the blood forsoke.
But they with gate direct to Lacon ran.
And first of all eche serpent doth enwrap
The bodies small of his two tender sonnes,   270
Whoes wretched limmes they byt, and fed theron.
Then raught they hym, who had his wepon caught
To rescue them; twise winding him about,
With folded knottes and circled tailes, his wast.
Their scaled backes did compasse twise his neck,   275
Wyth rered heddes aloft and stretched throtes.
He with his handes strave to unloose the knottes;
Whose sacred fillettes all besprinkled were
With filth of gory blod and venim rank.
And to the sterres such dredfull shoutes he sent,   280
Like to the sound the roring bull fourth loowes
Which from the altar wounded doth astart,
The swarving axe when he shakes from his neck.
The serpentes twain with hasted trail they glide
To Pallas temple and her towres of heighte;   285
Under the feete of which the goddesse stern,
Hidden behinde her targettes bosse, they crept.
New gripes of dred then pearse our trembling brestes.
They sayd Lacons desertes had derely bought
His hainous dede, that pearced had with stele   290
The sacred bulk, and throwen the wicked launce.
The people cried with sondry greeing shoutes
To bring the horse to Pallas temple blive,
In hope thereby the goddesse wrath t'appease.

We cleft the walles and closures of the towne,   295
Wherto all helpe, and underset the feet
With sliding rolles, and bound his neck with ropes.
This fatall gin thus overclambe our walles,
Stuft with armd men, about the which there ran
Children and maides that holly carolles sang;   300
And well were they whoes hands might touch the cordes.
With thretning chere thus slided through our town
The subtil tree, to Pallas temple ward.
O native land! Ilion! and of the goddes
The mansion place! O warrlik walles of Troy!   305
Fowr times it stopt in th'entrie of our gate,
Fowr times the harnesse clattred in the womb.
But we goe on, unsound of memorie,
And blinded eke by rage persever still.
This fatal monster in the fane we place.   310
  Cassandra then, inspired with Phebus sprite,
Her prophetes lippes, yet never of us leeved,
Disclosed eft, forespeking thinges to come.
We wretches, loe, that last day of our life,
With bowes of fest the town and temples deck.   315
  With this the skie gan whirle about the sphere;
The cloudy night gan thicken from the sea,
With mantells spred that cloked earth and skies
And eke the treason of the Grekish guile.
The watchemen lay disperst, to take their rest,   320
Whoes werried limmes sound slepe had then opprest.
When well in order comes the Grecian fleet
From Tenedon, toward the costes well knowne,
By frendly silence of the quiet moone.
When the kinges ship put fourth his mark of fire,   325
Sinon, preserved by froward destinie,
Let fourth the Grekes enclosed in the womb;
The closures eke of pine by stealth unpind
Whereby the Grekes restored were to aire,
With joy down hasting from the hollow tree.   330
With cordes let down did slide unto the ground
The great captaines: Sthenel, and Thesander,

43

The fierce Ulisses, Athamas, and Thoas,
Machaon first, and then king Menolae,
Opeas eke that did the engin forge;   335
And streight invade the town yburied then
With wine and sleep. And first the watch is slain,
Then gates unfold to let their fellowes in:
They joyne them selves with the conjured bandes.
    It was the time when, graunted from the godds,   340
The first slepe crepes most swete in wery folk.
Loe, in my dreame before mine eies, me thought,
With rufull chere I sawe where Hector stood:
Out of whoes eies there gushed streames of teares,
Drawn at a cart as he of late had be,   345
Distained with bloody dust, whoes feet were bowlne
With the streight cordes wherwith they haled him.
Ay me, what one! that Hector how unlike,
Which erst returnd clad with Achilles spoiles,
Or when he threw into the Grekish shippes   350
The Troian flame! so was his beard defiled,
His crisped lockes al clustred with his blood,
With all such wounds as many he received
About the walls of that his native town.
Whom franckly thus me thought I spake unto,   355
With bitter teres and dolefull deadly voice:
'O Troyan light! O only hope of thine!
What lettes so long thee staid? or from what costes,
Our most desired Hector, doest thou come?
Whom, after slaughter of thy many frends,   360
And travail of thy people and thy town,
Alweried, lord, how gladly we behold!
What sory chaunce hath staind thy lively face?
Or why see I these woundes, alas so wide?'
He answeard nought, nor in my vain demaundes   365
Abode, but from the bottom of his brest
Sighing he said: 'Flee, flee, O goddesse son,
And save thee from the furie of this flame.
Our enmies now ar maisters of the walles,
And Troye town now falleth from the top.   370

44

Sufficeth that is done for Priams reigne.
If force might serve to succor Troye town,
This right hand well mought have ben her defense.
But Troye now commendeth to thy charge
Her holy reliques and her privy gods.   375
Them joyne to thee, as felowes of thy fate.
Large walles rere thow for them: for so thou shalt,
After time spent in th'overwandred flood.'
This sayd, he brought fourth Vesta in his hands,
Her fillettes eke, and everlasting flame.   380

    In this meane while, with diverse plaint the town
Throughout was spred; and lowder more and more
The din resouned, with rattling of armes
(Although mine old father Anchisez house
Removed stood, with shadow hid of trees).   385
I waked; therwith to the house top I clambe,
And harkning stood I: like as when the flame
Lightes in the corne by drift of boisteous winde,
Or the swift stream that driveth from the hill
Rootes up the feldes and presseth the ripe corne   390
And plowed ground, and overwhelmes the grove,
The silly herdman all astonnied standes,
From the hye rock while he doth here the sound.

    Then the Grekes faith, then their deceit appered.
Of Deiphobus the palace large and great   395
Fell to the ground, all overspred with flash;
His next neighbour Ucalegon afire:
The Sygean seas did glister all with flame.
Upsprang the crye of men and trompettes blast.
Then, as distraught, I did my armure on,   400
Ne could I tell yet whereto armes availde.
But with our feres to throng out from the preasse
Toward the toure our hartes brent with desire.
Wrath prickt us fourth, and unto us it semed
A semely thing to dye armd in the feld.   405

    Wherwith Panthus, scapte from the Grekish dartes,
Otreus sonne, Phebus prest, brought in hand
The sacred reliques and the vanquisht gods,

45

And in his hand his little nephew led;
And thus, as phrentik, to our gates he ran.   410
'Panthus,' quod I, 'in what estate stand we?
Or for refuge what fortresse shall we take?'
Scarse spake I this when wailing thus he sayd:
'The later day and fate of Troye is come,
The which no plaint or prayer may availe.   415
Troyans we were, and Troye was somtime,
And of great fame the Teucrian glorie erst:
Fierce Jove to Grece hath now transposed all.
The Grekes ar lords over this fired town.
Yonder huge horse that stands amid our walles   420
Sheds armed men, and Sinon, victor now,
With scorne of us doth set all things on flame.
And rushed in at our unfolded gates
Are thousands moe than ever came from Grece.
And some with weapons watch the narrow stretes,   425
With bright swerdes drawn, to slaughter redy bent.
And scarse the watches of the gate began
Them to defend, and with blinde fight resist.'
    Through Panthus words and lightning of the gods
Amid the flame and armes ran I in preasse,   430
As furie guided me, and wher as I had heard
The crye greatest that made the ayre resound.
Into our band then fell old Iphytus,
And Rypheus, that met us by moonelight;
Dymas and Hypanis joyning to our side,   435
With yong Chorebus, Mygdonius son,
Which in those dayes at Troye did arive
Burning with rage of dame Cassandraes love,
In Priams ayd and rescue of his town.
Unhappy he, that wold no credit geve   440
Unto his spouses woords of prophecie.
        Whom when I saw assembled in such wise
So desperatly the battail to desire,
Then furthermore thus sayd I unto them:
'O ye yong men, of courage stout in vaine,   445
For nought ye strive to save the burning town.

46

What cruel fortune hath betid, ye see.
The gods out of the temples all ar fled,
Through whoes might long this empire was mainteind;
Their altares eke are left both wast and voyd.   450
But if your will be bent with me to prove
That uttermost that now may us befall
Then let us dye, and runne amid our foes.
To vanquisht folk despeir is only hope.'
    With this the yongmens courage did encrease,   455
And through the dark, like to the ravening wolves
Whom raging furie of their empty mawes
Drives from their den, leaving with hungry throtes
Their whelpes behinde, among our foes we ran,
Upon their swerdes, unto apparant death;   460
Holding alway the chiefe strete of the town,
Coverd with the close shadowes of the night.
    Who can expresse the slaughter of that night,
Or tell the nomber of the corpses slaine,
Or can in teres bewaile them worthely?   465
The auncient famous citie falleth down,
That many yeres did hold such seignorie.
With senslesse bodies every strete is spred,
Eche palace, and sacred porch of the gods.
Nor yet alone the Troyan blood was shed.   470
Manhod oft times into the vanquisht brest
Returnes, wherby some victors Grekes ar slain.
Cruel complaintes and terror every where,
And plentie of grisly pictures of death.
    And first with us Androgeus there met,   475
Fellowed with a swarming rout of Grekes,
Deming us, unware, of that feloship.
With frendly words whom thus he cald unto:
'Hast ye, my frendes! what slouth hath taried yow?
Your feers now sack and spoile the burning Troy.   480
From the tall ships are ye but newly come?'
When he had sayd, and heard no answer made
To him againe, wherto he might geve trust,
Finding himself chaunced amid his foes,

47

Mazde he withdrew his foote back with his word. 485
Like him that wandring in the bushes thick
Tredes on the adder with his rechlesse foote,
Rered for wrath, swelling her speckled neck,
Dismayd, geves back al sodenly for fere:
Androgeus so, feard of that sight, stept back. 490
And we gan rush amid the thickest rout,
When here and there we did them overthrow,
Striken with dred, unskilfull of the place.
Our first labor thus lucked well with us.

   Chorebus then, encouraged by his chaunce, 495
Rejoysing sayd: 'Hold fourth the way of health,
My feers, that hap and manhod hath us taught.
Change we our shields; the Grekes arms do we on.
Craft or manhod with foes, what reckes it which?
The slaine to us their armure they shall yeld.' 500
And with that word Androgeus crested helme
And the rich armes of his shield did he on;
A Grekish swerd he girded by his side.
Like gladly Dimas and Ripheus did.
The whole youth gan them clad in the new spoiles. 505
Mingled with Grekes, for no good luck to us,
We went, and gave many onsets that night,
And many a Greke we sent to Plutoes court.
Other there fled and hasted to their ships,
And to their costes of savegard ran againe. 510
And some there were, for shamefull cowardrie,
Clambe up againe unto the hugie horse,
And did them hide in his wellknowen womb.

   Ay me, bootelesse it is for any whight
To hope on ought against will of the gods. 515
Loe, where Cassandra, Priams daughter dere,
From Pallas chirch was drawn with sparkled tresse,
Lifting in vain her flaming eyen to heven:
Her eyen, for fast her tender wrestes were bound.
Which sight Chorebus raging could not bere, 520
Recklesse of death, but thrust amid the throng,
And after we through thickest of the swerdes.

Here were we first ybatred with the dartes
Of our own feers, from the hye temples top;
Wherby of us grete slaughter did ensue,   525
Mistaken by our Grekish armes and crestes.
Then flockt the Grekes moved with wrath and ire
Of the virgin from them so rescued:
The fell Ajax, and either Atrides,
And the great band cleped the Dolopes.   530
As wrastling windes, out of dispersed whirl,
Befight themselves, the west with southern blast,
And gladsome east proud of Auroraes horse;
The woods do whiz; and fomy Nereus,
Raging in furie, with threeforked mace   535
From bottoms depth doth weltre up the seas:
So came the Grekes. And such, as by deceit
We sparkled erst in shadow of the night,
And drave about our town, appered first.
Our fained shields and wepons then they found,   540
And by sound our discording voice they knew.
We went to wreck, with nomber overlayd.
And by the hand of Peneleus first
Chorebus fel before the altar dead
Of armed Pallas, and Rhypheus eke,   545
The justest man among the Troians all,
And he that best observed equitie.
But otherwise it pleased now the gods.
There Hipanis and Dimas both were slaine,
Throughpearced with the weapons of their feers.   550
Nor thee, Panthus, when thou wast overthrown,
Pitie, nor zele of good devocion,
Nor habit yet of Phebus hid from scathe.
Ye Troyan ashes, and last flames of mine,
I cal in witnesse, that at your last fall   555
I fled no stroke of any Grekish swerd,
And if the fates wold I had fallen in fight,
That with my hand I did deserve it wel.
With this from thense I was reculed back,
With Iphytus and Pelias alone: 560

Iphytus weke and feble all for age,
Pelias lamed by Ulissez hand.
To Priams palace crye did cal us then.
Here was the fight right hideous to behold,
As though there had no battail ben but there,   565
Or slaughter made els where throughout the town.
A fight of rage and furie there we saw.
The Grekes toward the palace rushed fast,
And, coverd with engines, the gates beset,
And rered up ladders against the walles;   570
Under the windowes scaling by their steppes,
Fenced with sheldes in their left hands, wheron
They did receive the dartes, while their right hands
Griped for hold th'embatel of the wall.
The Troyans on the tother part rend down   575
The turrets hye and eke the palace roofe:
With such weapons they shope them to defend,
Seing al lost, now at the point of death.
The gilt sparres and the beames then threw they down,
Of old fathers the proud and royal workes.   580
And with drawn swerds some did beset the gates,
Which they did watch, and kepe in routes full thick.
Our sprites restorde to rescue the kings house,
To help them, and to geve the vanquisht strength.

  A postern with a blinde wicket there was,   585
A common trade to passe through Priams house,
On the backside wherof wast houses stood:
Which way eftsithes, while that our kingdome dured,
Th'infortunate Andromache alone
Resorted to the parents of her make,   590
With yong Astyanax, his grandsire to see.
Here passed I up to the hyest toure,
From whense the wretched Troyans did throw down
Dartes, spent in wast. Unto a turret then
We stept, the which stood in a place aloft,   595
The top wherof did reache wellnere the sterres,
Where we were wont all Troye to behold,
The Grekish navie, and their tentes also.

With instrumentes of iron gan we pick,
To seke where we might finde the joyning shronk;   600
From that high seat which we razed and threw down:
Which falling gave fourthwith a rushing sound,
And large in breadth on Grekish routes it light.
But sone an other sort stept in theyr stede;
No stone unthrown, nor yet no dart uncast.   605
   Before the gate stood Pyrrhus in the porch
Rejoysing in his dartes, with glittring armes;
Like to the adder with venimous herbes fed,
Whom cold winter all bolne hid under ground,
And shining bright when she her slough had slong   610
Her slipper back doth rowle, with forked tong
And raised brest lift up against the sun.
With that together came great Periphas;
Automedon eke, that guided had somtime
Achilles horse, now Pyrrhus armure bare;   615
And eke with him the warlike Scyrian youth
Assayld the house, and threw flame to the top.
And he an axe before the formest raught,
Wherwith he gan the strong gates hew and break;
From whens he bet the staples out of brasse,   620
He brake the barres, and through the timber pearst
So large a hole wherby they might discerne
The house, the court, the secret chambers eke
Of Priamus and auncient kings of Troy,
And armed foes in th'entrie of the gate.   625
   But the palace within confounded was
With wayling, and with rufull shrikes and cryes;
The hollow halles did howle of womens plaint.
The clamor strake up to the golden sterres.
The frayd mothers, wandring through the wide house,   630
Embracing pillers, did them hold and kisse.
Pyrrhus assaileth with his fathers might,
Whom the closures ne kepers might hold out.
With often pushed ram the gate did shake;
The postes beat down, removed from their hookes.   635
By force they made the way, and th'entrie brake.

And now the Grekes let in, the formest slew,
And the large palace with soldiars gan to fill.
Not so fercely doth overflow the feldes
The foming flood, that brekes out of his bankes,   640
Whoes rage of waters beares away what heapes
Stand in his way, the coates, and eke the herdes,
As in th'entrie of slaughter furious
I saw Pyrrhus and either Atrides.

    There Hecuba I saw, with a hundred moe   645
Of her sons wyves, and Priam at the altar,
Sprinkling with blood his flame of sacrifice.
Fiftie bedchambers of his childrens wyves,
With losse of so great hope of his ofspring,
The pillers eke proudly beset with gold   650
And with the spoiles of other nations,
Fell to the ground; and whatso that with flame
Untouched was, the Grekes did all possesse.

    Parcase yow wold ask what was Priams fate.
When of his taken town he saw the chaunce,   655
And the gates of his palace beaten down,
His foes amid his secret chambers eke,
Th'old man in vaine did on his sholders then,
Trembling for age, his curace long disused,
His bootelesse swerd he girded him about,   660
And ran amid his foes ready to die.

    Amid the court under the heven all bare
A great altar there stood, by which there grew
An old laurel tree, bowing therunto,
Which with his shadow did embrace the gods.   665
Here Hecuba with her yong daughters all
About the altar swarmed were in vaine,
Like doves that flock together in the storme;
The statues of the gods embracing fast.
But when she saw Priam had taken there   670
His armure, like as though he had ben yong,
'What furious thought, my wretched spouse,' quod she,
'Did move thee now such wepons for to weld?
Why hastest thow? This time doth not require

Such succor, ne yet such defenders now; 675
No, though Hector my son were here againe.
Come hether; this altar shall save us all,
Or we shall dye together.' Thus she sayd.
Wherwith she drew him back to her, and set
The aged man down in the holy seat. 680
   But loe, Polites, one of Priams sons,
Escaped from the slaughter of Pyrrhus,
Comes fleing through the wepons of his foes,
Searching all wounded the long galleries
And the voyd courtes; whom Pyrrhus all in rage 685
Followed fast to reach a mortal wound,
And now in hand wellnere strikes with his spere.
Who fleing fourth till he came now in sight
Of his parentes, before their face fell down,
Yelding the ghost, with flowing streames of blood. 690
Priamus then, although he were half ded,
Might not kepe in his wrath, nor yet his words,
But cryeth out: 'For this thy wicked work,
And boldnesse eke such thing to enterprise,
If in the heavens any justice be 695
That of such things takes any care or kepe,
According thankes the gods may yeld to thee,
And send thee eke thy just deserved hyre,
That made me see the slaughter of my childe,
And with his blood defile the fathers face. 700
But he, by whom thow fainst thy self begot,
Achilles, was to Priam not so stern.
For loe, he tendring my most humble sute
The right and faith, my Hectors bloodlesse corps
Rendred for to be layd in sepulture, 705
And sent me to my kingdome home againe.'
Thus sayd the aged man, and therewithall
Forcelesse he cast his weake unweldy dart,
Which, repulst from the brasse where it gave dint,
Without sound hong vainly in the shieldes bosse. 710
Quod Pyrrhus: 'Then thow shalt this thing report.
On message to Pelide my father go.

53

Shew unto him my cruel dedes, and how
Neoptolem is swarved out of kinde.
Now shalt thow dye,' quod he. And with that word   715
At the altar him trembling gan he draw
Wallowing through the blodshed of his son;
And his left hand all clasped in his heare,
With his right arme drewe fourth his shining sword,
Which in his side he thrust up to the hilts.   720
Of Priamus this was the fatal fine,
The wofull end that was alotted him.
When he had seen his palace all on flame,
With ruine of his Troyan turrets eke,
That royal prince of Asie, which of late   725
Reignd over so many peoples and realmes,
Like a great stock now lieth on the shore;
His hed and sholders parted ben in twaine,
A body now without renome and fame.
    Then first in me entred the grisly feare.   730
Dismayd I was. Wherwith came to my minde
The image eke of my dere father, when
I thus beheld the king of equal age
Yeld up the sprite with wounds so cruelly.
Then thought I of Creusa left alone,   735
And of my house in danger of the spoile,
And the estate of young Iulus eke.
I looked back to seke what nomber then
I might discern about me of my feeres;
But weried they had left me all alone.   740
Some to the ground were lopen from above,
Some in the flame their irked bodies cast.
    There was no moe but I left of them all,
When that I saw in Vestaes temple sit
Dame Helen, lurking in a secret place   745
(Such light the flame did give as I went by,
While here and there I cast mine eyen about)
For she in dred least that the Troians shold
Revenge on her the ruine of their walles,
And of the Grekes the cruel wrekes also,   750

The furie eke of her forsaken make,
The common bane of Troy, and eke of Grece,
Hateful she sate beside the altars hid.
Then boyld my brest with flame and burning wrath
To revenge my town unto such ruine brought,   755
With worthy peines on her to work my will.
Thought I: 'Shall she passe to the land of Spart
All safe, and see Mycene her native land,
And like a quene returne with victorie
Home to her spouse, her parentes, and children,   760
Folowed with a traine of Troyan maides,
And served with a band of Phrigian slaves;
And Priam eke with iron murdred thus,
And Troy town consumed all with flame,
Whoes shore hath ben so oft forbathed in blood?   765
No, no: for though on wemen the revenge
Unsemely is, such conquest hath no fame,
To geve an end unto such mischief yet
My just revenge shal merit worthy praise;
And quiet eke my minde, for to be wroke   770
On her which was the causer of this flame,
And satisfie the cinder of my feers.'
    With furious minde while I did argue thus,
My blessed mother then appeard to me,
Whom erst so bright mine eyes had never seen,   775
And with pure light she glistred in the night,
Disclosing her in forme a goddesse like,
As she doth seme to such as dwell in heven.
My right hand then she toke, and held it fast,
And with her rosie lips thus did she say: 780
'Son, what furie hath thus provoked thee
To such untamed wrath? what ragest thou?
Or where is now become the care of us?
Wilt thou not first go see where thou hast left
Anchises, thy father fordone with age?   785
Doth Creusa live, and Ascanius thy son?
Whom now the Grekish bands have round beset,
And were they not defensed by my cure,

55

Flame had them raught and enmies swerd ere this.
Not Helens beautie hatefull unto thee,   790
Nor blamed Paris yet, but the gods wrath
Reft yow this wealth, and overthrew your town.
Behold, and I shall now the cloude remove
Which overcast thy mortal sight doth dim,
Whoes moisture doth obscure all thinges about: 795
And fere not thow to do thy mothers will,
Nor her advise refuse thow to performe.
Here where thow seest the turrets overthrown,
Stone bet from stone, smoke rising mixt with dust,
Neptunus there shakes with his mace the walles   800
And eke the loose foundations of the same,
And overwhelms the whole town from his seat.
And cruell Juno with the formest here
Doth kepe the gate that Scea cleped is,
Nere wood for wrath, whereas she standes, and calls   805
In harnesse bright the Grekes out of their ships.
And in the turrets hye behold where standes
Bright shining Pallas, all in warlike wede,
And with her shield where Gorgons hed apperes.
And Jupiter my father distributes   810
Avayling strength and courage to the Grekes;
Yet overmore, against the Troyan powr,
He doth provoke the rest of all the gods.
Flee then, my son, and geve this travail end.
Ne shall I thee forsake, in savegard till   815
I have thee brought unto thy fathers gate.'
This did she say; and therwith gan she hide
Her self in shadow of the close night.
    Then dredfull figures gan appere to me,
And great gods eke agreved with our town.   820
I saw Troye fall down in burning gledes,
Neptunus town clene razed from the soil.
Like as the elm forgrown in mountaines hye,
Rond hewen with axe, that husbandmen
With thick assaultes strive to teare up, doth threat;   825
And hackt beneath trembling doth bend his top,

56

Till yold with strokes, geving the latter crack,
Rent from the heighth with ruine it doth fall.
   With this I went, and guided by a god
I passed through my foes and eke the flame: 830
Their wepons and the fire eke gave me place.
And when that I was come before the gates
And auncient building of my fathers house,
My father, whom I hoped to convey
To the next hils, and did him thearto treat,   835
Refused either to prolong his life
Or bide exile after the fall of Troy.
'All ye', quod he, 'in whom yong blood is fresh,
Whose strength remaines entier and in full powr,
Take ye your flight.   840
For if the gods my life wold have proroged,
They had reserved for me this wonning place.
It was enough, alas, and eke to much,
To see the town of Troy thus razed ones,
To have lived after the citee taken.   845
When ye have sayd, this corps layd out forsake.
My hand shall seke my death, and pitie shal
Mine enmies move, or els hope of my spoile.
As for my grave, I wey the losse but light:
For I my yeres, disdainfull to the gods,   850
Have lingred fourth, unable to all nedes,
Sins that the sire of gods and king of men
Strake me with thonder and with levening blast.'
Such things he gan reherse, thus firmly bent.
But we besprent with teres; my tender son,   855
And eke my swete Creusa, with the rest
Of the houshold, my father gan beseche
Not so with him to perish all at ones,
Nor so to yeld unto the cruel fate.
Which he refused, and stack to his entent.   860
   Driven I was to harnesse then againe,
Miserably my death for to desire.
For what advise or other hope was left?
'Father, thoughtst thow that I may ones remove,'

Quod I, 'a foote, and leave thee here behinde? 865
May such a wrong passe from a fathers mouth?
If gods will be, that nothing here be saved
Of this great town, and thy minde bent to joyne
Both thee and thine to ruine of this town,
The way is plaine this death for to atteine. 870
Pyrrhus shall come besprent with Priams blood,
That gored the son before the fathers face,
And slew the father at the altar eke.
O sacred mother, was it then for this
That you me led through flame and wepons sharp, 875
That I might in my secret chaumber see
Mine enmies; and Ascanius my son,
My father, with Creusa my swete wife,
Murdred, alas, the one in th'others blood?
Why, servants, then, bring me my armes againe. 880
The latter day us vanquished doth call.
Render me now to the Grekes sight againe,
And let me see the fight begon of new.
We shall not all unwroken dye this day.'
   About me then I girt my swerd again, 885
And eke my shield on my left sholder cast,
And bent me so to rush out of the house.
Lo, in my gate my spouse, clasping my feet,
Foregainst his father yong Iulus set.
'If thow wilt go,' quod she, 'and spill thy self, 890
Take us with thee in all that may betide.
But as expert if thow in armes have set
Yet any hope, then first this house defend,
Whearas thy son, and eke thy father dere,
And I, somtime thine owne dere wife, ar left.' 895
Her shrill loud voice with plaint thus filld the house,
When that a sodein monstrous marvel fell.
For in their sight and woefull parents armes,
Behold, a light out of the butten sprang
That in the tip of Iulus cap did stand; 900
With gentle touch whoes harmlesse flame did shine
Upon his heare, about his temples spred.

And we afraid, trembling for dredfull fere,
Bet out the fire from his blasing tresse,
And with water gan quench the sacred flame.   905
Anchises glad his eyen lift to the sterres;
With handes his voice to heaven thus he bent:
'If by praier, almighty Jupiter,
Inclined thou mayst be, beholde us then
Of ruth; at least, if we so much deserve.   910
Graunt eke thine ayd, father, confirm this thing.'
    Scarse had the old man said, when that the hevens
With sodein noise thondred on the left hand.
Out of the skie, by the dark night there fell
A blasing sterre, dragging a brand of flame,   915
Which, with much light gliding on the house top,
In the forest of Ida hid her beames;
The which full bright cendleing a furrow shone,
By a long tract appointing us the way.
And round about of brimstone rose a fume.   920
    My father vanquist, then beheld the skies,
Spake to the gods, and th'holly sterre adored.
'Now, now,' quod he, 'no longer I abide.
Folow I shall where ye me guide at hand.
O native gods, your familie defend!   925
Preserve your line! This warning comes of you,
And Troy stands in your protection now.
Now geve I place, and wherso that thou goe
Refuse I not, my sonne, to be thy feer.'
    This did he say; and by that time more clere   930
The cracking flame was heard throughout the walles,
And more and more the burning heat drew nere.
'Why then, have done, my father dere,' quod I,
'Bestride my neck fourthwith, and sit theron,
And I shall with my sholders thee susteine;   935
Ne shal this labor do me any dere.
What so betide, come perill come welfare,
Like to us both and common there shal be.
Yong Iulus shall beare me company,
And my wife shal follow far of my steppes.   940

Now ye, my servantes, mark well what I say.
Without the town ye shall find, on an hill,
An old temple there standes, wheras somtime
Worship was don to Ceres the goddesse;
Biside which growes an aged cipresse tree,   945
Preserved long by our forefathers zele.
Behind which place let us together mete.
And thou, father, receive into thy handes
The reliques all, and the gods of the land,
The which it were not lawfull I should touch,   950
That come but late from slaughter and bloodshed,
Till I be washed in the running flood.'
    When I had sayd these wordes, my sholders brode
And laied neck with garments gan I spred,
And theron cast a yellow lions skin,   955
And therupon my burden I receive.
Yong Iulus, clasped in my right hand,
Followeth me fast with unegal pace,
And at my back my wife. Thus did we passe
By places shadowed most with the night.   960
And me, whom late the dart which enemies threw
Nor preasse of Argive routes could make amazde,
Eche whispring wind hath power now to fray,
And every sound to move my doutfull mind,
So much I dred my burden and my feer.   965
    And now we gan draw nere unto the gate,
Right well escapte the daunger, as me thought,
When that at hand a sound of feet we heard.
My father then, gazing throughout the dark,
Cried on me, 'Flee, son! They ar at hand.'   970
With that bright shelds and shene armours I saw.
But then I knowe not what unfrendly god
My trobled wit from me biraft for fere.
For while I ran by the most secret stretes,
Eschuing still the common haunted track,   975
From me catif, alas, bereved was
Creusa then, my spouse, I wot not how,
Whether by fate, or missing of the way,

Or that she was by werinesse reteind.
But never sithe these eies might her behold,   980
Nor did I yet perceive that she was lost,
Ne never backward turned I my mind,
Till we came to the hill wheras there stood
The old temple dedicate to Ceres.

   And when that we were there assembled all,   985
She was only away, deceiving us,
Her spouse, her son, and all her compainie.
What god or man did I not then accuse,
Nere wood for ire? or what more cruell chaunce
Did hap to me in all Troies overthrow?   990
Ascanius to my feeres I then betoke,
With Anchises, and eke the Troian gods,
And left them hid within a valley depe.
And to the town I gan me hye againe,
Clad in bright armes, and bent for to renew   995
Aventures past, to search throughout the town,
And yeld my hed to perils ones againe.

   And first the walles and dark entrie I sought
Of the same gate wherat I issued out,
Holding backward the steppes where we had come   1000
In the dark night, loking all round about.
In every place the ugsome sightes I saw,
The silence selfe of night agast my sprite.
From hense againe I past unto our house,
If she by chaunce had ben returned home.   1005
The Grekes were there, and had it all beset.
The wasting fire blown up by drift of wind
Above the roofes; the blazing flame sprang up,
The sound wherof with furie pearst the skies.
To Priams palace and the castel then   1010
I made; and there at Junous sanctuair,
In the void porches, Phenix, Ulisses eke,
Sterne guardens stood, watching of the spoile.
The richesse here were set, reft from the brent
Temples of Troy; the tables of the gods,   1015
The vessells eke that were of massy gold,

And vestures spoild, were gatherd all in heap.
The children orderly and mothers pale for fright
Long ranged on a rowe stode round about.
    So bold was I to showe my voice that night,   1020
With clepes and cries to fill the stretes throughout,
With Creuse name in sorrow, with vain teres,
And often sithes the same for to repete.
The town restlesse with furie as I sought,
Th'unlucky figure of Creusaes ghost,   1025
Of stature more than wont, stood fore mine eyen.
Abashed then I woxe. Therwith my heare
Gan start right up, my voice stack in my throte.
When with such words she gan my hart remove:
'What helps to yeld unto such furious rage,   1030
Sweet spouse?' quod she. 'Without wil of the gods
This chaunced not; ne lefull was for thee
To lead away Creusa hense with thee:
The king of the hye heven suffreth it not.
A long exile thou art assigned to bere,   1035
Long to furrow large space of stormy seas:
So shalt thou reach at last Hesperian land,
Wher Lidian Tiber with his gentle streme
Mildly doth flow along the frutfull felds.
There mirthful wealth, there kingdom is for thee,   1040
There a kinges child preparde to be thy make.
For thy beloved Creusa stint thy teres.
For now shal I not see the proud abodes
Of Myrmidons, nor yet of Dolopes;
Ne I, a Troyan lady and the wife   1045
Unto the sonne of Venus the goddesse,
Shall goe a slave to serve the Grekish dames.
Me here the gods great mother holdes.
And now farwell, and kepe in fathers brest
The tender love of thy yong son and myne.'   1050
    This having said, she left me all in teres,
And minding much to speake; but she was gone,
And suttly fled into the weightlesse aire.
Thrise raught I with mine arms t'accoll her neck,

Thrise did my handes vaine hold th'image escape,   1055
Like nimble windes, and like the flieng dreame.
So night spent out, returne I to my feers.
And ther wondring I find together swarmd
A new nomber of mates, mothers and men,
A rout exiled, a wreched multitude,   1060
From eche where flockte together, prest to passe,
With hart and goods, to whatsoever land
By sliding seas me listed them to lede.
And now rose Lucifer above the ridge
Of lusty Ide, and brought the dawning light.   1065
The Grekes held th'entries of the gates beset;
Of help there was no hope. Then gave I place,
Toke up my sire, and hasted to the hill."

42

The Aeneid, Book Four

But now the wounded quene with hevy care,
Throughout the veines she norisheth the playe,
Surprised with blind flame; and to hir mind
Gan eke resort the prowesse of the man
And honour of his race; while in her brest   5
Imprinted stack his wordes and pictures forme;
Ne to her limmes care graunteth quiet rest.
The next morow with Phebus laump the earth
Alightned clere, and eke the dawning day
The shadowes dank gan from the poale remove,   10
When all unsound her sister of like minde
Thus spake she to: 'O sister Ann, what dreames
Be these, that me tormented thus afray?
What new guest is this that to our realm is come?
What one of chere! how stout of hart in armes!   15
Truly I think (ne vain is my belefe)
Of goddish race some offspring shold he be:
Cowardry notes hartes swarved out of kind.
He driven, Lord, with how hard destiny!

What battailes eke atchived did he recount! 20
But that my mind is fixt unmoveably
Never with wight in wedlock ay to joyne
Sith my first love me left by death dissevered,
If geniall brands and bed me lothed not,
To this one gilt perchaunce yet might I yeld. 25
Anne, for I graunt, sith wretched Sichees death
My spouse, and house with brothers slaughter staind,
This onely man hath made my sences bend
And pricked foorth the mind that gan to slide.
Now feelingly I tast the steppes of mine old flame. 30
But first I wish the earth me swalow down,
Or with thunder the mighty Lord me send
To the pale gostes of hel and darknes deepe,
Ere I thee staine, shamefastnes, or thy lawes.
He that with me first coppled, tooke away 35
My love with him; enjoy it in his grave.'
  Thus did she say, and with supprised teares
Bained her brest. Wherto Anne thus replied:
'O sister, dearer beloved than the lyght,
Thy youth alone in plaint still wilt thou spill? 40
Ne children sweete, ne Venus giftes wilt know?
Cinders, thinkest thou, mind this? or graved ghostes?
Time of thy doole, thy spouse new dead, I graunt
None might the move: no, not the Libian king
Nor yet of Tire, Iarbas set so light, 45
And other princes mo whom the rich soile
Of Affrick breedes in honours triumphant.
Wilt thou also gainstand thy liked love?
Comes not to mind upon whoes land thou dwelst?
On this side, loe, the Getule town behold, 50
A people bold, unvanquished in warre;
Eke the undaunted Numides compasse thee;
Also the Sirtes, unfrendly harbroughe;
On th'other hand, a desert realme for thurst,
The Barceans, whose fury stretcheth wide. 55
What shall I touch the warres that move from Tire?
Or yet thy brothers threates?

By Gods purveiaunce it blewe, and Junos helpe,
The Troyaynes shippes, I think, to runn this course.
Sister, what town shalt thou see this become!   60
Throgh such allie how shal our kingdom rise!
And by the aid of Troyane armes how great!
How many wayes shal Cartages glorie grow!
Thou onely now besech the gods of grace
By sacrifice: which ended, to thy house   65
Receve him, and forge causes of abode;
Whiles winter frettes the seas, and watry Orion,
The shippes shaken, unfrendly the season.'
    Such wordes enflamed the kindled mind with love,
Loosed al shame, and gave the doubtfull hope.   70
And to the temples first they hast, and seeke
By sacrifice for grace, with hogreles of two yeares
Chosen, as ought, to Ceres that gave lawes,
To Phebus, Bachus, and to Juno chiefe
Which hath in care the bandes of mariage.   75
Faire Dido held in her right hand the cup,
Which twixt the hornes of a white cowe she shed
In presence of the gods, passing before
The aulters fatte, which she renewed oft
With giftes that day and beastes deboweled,   80
Gasing for counsell on the entrales warme.
Ay me, unskilfull mindes of prophesy!
Temples or vowes, what boote they in her rage?
A gentle flame the mary doth devoure,
Whiles in the brest the silent wound keepes life.   85
Unhappy Dido burns, and in her rage
Throughout the town she wandreth up and down,
Like to the striken hinde with shaft in Crete
Throughout the woods which chasing with his dartes
Aloofe, the shepheard smiteth at unwares   90
And leaves unwist in her the thirling head,
That through the groves and landes glides in her flight;
Amid whose side the mortall arrow stickes.
    Aeneas now about the walles she leades,
The town prepared and Cartage welth to shew.   95

Offring to speak, amid her voice, she whistes.
And when the day gan faile, new feastes she makes;
The Troyes travales to heare anew she listes
Inraged al, and stareth in his face
That tels the tale. And when they were al gone   100
And the dimme mone doth eft withold the light,
And sliding starres provoked unto sleepe,
Alone she mournes within her palace voide,
And sets her down on her forsaken bed.
And absent him she heares, when he is gone,   105
And seeth eke. Oft in her lappe she holdes
Ascanius, trapt by his fathers forme,
So to begile the love cannot be told.
   The turrettes now arise not, erst begonne;
Neither the youth weldes armes, nor they avaunce   110
The portes, nor other mete defence for warr.
Broken there hang the workes and mighty frames
Of walles high raised, threatning the skie.
Whom assoone as Joves deare wife sawe infect
With such a plage, ne fame resist the rage,   115
Saturnes daughter thus burdes Venus then:
'Great praise,' quod she, 'and worthy spoiles you win,
You and your son, great gods of memory,
By both your wiles one woman to devower.
Yet am not I deceived, that foreknew   120
Ye dread our walles and bildinges gan suspect
Of high Cartage. But what shalbe the ende?
Or wherunto now serveth such debate?
But rather peace and bridale bandes knit we,
Sith thou hast spede of that thy heart desired: 125
Dido doth burne with love, rage fretes her boones.
This people now, as common to us both,
With equal favour let us governe then.
Lefull be it to serve a Troyan spouse,
And Tirianes yeld to thy right hand in dowre.'   130
   To whom Venus replied thus, that knewe
Her wordes proceded from a fained minde,
To Libian coastes to turne th'empire from Rome:

'What wight so fond such offer to refuse?
Or yet with thee had lever strive in warr?   135
So be it fortune thy tale bring to effect.
But destenies I doubt: least Jove nill graunt
That folke of Tyre and such as came from Troye
Should hold one town, or graunt these nacions
Mingled to be, or joyned ay in leage.   140
Thou art his wife; lefull it is for the
For to attempt his fansie by request.
Passe on before and folow the I shall.'
    Quene Juno then thus tooke her tale againe:
'This travaile be it mine: but by what meane   145
Marke, in fewe wordes I shal thee lerne eftsones
This worke in hand may now be compassed.
Aeneas nowe and wretched Dido eke
To the forest a hunting minde to wende,
To morne as soon as Titan shall ascend   150
And with his beames hath overspred the world.
And whiles the winges of youth do swarm about,
And whiles they raunge to over set the groves,
A cloudie showr mingled with haile I shall
Poure down, and then with thonder shake the skies.   155
Th'assemble scattered the mist shall cloke.
Dido a cave, the Troyan prince the same
Shall enter to; and I will be at hand.
And if thy will sticke unto mine, I shall
In wedlocke sure knit and make her his own.   160
Thus shall the maryage be.' To whose request
Without debate Venus did seme to yeld,
And smyled soft, as she that found the wyle.
    Then from the seas the dawning gan arise.
The sun once up, the chosen youth gan throng   165
Out at the gates: the hayes so rarely knit,
The hunting staves with their brod heads of steele,
And of Masile the horsemen fourth they brake;
Of senting houndes a kenel huge likewise.
And at the threshold of her chaumber dore   170
The Carthage lords did on the quene attend.

67

The trampling steede with gold and purple trapt,
Chawing the fomie bit, there fercely stood.
Then issued she, awayted with great train,
Clad in a cloke of Tyre embradred riche.   175
Her quyver hung behinde her backe, her tresse
Knotted in gold, her purple vesture eke
Butned with gold. The Troyans of her train
Before her go, with gladsome Iulus.
Aeneas eke, the goodliest of the route,   180
Makes one of them, and joyneth close the throngs:
Like when Apollo leaveth Lycia,
His wintring place, and Xanthus floods likewise,
To viset Delos his mothers mansion,
Repairing eft and furnishing her quire;   185
The Candians and folkes of Driopes
With painted Agathyrsies shoute and crye
Environing the alters roundabout,
When that he walks upon mount Cynthus top:
His sparkled tresse represt with garlandes soft   190
Of tender leaves, and trussed up in gold;
His quivering dartes clattring behinde his back:
So fresh and lustie did Aeneas seme,
Such lordly port in countenaunce present.

    But to the hils and wilde holtes when they came   195
From the rocks top the driven savage rose,
Loe from the hill above on th'other side
Through the wyde lawnds they gan to take their course.
The harts likewise, in troupes taking their flight,
Raysing the dust, the mountain fast forsake.   200
The childe Iulus, blithe of his swift steede,
Amids the plain now pricks by them, now thes,
And to encounter wisheth oft in minde
The foming bore in steede of ferefull beasts,
Or lion brown might from the hill descend.   205

    In the meane while the skies gan rumble sore;
In tayle therof a mingled showr with hayle.
The Tyrian folk and eke the Troyans youth
And Venus nephew the cotages for feare

Sought round about; the floods fell from the hils.   210
Dido a den, the Troyan prince the same,
Chaunced upon. Our mother then the earth,
And Juno that hath charge of mariage,
First tokens gave with burning gledes of flame,
And privie to the wedlock lightning skies;   215
And the nymphes yelled from the mountains top.
Ay me, this was the first day of their mirth,
And of their harmes the first occasion eke.
Respect of fame no longer her withholdes,
Nor museth now to frame her love by stelth.   220
Wedlock she cals it; under the pretence
Of which fayre name she cloketh now her faut.
   Forthwith Fame flieth through the great Libian towns:
A mischefe Fame, there is none els so swift:
That moving growes, and flitting gathers force;   225
First small for dred, sone after climes the skies,
Stayeth on earth, and hides her hed in cloudes.
Whom our mother the earth, tempted by wrath
Of gods, begat: the last sister (they write)
To Caeus, and to Enceladus eke;   230
Spedie of foote, of wyng likewise as swift;
A monster huge, and dredfull to descrive.
In every plume that on her body sticks
(A thing in dede much marvelous to heare)
As many waker eyes lurk underneath,   235
So many mouthes to speake, and listning eares.
By night she flies amid the cloudie skie,
Shriking by the dark shadow of the earth,
Ne doth decline to the swete sleepe her eyes.
By day she sits to mark on the house top,   240
Or turretts hye, and the great towns afraies,
As mindefull of yll and lyes as blasing truth.
This monster blithe with many a tale gan sow
This rumor then into the common eares,
As well things don as that was never wrought: 245
As, that there comen is to Tyrians court
Aeneas, one outsprong of Troyan blood,

To whom fair Dido wold her self be wed,
And that the while the winter long they passe
In foule delight, forgetting charge of reigne,⁣ 250
Led against honour with unhonest lust.
   This in eche mouth the filthie goddesse spreds,
And takes her course to king Hiarbas straight;
Kindling his minde, with tales she feedes his wrath.
Gotten was he by Ammon Jupiter⁣ 255
Upon the ravisht nymph of Garamant.
An hundred hugie great temples he built
In his farre stretching realmes to Jupiter,
Altars as many kept with waking flame
A watche alwayes upon the gods to tend;⁣ 260
The floores embrude with yelded blood of beastes,
And threshold spred with garlands of strange hue.
He wood of minde, kindled by bitter brute,
Tofore th'altars, in presence of the gods,
With reared hands gan humbly Jove entreate:⁣ 265
'Almighty God, whom the Moores nacion,
Fed at rich tables, presenteth with wine,
Seest thou these things? or feare we thee in vaine
When thou lettest flye thy thonder from the cloudes?
Or do those flames with vaine noyse us affray?⁣ 270
A woman that wandring in our coastes hath bought
A plot for price, where she a citie set,
To whom we gave the strond for to manure
And lawes to rule her town: our wedlock lothed,
Hath chose Aeneas to commaund her realme.⁣ 275
That Paris now, with his unmanly sorte,
With mitred hats, with oynted bush and beard,
His rape enjoyth: whiles to thy temples we
Our offrings bring, and folow rumors vaine.'
   Whom praing in such sort, and griping eke⁣ 280
The altars fast, the mighty father heard;
And writhed his loke toward the royal walls
And lovers eke forgetting their good name.
To Mercurie then gave he thus in charge:
'Hense son in hast, and call to thee the windes:⁣ 285

Slide with thy plumes, and tell the Troyan prince
That now in Carthage loytreth, rechlesse
Of the towns graunted him by destenye:
Swift through the skies see thow these words convey.
His faire mother behight him not to us   290
Such one to be, ne therefore twyse him saved
From Grekish arms; but such a one
As mete might seme great Italie to rule,
Dreedfull in arms, charged with seigniorie,
Shewing in profe his worthy Teucrian race,   295
And under lawes the whole world to subdue.
If glorie of such things nought him enflame,
Ne that he listes seke honour by som paine,
The towers yet of Rome, being his sire,
Doth he envie to yong Ascanius?   300
What mindeth he to frame? or on what hope
In enmies land doth he make hys abode,
Ne his offspring in Italie regardes,
Ne yet the land of Lavin doth behold?
Bid him make sayle: have here the sum and end.   305
Our message thus report.' When Jove had sayd,
Then Mercurie gan bend him to obey
His mightie fathers will; and to his heeles
His golden wings he knits, which him transport
With a light winde above the earth and seas.   310
And then with him his wande he toke, whereby
He calles from hell pale gostes, and other some
Thether also he sendeth comfortlesse;
Wherby he forceth sleepes, and them bereves,
And mortall eyes he closeth up in deth.   315
By power wherof he drives the windes away,
And passeth eke amid the troubled cloudes
Till in his flight he gan descrie the top
And the stepe flankes of rocky Atlas hill
That with his crowne susteines the welkin up;   320
Whose head forgrowen with pine, circled alway
With misty cloudes, beaten with wind and storme;
His shoulders spred with snow, and from his chin

71

The springes descend, his beard frosen with yse.
Here Mercury with equal shining winges   325
First touched, and, with body headling bente,
To the water thence tooke he his discent,
Like to the foule that endlong costes and strondes,
Swarming with fysh, flyes sweping by the sea.
Cutting betwixt the windes and Libian landes,   330
From his graundfather by the mothers side,
Cillenes child so came, and then alight
Upon the houses with his winged feete,
To fore the towers, where he Aeneas saw
Foundacions cast, arering lodges new,   335
Girt with a swearde of jasper starry bright;
A shining parel, flamed with stately die
Of Tirian purple, hong his shoulders down,
The gift and work of wealthy Didoes hand,
Stripped throughout with a thin thred of gold.   340
   Thus he encounters him: 'Oh careles wight
Both of thy realme and of thine own affaires:
A wifebound man now dost thou reare the walles
Of high Cartage, to build a goodly town?
From the bright skies the ruler of the gods   345
Sent me to thee, that with his beck commaundes
Both heven and earth; in hast he gave me charge
Through the light aire this message thee to say:
What framest thou? or on what hope thy time
In idleness doth wast in Affrick land?   350
Of so great things if nought the fame thee stirr,
Ne list by travaile honour to pursue,
Ascanius yet, that waxeth fast behold
And the hope of Iulus seede thine heir,
To whom the realme of Italy belonges   355
And soile of Rome.' When Mercury had said,
Amid his tale far of from mortall eyes
Into light aire he vanisht out of sight.
   Aeneas, with that vision striken domm,
Well nere bestraught, upstart his heare for dread; 360
Amid his throtal his voice likewise gan stick.

For to depart by flight he longeth now,
And the sweet land to leave, astoined sore
With this advise and message of the gods.
What may he do, alas? or by what words 365
Dare he persuade the raging quene in love?
Or in what sort may he his tale beginne?
Now here now there his recklesse minde gan run
And diversly him drawes, discoursing all.
After long doutes this sentence semed best: 370
Mnestheus first, and strong Cloanthus eke,
He calles to him, with Sergest; unto whom
He gave in charge his navie secretly
For to prepare, and drive to the sea coast
His people, and their armour to addresse, 375
And for the cause of change to faine excuse;
And that he, when good Dido least foreknew
Or did suspect so great a love could break,
Wold wait his time to speke therof most meete,
The nearest way to hasten his entent. 380
Gladly his wil and biddings they obey.
   Ful soone the quene this crafty sleight gan smell,
(Who can deceive a lover in forecast?)
And first foresaw the motions for to come,
Things most assured fearing; unto whom 385
That wicked Fame reported how to flight
Was armde the fleet, all redy to avale.
Then ill bested of counsell rageth she,
And whisketh through the town like Bachus nunne,
As Thias stirres, the sacred rites begon, 390
And when the wonted third yeres sacrifice
Doth prick her fourth, hering Bachus name hallowed,
And that the festful night of Citheron
Doth call her fourth with noyes of dauncing.
   At length her self bordeth Aeneas thus: 395
'Unfaithfull wight, to cover such a fault
Coldest thou hope? unwist to leve my land?
Not thee our love, nor yet right hand betrothed,
Ne cruell death of Dido may withhold?

73

But that thou wilt in winter shippes prepare, 400
And trie the seas in broile of whorling windes?
What if the land thou seekest were not straunge,
If not unknowen, or auncient Troye yet stoode,
In rough seas yet should Troye towne be sought?
Shunnest thou me? By these teares and right hand, 405
(For nought els have I wretched lefte my selfe)
By our spousals and mariage begonne,
If I of thee deserved ever well
Or thing of mine were ever to thee leefe,
Rue on this realme whoes ruine is at hand! 410
If ought be left that prayer may availe,
I thee beseche to do away this minde.
The Libians and tirans of Nomadane
For thee me hate; my Tirians eke for thee
Ar wroth; by thee my shamefastnes eke stained, 415
And good renoume, wherby up to the starres
Perelesse I clame. To whom wilt thou me leave,
Redy to dye, my swete guest? sithe this name
Is all as nowe that of a spouse remaines.
But wherto now shold I prolong my death? 420
What? until my brother Pigmalion
Beate downe my walles? or the Getulian king
Hiarbas yet captive lead me away?
Before thy flight a child had I ones borne,
Or sene a yong Aeneas in my court 425
Play up and down, that might present thy face,
All utterly I could not seeme forsaken.'
　　Thus sayd the quene. He, to the gods advise,
Unmoved held his eyes, and in his brest
Represt his care, and strove against his wil. 430
And these few wordes at last then forth he cast:
'Never shall I denie, quene, thy deserte
Greater than thou in wordes may well expresse.
To thinke on thee ne irke me aye it shall
Whiles of my selfe I shall have memory, 435
And whiles the spirit these limmes of mine shal rule.
For present purpose somwhat shal I say.

74

Never ment I to clok the same by stealth
(Sclaunder me not), ne to escape by flight.
Nor I to thee pretended mariage,   440
Ne hyther cam to joine me in such leage.
If desteny at mine own liberty
To lead my life would have permitted me
After my wil my sorow to redoub,
Troy and the remainder of our folke   445
Restore I shold, and with these scaped handes
The walles againe unto the vanquished
And palace high of Priam eke repaire.
But now Apollo called Grineus
And prophecies of Licia me advise   450
To sease upon the realme of Italy;
That is my love, my country, and my land.
If Cartage turrettes thee, Phenician borne,
And of a Libian town the sight deteine,
To us Troyans why doest thou then envy   455
In Italy to make our risting seat?
Lefull is eeke for us straunge realmes to seeke.
As ofte as night doth cloke with shadowes danke
The earth, as oft as flaming starres apere,
The troubled ghost of my father Anchises   460
So oft in sleepe doth fray me and advise
The wronged hed by me of my deare sonne,
Whom I defraud of the Hisperian crown
And landes alotted him by desteny.
The messenger eke of the gods but late   465
Sent down from Jove (I sware by eyther hed)
Passing the ayre, did this to me report.
In bright day light the god my selfe I saw
Entre these walles, and with these eares him heard.
Leve then with plaint to vexe both the and me.   470
Against my will to Italy I go.'
    Whiles in this sort he did his tale pronounce,
With wayward looke she gan him ay behold,
And roling eyes that moved to and fro,
With silent looke discoursing over al.   475

75

And foorth in rage at last thus gan she brayde:
'Faithlesse, forsworn, ne goddesse was thy dam,
Nor Dardanus beginner of thy race,
But of hard rockes mount Caucase monstruous
Bred thee, and teates of tyger gave thee suck.   480
But what should I dissemble now my chere,
Or me reserve to hope of greater things?
Mindes he our teares or ever moved his eyen?
Wept he for ruth, or pitied he our love?
What shall I set before, or where begin?   485
Juno nor Jove with just eyes this beholds.
Faith is no where in suretie to be found.
Did I not him, thrown up upon my shore,
In neede receive, and fonded eke invest
Of halfe my realme? his navie lost repair?   490
From deathes daunger his fellowes eke defend?
Ay me, with rage and furies loe I drive!
Apollo now, now Lycian prophesies,
Another while the messenger of gods,
(He sayes) sent down from mighty Jove himself,   495
The dredfull charge amid the skies hath brought.
As though that were the travil of the gods
Or such a care their quietnes might move.
I hold thee not, nor yet gainsay thy words:
To Italie passe on by helpe of windes,   500
And through the floods go searche thy kingdom new.
If ruthfull gods have any power, I trust
Amid the rocks thy guerdon thou shalt finde,
When thou shalt clepe full oft on Didos name.
With burial brandes I absent shall thee chase,   505
And when cold death from life these lims devides,
My gost eche where shall still on thee awaite.
Thou shalt abye, and I shall here thereof;
Among the soules below thy brute shall come.'
    With such like wordes she cut of half her tale,   510
With pensive hart abandoning the light,
And from his sight her self gan farre remove,
Forsaking him, that many things in fere

76

Imagened, and did prepare to say.
Her swouning lims her damsels gan releve,   515
And to her chamber bare of marble stone,
And layd her on her bed with tapets spred.
   But just Aeneas, though he did desire
With comfort swet her sorows to appease
And with his words to banish all her care,   520
Wailing her much, with great love overcome,
The gods will yet he woorketh, and resortes
Unto his navie, where the Troyans fast
Fell to their worke, from the shore to unstock
High rigged ships. Now fleetes the talowed kele.   525
Their oares with leaves yet grene from wood they bring,
And mastes unshave, for hast to take their flight.
You might have sene them throng out of the town
Like ants, when they do spoile the bing of corn,
For winters dred, which they beare to their den,   530
When the black swarm creeps over all the fields,
And thwart the grasse by strait pathes drags their pray;
The great graines then som on their shoulders trusse,
Some drive the troupe, som chastice eke the slow,
That with their travaile chafed is eche pathe.   535
   Beholding this, what thought might Dido have?
What sighes gave she? when from her towers hye
The large coasts she saw haunted with Troyans workes,
And in her sight the seas with din confounded.
O witlesse love, what thing is that to do   540
A mortal minde thou canst not force thereto!
Forced she is to teares ay to returne,
With new requestes, to yeld her hart to love.
And least she should before her causelesse death
Leave any thing untried, 'O sister Anne,'   545
Quoth she, 'behold the whole coast round about,
How they prepare assembled every where;
The streming sailes abiding but for wynde;
The shipmen crowne theyr ships with bows for joy.
O sister, if so great a sorow I   550
Mistrusted had, it were more light to beare.

77

Yet nathelesse this for me wretched wight,
Anne, shalt thou do, for faithles, thee alone
He reverenced, thee eke his secretes tolde.
The metest time thou knewest to borde the man.   555
To my proud foe thus sister humbly say:
I with the Grekes within the port Aulide
Conjured not the Troyans to destroy,
Nor to the walles of Troy yet sent my fleete,
Nor cynders of his father Anchises   560
Disturbed have out of his sepulture.
Why lettes he not my wordes sinke in his eares
So harde to overtreate? whither whirles he?
This last boone yet graunt he to wretched love:
Prosperous windes for to depart with ease   565
Let him abide. The foresayde mariage now,
That he betraied, I do not him require,
Nor that he should faire Italy forgo.
Neither I would he should his kingdom leave:
Quiet I aske, and a time of delay,   570
And respite eke my furye to asswage,
Til my mishap teach me all comfortlesse
How for to wayle my grief. This latter grace
Sister I crave; have thou remorse of me:
Whiche, if thou shalt vouchsafe, with heapes I shall   575
Leave by my death redoubled unto thee.'
    Moisted with teares thus wretched gan she playne;
Which Anne reportes, and answere bringes againe.
Nought teares him move, ne yet to any wordes
He can be framed with gentle minde to yelde.   580
The werdes withstande, and God stops his meke eares.
Like to the aged boysteous bodied oke,
The which among the Alpes the northerne windes
Blowyng now from this quarter now from that
Betwixt them strive to overwhelme with blastes;   585
The whistlyng ayre among the braunches rores,
Which all at once bow to the earth ther croppes,
The stock once smit, whiles in the rockes the tree
Stickes fast; and loke, how hye to the heaven her toppe

78

Reares up, so deepe her roote spredes down to hell: 590
So was this lorde now here now there beset
With wordes, in whose stout brest wrought many cares.
   But still his minde in one remaines, in vaine
The teares were shed. Then Dido frayde of fates,
Wisheth for death, irked to see the skyes.   595
And that she might the rather worke her will
And leave the light (a grisely thing to tell),
Upon the altars burnyng full of cense
When she set giftes of sacrifice, she saw
The holy water stocks waxe blacke within;   600
The wine eke shed, chaunge into filthy gore.
This she to none, not to her sister told.
A marble temple in her palace eke
In memory of her old spouse there stood,
In great honour and worship which she held,   605
With snowwhite clothes deckt and with bows of feast;
Wherout was heard her husbandes voyce and speche
Cleping for her, when dark night hid the earth.
And oft the owle with rufull song complaind
From the house top, drawing long dolefull tunes.   610
And many things, forspoke by prophets past,
With dredfull warning gan her now affray;
And stern Aeneas semed in her slepe
To chase her stil about, distraught in rage;
And still her thought that she was left alone   615
Uncompanied great viages to wende,
In desert land her Tyrian folk to seeke:
Like Pentheus, that in his madnes saw
Swarming in flocks the furies all of hell,
Two suns remove, and Thebes town shew twain;   620
Or like Orestes Agamemnons son,
In tragedies who represented aye
Driven about, that from his mother fled
Armed with brands, and eke with serpents black;
That sitting found within the temples porche   625
The uglie furies his slaughter to revenge.
   Yelden to wo, when phrensie had her caught,

Within her selfe then gan she well debate,
Full bent to dye, the time and eke the meane;
And to her wofull sister thus she sayd,   630
In outward chere dissembling her entent,
Presenting hope under a semblant glad:
'Sister rejoyce, for I have found the way
Him to returne, or lose me from his love.
Toward the end of the great ocean flood   635
Where as the wandring sun discendeth hence,
In the extremes of Ethiope, is a place
Where huge Atlas doth on his sholders turne
The sphere so rund, with flaming starres beset;
Borne of Massyle I heare, should be a nunne   640
That of th'Hesperian sisters temple old
And of their goodly garden keper was,
That geves unto the dragon eke his foode,
That on the tree preserves the holy fruit,
That honie moyst and sleping poppey castes.   645
This woman doth avaunt, by force of charme,
What hart she list to set at libertie,
And other some to perce with hevy cares,
In running flood to stop the waters course,
And eke the sterres their mevings to reverse,   650
T'assemble eke the gostes that walk by night;
Under thy feete th'earth thou shalt behold
Tremble and rore, the okes come from the hill.
The gods and thee dere sister, now I call
In witnes, and thy hed to me so sweete: 655
To magike artes against my will I bend.
Right secretly within our inner court
In open ayre reare up a stack of wood,
And hang theron the weapon of this man,
The which he left within my chamber sticke.   660
His weedes dispoiled all, and bridal bed,
Wherein, alas sister, I found my bane,
Charge thereupon; for so the nunne commaundes,
To do away what did to him belong,
Of that false wight that might remembraunce bring.'   665

Then whisted she; the pale her face gan staine,
Ne could yet Anne beleve her sister ment
To cloke her death by this new sacrifice,
Nor in her brest such furie did conceive;
Neither doth she now dred more grevous thing   670
Then folowed Sichees death; wherefore
She put her will in ure. But then the quene,
When that the stak of wood was reared up
Under the ayre within the inward court,
With cloven oke and billettes made of fyrre,   675
With garlandes she doth all beset the place,
And with grene bows eke crown the funerall;
And therupon his wedes and swerd yleft,
And on a bed his picture she bestowes,
As she that well foreknew what was to come.   680
The altars stande about, and eke the nunne
With sparkeled tresse, the which thre hundred gods
With a loude voice doth thunder out at once,
Erebus the grisely, and Chaos huge,
And eke the threefolde goddesse Hecate,   685
And three faces of Diana the virgin;
And sprinkles eke the water counterfet
Like unto blacke Avernus lake in hell.
And springyng herbes reapt up with brasen sithes
Were sought, after the right course of the moone;   690
The venim blacke intermingled with milke;
The lumpe of fleshe twene the new borne foales eyen
To reve, that winneth from the damme her love.
She with the mole all in her handes devout
Stode neare the aulter, bare of the one foote,   695
With vesture loose, the bandes unlaced all;
Bent for to dye, calls the gods to recorde,
And gilty starres eke of her desteny.
And if there were any god that had care
Of lovers hartes not moved with love alike,   700
Him she requires of justice to remember.
    It was then night; the sounde and quiet slepe
Had through the earth the weried bodyes caught;

The woodes, the ragyng seas were falne to rest;
When that the starres had halfe their course declined;   705
The feldes whist; beastes and fowles of divers hue,
And what so that in the brode lakes remainde
Or yet among the bushy thickes of bryar
Laide down to slepe by silence of the night,
Gan swage their cares, mindlesse of travels past.   710
Not so the spirite of this Phenician:
Unhappy she, that on no slepe could chance,
Nor yet nightes rest enter in eye or brest.
Her cares redoble; love doth rise and rage againe,
And overflowes with swellyng stormes of wrath.   715
Thus thinkes she then, this roules she in her mind:
'What shall I do? shall I now beare the scorne
For to assaye mine olde woers againe,
And humbly yet a Numid spouse require
Whose mariage I have so oft disdayned?   720
The Troyan navy and Teucrian vile commaundes
Folow shall I? as though it shoulde availe
That whilom by my helpe they were releved.
Or for because with kinde and mindfull folke
Right well doth sit the passed thankefull dede?   725
Who would me suffer (admit this were my will)
Or me scorned to their proude shippes receive?
Oh wo begone: full little knowest thou yet
The broken othes of Laomedons kinde!
What then? alone on mery mariners   730
Shall I awaite? or borde them with my power
Of Tyrians assembled me about?
And such as I with travaile brought from Tyre
Drive to the seas, and force them saile againe?
But rather dye, even as thou hast deserved,   735
And to this wo with iron geve thou ende.
And thou, sister, first vanquisht with my teares,
Thou in my rage with all these mischiefes first
Didst burden me, and yelde me to my foe.
Was it not graunted me, from spousals free,   740
Like to wilde beastes, to live without offence,

Without taste of such cares? Is there no fayth
Reserved to the cinders of Sychee?'
   Such great complaints brake forth out of her brest,
Whiles Aeneas full minded to depart,   745
All thinges prepared, slept in the poupe on high.
To whom in slepe the wonted godheds forme
Gan aye appere, returnyng in like shape
As semed him, and gan him thus advise,
Like unto Mercury in voyce and hue,   750
With yelow bushe, and comely lymmes of youth:
'O goddesse sonne, in such case canst thou sleepe?
Ne yet bestraught the daungers doest forsee
That compasse thee? nor hearst the faire windes blowe?
Dido in minde roules vengeance and desceite;   755
Determd to dye, swelles with unstable ire.
Wilt thou not flee whiles thou hast time of flight?
Straight shalt thou see the seas covered with sayles,
The blasyng brondes, the shore all spred with flame
And if the morow steale upon thee here.   760
Come of, have done, set all delay aside,
For full of change these women be alway.'
This sayd, in the dark night he gan him hide.
   Aeneas of this sodain vision
Adred, starts up out of his sleepe in hast,   765
Cals up his feers: 'Awake! get up my men!
Abord your ships, and hoyse up sayl with speede!
A god me wills, sent from above againe
To hast my flight and writhen cabels cut.
Oh holy god, what so thou art, we shall   770
Folow thee, and all blithe obey thy will.
Be at our hand, and frendly us assist!
Addresse the sterres with prosperous influence!'
And with that word his glistering sword unshethes,
With which drawen he the cabels cut in twaine.   775
The like desire the rest embraced all.
All thing in hast they cast and fourth they whurle.
The shores they leave, with ships the seas ar spred,
Cutting the fome by the blew seas they swepe.

Aurora now from Titans purple bed   780
With new day light hath overspred the earth,
When by her windowes the quene the peping day
Espyed, and navie with splaid sailes depart
The shore, and eke the port of vessels voyde.
Her comly brest thrise or foure times she smote   785
With her own hand, and tore her golden tresse.
'Oh Jove,' quoth she, 'shall he then thus depart
A straunger thus and scorne our kingdom so?
Shall not my men do on theyr armure prest,
And eke pursue them throughout all the town?   790
Out of the rode some shall the vessells warpe?
Hast on, cast flame, set sayle and welde your owers!
What said I? but where am I? what phrensie
Alters thy minde? Unhappy Dido, now
Hath thee beset a froward destenie.   795
Then it behoved, when thou didst geve to him
The scepter. Lo, his faith and his right hand,
That leades with him (they say) his countrie godes,
That on his back his aged father bore.
His body might I not have caught and rent?   800
And in the seas drenched him and his feers?
And from Ascanius his life with iron reft,
And set him on his fathers bord for meate?
Of such debate perchaunce the fortune might
Have bene doubtfull: would God it were assayed!   805
Whom should I feare, sith I my selfe must die?
Might I have throwen into that navy brandes,
And filled eke their deckes with flaming fire,
The father, sonne, and all their nacion
Destroyed, and falln my self ded over al.   810
Sunne, with thy beames that mortall workes discries,
And thou Juno, that wel these travailes knowest,
Proserpine thou, upon whom folk do use
To houle, and call in forked wayes by night,
Infernal furies, ye wreakers of wrong,   815
And Didos gods, who standes at point of death,
Receive these wordes, and eke your heavy power

Withdraw from me, that wicked folk deserve,
And our request accept, we you beseche.
If so that yonder wicked head must needes   820
Recover port, and saile to land of force,
And if Joves wil have so resolved it
And such ende set as no wight can fordoe,
Yet at the least asailed mought he be
With armes and warres of hardy nacions,   825
From the boundes of his kingdom farre exiled,
Iulus eke rashed out of his armes,
Driven to call for helpe, that he may see
The giltles corpses of his folke lie dead.
And after hard condicions of peace,   830
His realme nor life desired may he brooke,
But fall before his time, ungraved amid the sandes.
This I require, these wordes with blood I shed.
And Tirians, ye his stocke and all his race
Pursue with hate, rewarde our cinders so.   835
No love nor leage betwixt our peoples be.
And of our bones some wreaker may there spring,
With sword and flame that Troyans may pursue.
And from hencefoorth, when that our powr may stretch,
Our costes to them contrary be for aye,   840
I crave of God, and our streames to their fluddes,
Armes unto armes, and offspring of eche race
With mortal warr eche other may fordoe.'
     This said, her mind she writhed on al sides,
Seking with spede to end her irksome life.   845
To Sichees nurse Barcen then thus she said
(For hers at home in ashes did remaine):
'Cal unto me, deare nurse, my sister Anne.
Bid her in hast in water of the fludde
She sprinckle the body, and bring the beastes   850
And purging sacrifice I did her shewe.
So let her come; and thou thy temples bind
With sacred garlandes; for the sacrifice
That I to Pluto have begonne, my mind
Is to performe, and geve end to these cares;   855

And Troyan statue throw into the flame.'
When she had said, redouble gan her nurse
Her steppes, forth on an aged womans trot.
    But trembling Dido egerly now bent
Upon her sterne determinacion,   860
Her bloodshot eyes roling within her head,
Her quivering chekes flecked with deadly staine,
Both pale and wan to think on death to come,
Into the inward wardes of her palace
She rusheth in, and clam up as distraught   865
The buriall stack, and drew the Troyan swerd,
Her gift sometime, but ment to no such use.
Where when she saw his weed and wel knowen bed,
Weping a while, in study gan she stay,
Fell on the bed, and these last words she said: 870
'Swete spoiles, whiles God and destenies it wold,
Receve this sprite, and rid me of these cares.
I lived and ranne the course fortune did graunt,
And under earth my great gost now shall wende.
A goodly town I built, and saw my walles,   875
Happy, alas to happy, if these costes
The Troyan shippes had never touched aye.'
    This said, she laid her mouth close to the bed.
'Why then,' quoth she, 'unwroken shall we die?
But let us die, for thus and in this sort   880
It liketh us to seeke the shadowes darck.
And from the seas the cruel Troyans eyes
Shall wel discern this flame, and take with him
Eke these unlucky tokens of my death.'
    As she had said, her damsells might perceve   885
Her with these wordes fal pearced on a sword,
The blade embrued, an hands besprent with gore.
The clamor rang unto the pallace toppe,
The brute ranne throughout al th'astoined towne.
With wailing great and womens shril yelling   890
The roofes gan roare, the aire resound with plaint,
As though Cartage or th'auncient town of Tyre
With prease of entred enemies swarmed full,

Or when the rage of furious flame doth take
The temples toppes and mansions eke of men.   895
   Her sister Anne, spritelesse for dread to heare
This fearefull sturre, with nailes gan teare her face.
She smote her brest, and rushed through the rout
And her dyeng she cleapes thus by her name:
'Sister, for this with craft did you me bourd?   900
The stak, the flame, the altars, bred they this?
What shall I first complaine, forsaken wight?
Lothest thou in death thy sisters felowship?
Thou shouldst have calld me to like destiny:
One wo, one sword, one houre mought end us both.   905
This funerall stak built I with these handes
And with this voice cleped our native gods,
And cruel so absentest me from thy death?
Destroyd thou hast, sister, both thee and me,
Thy people eke, and princes borne of Tyre.   910
Geve here: I shall with water washe her woundes,
And suck with mouth her breath, if ought be left.'
   This said, unto the high degrees shee mounted,
Embracing fast her sister now half dead,
With wailefull plaint, whom in her lap she layd,   915
The black swart gore wiping dry with her clothes.
But Dido striveth to lift up againe
Her heavy eyen, and hath no power thereto:
Deepe in her brest that fixed wound doth gape.
Thrise leaning on her elbow gan she raise   920
Her self upward, and thrise she overthrewe
Upon the bed, ranging with wandring eyes
The skies for light, and wept when she it found.
   Almighty Juno having ruth by this
Of her long paines and eke her lingring death,   925
From heaven she sent the goddesse Iris downe,
The throwing sprit and jointed limmes to loose.
For that neither by lot of destiny
Nor yet by kindly death she perished,
But wretchedly before her fatall day,   930
And kindled with a sodein rage of flame;

Prosperpine had not from her head bereft
The golden heare, nor judged her to hell.
The dewye Iris thus with golden wings,
A thousand hues shewing against the sunne,   935
Amid the skies then did she flye adowne,
On Didos head where as she gan alight:
'This heare,' quod she, 'to Pluto consecrate,
Commaunded I reve, and thy spirit unloose
From this body.' And when she thus had said,   940
With her right hand she cut the heare in twaine,
And therwith al the kindly heat gan quench
And into wind the life foorthwith resolve.

BIBLICAL PARAPHRASES

43

Ecclesiastes, Chapter One

I Salamon, Davids sonne, King of Jerusalem,
Chossen by God to teach the Jewes and in his lawes to leade them,
  Confesse under the sonne that every thing is vayne,
The world is false, man he is fraile, and all his pleasures payne.
  Alas, what stable frute may Adams childeren fynde   5
In that they seke by sweate of browes and travill of their mynde?
  We that live on the earthe drawe toward our decay;
Ower childeren fill our place a whille, and then they fade awaye.
  Such chaunges maks the earthe, and doth remove for none,
But sarves us for a place too play our tragedes uppon.   10
  When that the restles sonne westwarde his course hathe ronne,
Towards the east he hasts as fast to ryse where he begonne.
  When hoorrey Boreas hathe blowen his frosen blaste,
Then Zephirus with his gentill breathe dissolves the ise as fast.
  Fludds that drinke upp smale broks and swell by rage of
    rayne   15
Discharge in sees which them repulse and swallowe strayte againe.
  These worldly pleasures, Lord, so swifte they ronne their race
That skace our eyes may them discerne, they bide so littell space.

What hathe bin, but is now, the like hereafter shall.
What new device grounded so suer, that dreadeth not the fall? 20
    What may be called new, but suche things in tymes past
As time buryed and dothe revive, and tyme agayne shall waste?
    Things past right worthey fame have now no brute at all.
Even so shall dey suche things as now the simple wounders call.
    I that in Davides seate sit crowned and rejoyce,   25
That with my septer rewle the Jewes and teache them with my
        voyce,
    Have serchied long to know all things under the sonne
To see how, in this mortall lyef, a suerty might be wonne.
    This kyndled will to knowe, straunge things for to desyer,
God hath grafte in our gredye breasts, a torment for our hier. 30
    The end of eache travell furthwith I sought to knoo:
I found them vaine, mixed with gall, and burdend with muche
        woo.
    Defaults of natures wourke no mans hand may restore,
Whiche be in nomber like the sandes uppon the salte floods shore.
    Then, vaunting in my witte, I gan call to my mynd   35
What rewles of wysdom I hadde taught, that elders could not
        find;
    And as, by contraries, to treye most things we use,
Mens follies and ther errors eke I gan them all peruse,
    Thyerby with more delight to knowledge for to clime:
But this I found an endles wourke of payne and losse of tyme. 40
    For he to wisdomes skoole that doth applie his mynd,
The further that he wades ther in, the greater doubts shall find.
    And such as enterprice to put newe things in ure
Of some that shall skorne their devise may well them selfes assure.

44

Ecclesiastes, Chapter Two

    From pensif fanzies then, I gan my hart revoke,
And gave me to suche sporting plaies as laughter myght provoke.
    But even such vain delights, when they moste blinded me,
Allwayes me thought with smiling grace a king did yll agre.

Then sought I how to please my belly with muche wine,   5
To feede me fatte with costely feasts of rare delights and fine,
    And other plesures eke, too purchace me with rest,
In so great choise to finde the thing that might content me best.
    But, Lord, what care of mynde, what soddaine stormes of ire,
With broken slepes enduryd I, to compasse my desier!   10
    To buylde my howses faier then sett I all my cure:
By princely acts thus strave I still to make my fame indure.
    Delicius gardens eke I made to please my sight,
And grafte therin all kindes of fruts that might my mouthe delight.
    Condits, by lively springs, from their owld course I drewe   15
For to refreshe the frutfull trees that in my gardynes grewe.
    Of catell great encreace I bred in littell space.
Bondmen I bought, I gave them wifes, and sarved me with ther
    race.
    Great heapes of shining gold by sparing gan I save,
With things of price so furnyshed as fitts a prince to have.   20
    To heare faier women sing sometyme I did rejoyce;
Ravyshed with ther pleasannt tunes and swetnes of their voyce.
    Lemans I had, so faier and of so lively hewe
That who so gased in their face myght well their bewtey rewe.
    Never erste sat theyr king so riche in Davyds seate: 25
Yet still me thought for so smale gaine the travaile was to great.
    From my desirous eyes I hyd no pleasannt sight,
Nor from my hart no kind of myrth that might geve them
    delyght;
    Which was the only freute I rept of all my payne:
To feade my eyes and to rejoyce my hart with all my gaine.   30
    But when I made my compte, with howe great care of mynd
And hertes unrest that I had sought so wastfull frutt to fynde,
    Then was I streken strayte with that abused fier,
To glorey in that goodly witte that compast my desyer.
    But freshe before myne eyes grace did my fawlts renewe: 35
What gentill callings I hadd fledd, my ruyne to purswe,
    What raging pleasurs past, perill and hard eskape,
What fancis in my hed had wrought the licor of the grape.
    The erroure then I sawe that their fraile harts dothe move,   39
Which strive in vaine for to compare with him that sitts above;

In whose most perfect worcks suche craft apperyth playne
That to the least of them their may no mortall hand attayne.
  And like as lightsome day dothe shine above the night,
So darke to me did folly seme, and wysdomes beames as bright.
  Whose eyes did seme so clere, mots to discern and fynde;   45
But will had clossed follies eyes, which groped like the blynde.
  Yet death and time consume all witt and worldly fame,
And looke what ende that folly hath, and wisdome hath the same.
  Then sayd I thus: Oh Lord, may not they wisdome cure
The waylfull wrongs and hard conflicts that folly doth endure?   50
  To sharpe my witt so fine then why toke I this payne?
Now finde I well this noble serche may eke be called vayne.
  As slanders lothsome brute soundes follies just rewarde,
Is put to silence all be time, and brought in smale regarde,
  Evn so dothe tyme devoure the noble blast of fame,   55
Which showld resounde their glories great that doo desarve the
    same.
  Thus present changes chase away the wonders past,
Ne is the wise mans fattal thred yet lenger spunne to last.
  Then in this wredtched vale our lief I lothed playne
When I beheld our frutles paynes to compasse pleassurs vayne.   60
  My travayll this availe hath me produced, loo!
An heire unknowen shall reape the frute that I in sede did sowe.
  But wherunto the Lord his nature shall inclyne
Who can fore knowe, into whose handes I must my goods resine?
  But, Lord, how pleasannt swete then seamd the idell liefe,   65
That never charged was with care, nor burdened with stryefe,
  And vile the gredye trade of them that toile so sore
To leave to suche ther travells frute that never swet therfore.
  What is that pleasant gaine, which is that swet relief,
That showld delay the bitter tast that we fele of our gref?   70
  The gladsome dayes we passe to serche a simple gaine,
The quiete nights, with broken slepes, to fead a resteles brayne.
  What hope is left us then, what comfort dothe remayne?
Our quiet herts for to rejoyce with the frute of our payne.
  Yf that be trew, who may him selfe so happy call   75
As I, whose free and sumptius spence dothe shyne beyonde them
    all?

Sewerly it is a gift and favor of the Lorde
Liberally to spend our goods, the ground of all discorde,
    And wretched herts have they that let their tressurs mold,
And carrey the roodde that skorgeth them that glorey in their
        gold.   80
    But I doo knowe by proofe, whose ryches beres suche brute,
What stable welthe may stand in wast, or heping of suche frute.

45

Ecclesiastes, Chapter Three

    Like to the stereles boote that swerves with every wynde,
The slipper topp of worldley welthe by crewell prof I fynde.
    Skace hath the seade, wherof that naure foremethe man,
Recevid lief, when deathe him yeldes to earth wher he began.
    The grafted plants with payn, wherof wee hoped frute,   5
To roote them upp, with blossomes sprede, then is our chief
        porsute.
    That erst we rered upp we undermyne againe,
And shred the spraies whose grouthe some tyme we laboured
        with paine.
    Eache frowarde thretning chere of fortune maiks us playne,
And every plesant showe revives our wofull herts againe.   10
    Auncient walles to race is our unstable guyse,
And of their wetherbeten stones to buylde some new devyse.
    New fanzes dayly spring, which vaade returning moo;
And now we practyse to optaine that strayt we must forgoo.
    Some tyme we seke to spare that afterward we wast,   15
And that we travelid sore to knitt for to unclose as fast.
    In sober sylence now our quiet lipps we closse,
And with unbrydled toungs furth with our secret herts disclosse.
    Suche as in folded armes we did embrace, we haate;
Whom strayte we reconsill againe and banishe all debate.   20
    My sede with labour sowne suche frute produceth me
To wast my lief in contraries that never shall agree.
    From God these hevy cares ar sent for our unrests,
And with suche burdens for our welth he frauteth full our brests.

All that the Lord hathe wrought hath bewtey and good
    grace,   25
And to eache thing assined is the proper tyme and place.
  And graunted eke to man, of all the worldes estate
And of eache thinge wrought in the same, to argue and debate.
  Which arte though it approche the hevenly knowlege most
To serche the naturall grounde of things, yet all is labor loste. 30
  But then the wandering eyes, that longe for suertey sought,
Founde that by paine no certayne welth might in this world be
    bought.
  Who liveth in delight and seks no gredy thryfte,
But frely spends his goods, may thinke it as a secret gifte.
  Fullfilled shall it be, what so the Lorde intende,   35
Which no device of mans witt may advaunce, nor yet defende;
  Who made all thing of nought, that Adams chyldren might
Lerne how to dread the Lord, that wrought suche wonders in
    their sight.
  The gresly wonders past, which tyme wearse owt of mynde,
To be renewed in our dayes the Lord hath so assynde.   40
  Lo, thuse his carfull skourge doth stele on us unware,
Which, when the fleshe hath clene forgott, he dothe againe
    repaire.
  When I in this vaine serche had wanderyd sore my witt,
I saw a roiall throne wheras that Justice should have sitt;
  In stede of whom I saw, with fyerce and crwell mode,   45
Wher Wrong was set, that blody beast, that drounke the giltles
    blode.
  Then thought I thus: One day the Lord shall sitt in dome,
To vewe his flock and chose the pure: the spotted have no rome.
  Ye be suche skourges sent that eache agrevid mynde,
Lyke the brute beasts that swell in rage and fury by ther kynde, 50
  His erroure may confesse, when he hath wreasteled longe;
And then with pacience may him arme, the sure defence of
    wronge.
  For death, that of the beaste the carion doth devoure,
Unto the noble kynde of man presents the fatall hower.
  The perfitt forme that God hathe geven to ether man   55
Or other beast, dissolve it shall to earth wher it began.

And who can tell yf that the sowle of man ascende,
Or with the body if it dye, and to the ground decende?
  Wherfore eache gredy hart that riches seks to gayne,
Gather may he that savery frutte that springeth of his payne.　60
  A meane convenient welth I meane to take in worth,
And with a hand of larges eke in measure poore it fourth.
  For treasure spent in lyef the bodye dothe sustayne;
The heire shall waste the whourded gold amassed with muche
     payne.
  Ne may foresight of man suche order geve in lyef　　65
For to foreknow who shall rejoyce their gotton good with stryef.

46

Ecclesiastes, Chapter Four

  When I be thought me well, under the restles soon
By foolke of power what crewell wourks unchastyced were doon,
  I saw wher stoode a heard by power of suche opprest,
Oute of whose eyes ran floods of teares that bayned all ther brest;
  Devoyde of comfort clene, in terroure and distresse,　　5
In whose defence none wolde aryse, suche rigor to represse.
  Then thought I thus: Oh Lord, the dead, whose fatall hower
Is clene roune owt, more happy ar, whom that the wormes
     devoure;
  And happiest is the sede that never did conceve,
That never felt the waylfull wrongs that mortall folke receve.　10
  And then I saw that welth and every honest gayne
By travill woune and swete of browes gan grow into disdayne
  Throughe slouthe of carles folke, whom ease so fatt dothe
     feade,
Whose idell hands doo noght but waast the frute of other seade;
  Which to them selves perswade that little gott with ease　15
More thankefull is then kyndomes woon by travayle and disceace.
  A nother sort I saw, with out bothe frend or kynne,
Whose gredy wayes yet never sought a faithfull frend to winne;
  Whose wretched corps no toile yet ever wery could,
Nor glutted ever wer their eyne with heaps of shyning gould.　20

94

But yf it might appeare to ther abused eyne
To whose a vaile they travill so, and for whose sake they pyne,
    Then should they see what cause they have for to repent
The frutles paynes and eke the tyme that they in vayne have
        spent.
    Then gan I thus resolve: More pleasant is the lyef   25
Of faythefull frends that spends their goods in commone, with
        out stryef.
    For as the tender frend appeasith every gryef,
So, yf he fall that lives alone, who shalbe his relyef?
    The frendly feares ly warme, in armes embraced faste;
Who sleapes aloone at every tourne dothe feale the winter
        blast.   30
    What can he doo but yeld that must resist aloone?
Yf ther be twaine, one may defend the tother over throwne.
    The single twyned cordes may no such stresse indure
As cables brayded thre fould may, together wrethed swer.
    In better far estate stande children, poore and wyse,   35
Then aged kyngs wedded to will that worke with out advice.
    In prison have I sene or this a wofull wyght
That never knewe what fredom ment, nor tasted of delyght;
    With such, unhoped happ in most dispaier hath mete,
With in the hands that erst ware gives to have a septre sett. 40
    And by conjures the seade of kyngs is thrust from staate,
Wheron agrevyd people worke ofteymes their hidden haat.
    Other with out respect I saw, a frend or foo,
With feat worne bare in tracing such wheras the honours groo.
    And at change of a prynce great rowtes revived strange   45
Which, faine theare owlde yoke to discharg, rejoyced in the
        change.
    But when I thought, to theise as hevy even or more
Shalbe the burden of his raigne as his that went before,
    And that a trayne like great upon the deade depend,
I gan conclude eache gredy gayne hath his uncertayne end.   50
    In humble spritte is sett the temple of the Lorde;
Wher yf thou enter, loke thy mouth and conscyence may accorde.
    Whose churtche is buylte of love, and decte with hoote desyre
And simple fayth; the yolden hoost his marcy doth requyre.

95

Wher perfectly for aye he in his woord dothe rest,　55
With gentill care to heare thy sute and graunt to thy request.
　In boost of owtwarde works he taketh no delight,
Nor wast of wourds; suche sacryfice unsavereth in his sight.

47

Psalm Eight

　Thie name, O Lord, howe greate is fownd before our sight!
Yt fills the earthe and spreades the ayre, the great workes of thie
　　might.
　For even unto thie powre the hevens have geven a place,
And closyd it above their heades, a mightie lardge compace.
　Thye praise what clowde can hyde, but it will sheene agayne,　5
Synce yonge and tender sucking babes have powre to shew it
　　playne;
　Whiche, in dispight of those that wold thie glorye hide,
Hast put into such Infantes mowthes for to confounde their
　　pryde.
　Wherefore I shall beholde thy fygurde heaven so hye,
Whiche shews suche printes of dyvers formes within the clowdye
　　skye　　　　　　　　　　　　　　　　　　　　　　　10
　As hills and shapes of men, eke beastes of sondrie kynde,
Monstruous to our outward sight and fancyes of our mynde;
　And eke the wanishe moone which sheenes by night also,
And eache one of the wondring sterres whiche after her doth goe;
　And how to kepe their course, and which are those that
　　stands,　　　　　　　　　　　　　　　　　　　　　15
Because they be thie wonderous workes and labours of thie
　　hands.
　But yet among all theise I aske: What thing is man,
Whose tourne to serve in his poore neede this worke thow first
　　began?
　Or whate is Adames sonne that beares his fathers marke,
For whose delyte and compforte eke thow hase wrought all this
　　warke?　　　　　　　　　　　　　　　　　　　　　20

96

I see thow mindest hym moche that doste rewarde hym so,
Being but earthe, to rule the earthe wheare on hymself doth go.
From aungells substaunce eke thow madeste hym differ small,
Save one dothe chaunge his lif awhyle, the other not at all.
The Sonne and Moone also, thow madeste to geve hym light, 25
And eache one of the wandring sterrs to twynckle sparkles bright.
The ayre to geve hym breathe, the water for his health,
The earth to bring forth grayne and frute for to encrease his wealth.
And many metalls to, for pleasure of the eye,
Which in the hollow sowndyd grownd in previe vaynes do lye. 30
The sheepe to geve his wool, to wrapp his boddie in,
And for suche other needefull thynges the oxe to spare his skynne.
The horse, even at his will, to bear hym to and fro,
And as hym list eache other beaste to serve his turne also.
The fysshes of the sea lykewyse to feede hym ofte, 35
And eke the birdes, whose feathers serve to make his sydes lye softe.
On whose head thow hast sett a Crowne of Glorye to,
To whom also thow didest appoint that honour shuld be do.
And thus thow madeste hym Lord of all this worke of thyne:
Of man that goes; of beast that creapes, whose lookes dothe downe declyne; 40
Of fysshe that swymme below; of fowles that flyes on hye;
Of sea that fyndes the ayre his rayne; and of the land so drye.
And underneath his feet thow hast sett all this same
To make hym know and playne confesse that marveilous is thie name.
And Lord, whiche art our Lord, how merveilouse is it fownd 45
The heavens doth shew, the earth doth tell, and eke the world so rownd.
Glorie therefore be geven to thee first, whiche art three,
And yet but one almightie God, in substaunce and degree.
As first it was when thow the darcke confused heape

Clottid in one, didest part in fowre, which Elements wee
cleape,   50
    And as the same is now, even heare within our tyme,
And ever shall here after be, when we be filth and slyme.

48

Psalm Eighty-eight

Oh Lorde, uppon whose will dependeth my welfare,
To call uppon thy hollye name syns daye nor night I spare,
    Graunt that the just request of this repentaunt mynd
So perce thyne eares that in thy sight som favour it may find.
    My soule is fraughted full with greif of follies past;   5
My restles bodye doth consume and death approcheth fast;
    Lyke them whose fatall threde thy hand hath cut in twayne,
Of whome ther is no further brewte, which in their graves
remayne.
    Oh Lorde, thow hast cast me hedling to please my fooe,
Into a pitt all botomeles, whear as I playne my wooe.   10
    The burden of thy wrath it doth me sore oppresse,
And sundrye stormes thow hast me sent of terrour and distresse.
    The faithfull frends ar fled and bannyshed from my sight,
And such as I have held full dere have sett my frendshipp light.
    My duraunce doth perswade of fredom such dispaire   15
That, by the teares that bayne my brest, myne eye sight doth
appaire.
    Yet did I never cease thyne ayde for to desyre,
With humble hart and stretched hands for to appease thy yre.
    Wherfore dost thow forbeare, in the defence of thyne,
To shewe such tokens of thy power, in sight of Adams lyne,   20
    Wherby eche feble hart with fayth might so be fedd
That in the mouthe of thy elect thy mercyes might be spredd?
    The fleshe that fedeth wormes can not thy love declare,
Nor suche sett forth thy faith as dwell in the land of dispaire.
    In blind endured herts light of thy lively name   25
Can not appeare, as can not judge the brightnes of the same.

Nor blasted may thy name be by the mouth of those
Whome death hath shutt in sylence, so as they may not disclose.
    The livelye voyce of them that in thy word delight
Must be the trumppe that must resound the glorye of thy
        might.   30
    Wherfore I shall not cease, in chief of my distresse,
To call on the till that the sleape my weryd lymes oppresse.
    And in the morning eke, when that the slepe is fledd,
With floods of salt repentaunt teres to washe my restles bedd.
    Within this carefull mynd, bourdnyd with care and greif, 35
Why dost thou not appere, Oh Lord, that sholdest be his relief?
    My wretched state beholde, whome death shall strait assaile;
Of one from youth afflicted still, that never did but waile.
    The dread, loo, of thyne yre hath trod me under feet;
The scourgis of thyne angrye hand hath made deth seme full
        sweet.   40
    Like to the roring waves the sunken shipp surrounde,
Great heaps of care did swallow me and I no succour found.
    For they whome no myschaunce could from my love devyde
Ar forced, for my greater greif, from me their face to hyde.

49

Psalm Seventy-three

Thoughe, Lorde, to Israell thy graces plentuous be:
I meane to such with pure intent as fixe their trust in the;
    Yet whiles the faith did faynt that shold have ben my guyde,
Lyke them that walk in slipper pathes my feet began to slyde,
    Whiles I did grudge at those that glorey in ther golde, 5
Whose lothsom pryde rejoyseth welth, in quiet as they wolde.
    To se by course of yeres what nature doth appere,
The pallayces of princely fourme succede from heire to heire;
    From all such travailes free as longe to Adams sede;
Neither withdrawne from wicked works by daunger nor by
        dread,   10
    Wherof their skornfull pryde; and gloried with their eyes,
As garments clothe the naked man, thus ar they clad in vyce.

Thus as they wishe succeds the mischief that they meane,
Whose glutten cheks slouth feads so fatt as scant their eyes be sene.
    Unto whose crewell power most men for dred ar fayne   15
To bend and bow with loftye looks, whiles they vawnt in their
    rayne
    And in their bloody hands, whose creweltye doth frame
The wailfull works that skourge the poore with out regard of
    blame.
    To tempt the living God they thinke it no offence,   19
And perce the symple with their tungs that can make no defence.
    Suche proofes bifore the just, to cawse the harts to waver,
Be sett lyke cups myngled with gall, of bitter tast and saver.
    Then saye thy foes in skorne, that tast no other foode,
But sucke the fleshe of thy elect and bath them in their bloode:
    'Shold we beleve the Lorde doth know and suffer this?   25
Foled be he with fables vayne that so abused is.'
    In terrour of the just thus raignes iniquitye,
Armed with power, laden with gold, and dred for crueltye.
    Then vayne the warr might seme that I by faythe mayntayne
Against the fleshe, whose false effects my pure hert wold dis-
    tayne.   30
    For I am scourged still, that no offence have doon,
By wrathes children; and from my birth my chastesing begoon.
    When I beheld their pryde and slacknes of thy hand,
I gan bewaile the woful state wherin thy chosen stand.
    And as I sought wherof thy sufferaunce, Lord, shold groo,   35
I found no witt cold perce so farr, thy holly domes to knoo,
    And that no mysteryes nor dought could be distrust
Till I com to the holly place, the mansion of the just,
    Where I shall se what end thy justice shall prepare
For such as buyld on worldly welth, and dye ther colours faire.   40
    Oh, how their ground is false and all their buylding vayne!
And they shall fall, their power shall faile that did their pryde
    mayntayne.
    As charged harts with care, that dreme some pleasaunt tourne,
After their sleape fynd their abuse, and to their plaint retourne,
    So shall their glorye faade; thy sword of vengeaunce shall   45
Unto their dronken eyes, in blood disclose their errours all.

And when their golden fleece is from their backe yshorne,
The spotts that under neth wer hidd, thy chosen shepe shall
   skorne.
And till that happye daye my hert shall swell in care,   49
My eyes yeld teares, my yeres consume bitwne hope and dispayre.
Loo, how my sprits ar dull, and all thy judgments darke;
No mortall hedd may skale so highe, but wunder at thy warke.
Alas, how oft my foes have framed my decaye;
But when I stode in drede to drenche, thy hands still did me stay.
And in eache voyage that I toke to conquer synne,   55
Thow wert my guyd, and gave me grace to comfort me therin.
And when my withered skyn unto my bones did cleve,
And fleshe did wast, thy grace did then my simple sprits releve.
In other succour then, Oh Lord, why should I trust,
But onely thyn, whom I have found in thy behight so just.   60
And suche for drede or gayne, as shall thy name refuse,
Shall perishe with their golden godds that did their harts seduce.
Where I, that in thy worde have set my trust and joye,
The highe reward that longs therto shall quietlye enjoye.
And my unworthye lypps, inspired with thy grace,   65
Shall thus forespeke thy secret works in sight of Adams race.

50

Psalm Fifty-five

Give eare to my suit, Lord, fromward hide not thy face.
Beholde, herking in grief, lamenting how I praye.
My fooes they bray so lowde, and eke threpe on so fast,
Buckeled to do me scathe, so is their malice bent.
Care perceth my entrayles and traveyleth my sprite;   5
The greslye feare of death envyroneth my brest;
A tremblynge cold of dred clene overwhelmeth my hert.
'O', thinke I, 'hadd I wings like to the symple dove,
This peryll myght I flye, and seke some place of rest
In wylder woods, where I might dwell farr from these cares.'   10
What speady way of wing my playnts shold thei lay on,
To skape the stormye blast that treatned is to me!

Rayne those unbrydled tungs! breake that conjured league!
For I decyphred have amydd our towne the stryfe: 14
Gyle and wrong kept the walles, they ward both day and night;
And whiles myscheif with care doth kepe the market stede;
Whilst wickidnes with craft in heaps swarme through the strete.
Ne my declared foo wrought me all this reproche;
By harme so loked for, yt wayeth halfe the lesse.
For though myne ennemyes happ had byn for to prevaile,   20
I cold have hidd my face from venym of his eye.
It was a frendly foo, by shadow of good will,
Myne old fere and dere frende, my guyde, that trapped me;
Where I was wont to fetche the cure of all my care,
And in his bosome hyde my secreat zeale to God.   25
Such soden surprys quicke may them hell devoure,
Whilst I invoke the Lord, whose power shall me defend.
My prayer shall not cease from that the sonne disscends
Till he his haulture wynn and hyde them in the see.
With words of hott effect, that moveth from hert contryte,   30
Such humble sute, O Lord, doth perce thy pacyent eare.
It was the Lord that brake the bloody compackts of those
That preloked on with yre to slaughter me and myne.
The everlasting God whose kingdom hath no end,
Whome, by no tale to dred he cold divert from synne,   35
The conscyence unquiet he stryks with hevy hand,
And proves their force in fayth whome he sware to defend.
Butter fales not so soft as doth hys pacyence longe,
And over passeth fine oyle, running not halfe so smothe.
But when his suffraunce fynds that brydled wrath provoks,   40
He thretneth wrath, he whets more sharppe then any toole can
    fyle.
Friowr, whose harme and tounge presents the wicked sort
Of those false wolves, with cootes which doo their ravin hyde,
That sweare to me by heaven, the fotestole of the Lord,
Who though force had hurt my fame, they did not touche my
    lyfe: 45
Such patching care I lothe as feeds the welth with lyes.
But in the th'other Psalme of David fynd I ease:
Iacta curam tuam super dominum et ipse te enutriet.

NOTES

1. *When ragyng love with extreme payne*

28. *draweth in ure*: 'comes into existence', 'comes in'.

2. *The soote season, that bud and blome furth bringes*

This is not a translation but a variation on the theme of Petrarch's sonnet *In Morte di Madonna Laura* cccx. (References for Petrarchan sonnets and *canzoni* are to the edition of the *Rime* by Carducci and Ferrari; recension of 1957.)

> Zefiro torna, e 'l bel tempo rimena,
>   E i fior e l'erbe, sua dolce famiglia,
>   E garrir Progne e pianger Filomena,
>   E primavera candida e vermiglia.
> Ridono i prati e 'l ciel si rasserena;
>   Giove s'allegra di mirar sua figlia;
>   L'aria e l'acqua e la terra è d'amor piena;
>   Ogni animal d'amar si riconsiglia.
> Ma per me, lasso! tornano i piú gravi
>   Sospiri, che del cor profondo tragge
>   Quella ch'al ciel se ne portò le chiavi;
> E cantar augelletti e fiorir piagge
>   E 'n belle donne oneste atti soavi
>   Sono un deserto e fere aspre e selvagge.

Petrarch's sonnet was a popular one, and inspired a number of imitations, e.g. the sonnet 'Zephyro spira e col so dolce fiato' by Pamphilo Sasso (*c.* 1455–1527) (no. xcvii, 1511 edn.), which in its realistic details is closer to Surrey's than Petrarch's. Its eighth line reads: 'La serpa va col capo al ciel levato' ('The serpent moves with head lifted towards the sky'). A translation of Petrarch's sonnet appears in *England's Helicon* (1600), beginning 'Zephirus brings the time that sweetly senteth'.

'The soote season' is a tissue of traditional phrasing drawn from English medieval poetry, e.g. for 'soote season' cf. *Canterbury Tales*, v. 389, for 'Somer is come' cf. *English Lyrics of the XIIIth Century*, ed. Carleton Brown, nos. 6, 52, and 54. Alliteration and archaism, used perhaps playfully, are prominent features of the poem.

1. *The soote season.* For a suggested semantic difference between *swete* and *swote* or *soote* see J. H. Fisher's article 'Chaucer's Use of *Swete* and *Swote*', *J.E.G.P.* l (1951).

9. *The adder . . . slinges*: cf. 41. 610.

10. *The swift . . . smale*: cf. Chaucer, *Parliament of Fowls*, ll. 353–4:

> The swalwe, mortherere of the foules smale
> That maken hony of floures freshe of hewe

11. *minges*: see Glossary.

14. *springes*: cf. *springes*, l. 5. The repetition of the rhyme word is perhaps to be explained according to the principle of *equivocatio* given in medieval Latin rhyming treatises. If the poet was in difficulties over finding a rhyme, he was allowed to take the same word provided it was used either in a different sense or as a different part of speech. This had become traditional English practice. See J. M. Berdan, *Early Tudor Poetry* (1939), p. 136. But sometimes no such explanation is possible (cf. 4. 5, 12).

3. *Set me wheras the sonne dothe perche the grene*

Translated from Petrarch's sonnet *In Vita* cxlv:

> Pommi ove 'l sole occide i fiori e l'erba
>   O dove vince lui il ghiaccio e la neve;
>   Pommi ov'è 'l carro suo temprato e leve
>   Et ov'è chi ce 'l rende o chi ce 'l serba:
> Pommi in umil fortuna od in superba,
>   Al dolce aere sereno al fosco e greve;
>   Pommi a la notte, al dí lungo ed al breve,
>   A la matura etate od a l'acerba:
> Pommi in cielo od in terra od in abisso,
>   In alto poggio in valle ima e palustre,
>   Libero spirto od a' suoi membri affisso:
> Pommi con fama oscura o con illustre:
>   Sarò qual fui, vivrò com'io visso,
>   Continuando il mio sospir trilustre.

Petrarch's sources are Horace, *Odes* i. 22. 17–24 and possibly *Satires* ii. 1. 57–60; and for l. 13 cf. Propertius, ii. 15. 36: 'huius ero vivus, mortuus huius ero'.

This is an example of the so-called Shakespearian sonnet, which Surrey was the first to devise. It divides into three quatrains and a concluding couplet, and its rhyme scheme is abab, cdcd, efef, gg.

4. *With prowde . . . wyse*: a departure from Petrarch which disrupts the development of the quatrain.

14. Petrarch's reference to the fifteen years' duration of his love ('trilustre') is suppressed.

4. *Love that doth raine and live within my thought*

Translated from Petrarch's sonnet *In Vita* cxl:

> Amor, che nel penser mio vive e regna
> E 'l suo seggio meggior nel mio cor tene,
> Tal or armato ne la fronte vène,
> Ivi si loca et ivi pon sua insegna.
> Quella ch'amare e sofferir ne 'nsegna,
> E vòl che 'l gran desio, l'accesa spene,
> Ragion, vergogna e reverenza affrene,
> Di nostro ardir fra sé stessa si degna.
> Onde Amor paventoso fugge al core
> Lasciando ogni sua impresa, e piange e trema;
> Ivi s'asconde e non appar piú fòre.
> Che poss'io far, temendo il mio signore,
> Se non star seco in fin a l'ora estrema?
> Ché bel fin fa chi ben amando more.

Wyatt translated the same sonnet ('The longe love, that in my thought doeth harbar', ed. Kenneth Muir, no. 4).

13. *shall not my foote remove*: cf. 41. 864–6, where Virgil has 'mene efferre pedem, genitor, te posse relicto / sperasti . . .'. Surrey is perhaps recalling Virgil's phrase and its context of loyal military service.

5. *In Cypres springes, wheras dame Venus dwelt*

The source is probably Ariosto, *Orlando Furioso*, i. 78:

> E questo hanno causato due fontane
> Che di diverso effetto hanno liquore,
> Ambe in Ardenna, e non sono lontane:
> D'amoroso desio l'una empie il core;
> Chi bee de l'altra, senza amor rimane,
> E volge tutto in ghiaccio il primo ardore.
> Rinaldo gustò d'una, e amor lo strugge;
> Angelica de l'altra, e l'odia e fugge.

4–6. H. A. Mason points out (*T.L.S.*, 6 Mar. 1953) the debts in phrasing to Wyatt's first Prologue to his Penitential Psalms (ed. Muir, no. 200): *creping fyre* (l. 8) and

> And when he saw that kendlid was the flame,
> The moyst poyson in his hert he launcyd. (ll. 9–10)

6. *I never saw youe, madam, laye aparte*

Translated from Petrarch's *ballata In Vita* xi:

> Lassare il velo o per sole o per ombra,
> Donna, non vi vid'io,
> Poi che in me conosceste il gran desio
> Ch'ogni altra voglia d'entr'al cor mi sgombra.
> Mentr'io portava i be' pensier celati
> C'hanno la mente desïando morta,
> Vidivi di pietate ornare il volto;
> Ma, poi ch'Amor di me vi fece accorta,
> Fuor i biondi capelli allor velati,
> E l'amoroso sguardo in sé raccolto.
> Quel ch'i' piú desïava in voi, m'è tolto;
> Sí mi governa il velo,
> Che per mia morte et al caldo et al gelo
> De' be' vostri occhi il dolce lume adombra.

Line 10 is omitted in the MS. Tottel reads: 'Her smilyng lokes that hid thus euermore.' Padelford's conjectural adaptation of his reading is followed in the text.

2. *cornet*: a kind of head-dress with a veil or shade to protect the complexion against the sun.

12. *governe*: cf. Petrarch's *governa*. Surrey misses the idiomatic force of the Italian word, which means 'ill-treat'.

7. *Alas, so all thinges nowe doe holde their peace*

Adapted from Petrarch's sonnet *In Vita* clxiv:

> Or che 'l ciel e la terra e 'l vento tace
> E le fere e gli augelli il sonno affrena,
> Notte il carro stellato in giro mena
> E nel suo letto il mar senz'onda giace;

Vegghio, penso, ardo, piango; e chi mi sface
 Sempre m'è inanzi per mia dolce pena:
 Guerra è 'l mio stato, d'ira e di duol piena;
 E sol di lei pensando ho qualche pace.
Cosí sol d'una chiara fonte viva
 Move 'l dolce e l'amaro ond'io mi pasco;
 Una man sola mi risana e punge.
E perché 'l mio martír non giunga a riva,
 Mille volte il dí moro e mille nasco;
 Tanto da la salute mia son lunge.

Surrey's sonnet falls into three parts: ll. 1–4, ll. 5–9, and ll. 10–14. Cf. No. 10.

 2. *nothing*: stressed on the second syllable.

 3. *ayer*: 'wind'. It renders *vento* in Petrarch's l. 1. For this use of the word, cf. Shakespeare, *Timon of Athens*, IV. iii. 222: 'the bleake ayre, thy boysterous Chamberlaine'. Nott objected to this line: 'It cannot be said of the beasts and of the air, that like the birds they "*cease their song*"; and yet as the passage now stands, there is nothing else with which those nominatives can agree.'

 4. *The nightes chare . . . bring*. Cf. Sackville, *Induction*, ll. 46–49:

> When that the stars fraught in the heavens face
> With twinckeling light shone on the earth apace
> That, while they brought about the nightes chare,
> The darke had dimd the daie er I was ware.

As Nott points out, this passage shows that *nightes* is used by Surrey as a disyllable and that *the starres* is the subject of the sentence, despite the singular verb *dothe bring*.

 5. *Calme . . . lesse*. Cf. 42. 704:

> The woodes, the ragyng seas were falne to rest.

Virgil's famous night-piece in *Aeneid* iv. 522–8 was the chief source of Petrarch's sonnet; Surrey's versions of both poets are worth comparing.

 13. *againe*: to be construed with 'When that I thinke'.

8. *The golden gift that Nature did thee geve*

No source is known, but with l. 4 cf. Petrarch, *In Vita* clix. 1–4:

> In qual parte del ciel, in quale idea
> Era l'essempio onde natura tolse

Quel bel viso leggiadro, in ch'ella volse
Mostrar qua giú quanto là su potea?

5. *Whose*: i.e. Nature's.
6. *lively domes*: 'quick judgments'.

9. *From Tuscan cam my ladies worthi race*

The 'Geraldine' of this sonnet and her relationship to Surrey have been the subject of extensive romantic speculation. The essential facts are as follows. Lady Elizabeth Fitzgerald ('Geraldine'), the grand-daughter of Gerald Fitzgerald, ninth Earl of Kildare, was born in Ireland in or about 1528 and was brought to England in 1533. Probably in 1539 she entered the service of Princess Elizabeth, and seems to have been transferred to that of Queen Catherine Howard in 1540. She was married in December 1542 to Sir Anthony Browne, Master of the Horse. She was then fourteen or fifteen, he was about sixty.

The tradition that Surrey and 'Geraldine' were lovers took its origin from Nashe's *Unfortunate Traveller* (1594). According to this picaresque romance, 'Geraldine' was the object of Surrey's passion. For her Surrey wrote his love-poems and for her he entered the lists at Florence to defend her beauty against all comers. Drayton used Nashe's fiction in *Englands Heroicall Epistles, Henry Howard Earle of Surrey to Geraldine* (1597), and it was subsequently accepted as fact by scholars and romancers for over two centuries. The legend reached its high point of elaboration in G. F. Nott's otherwise admirable edition of Surrey in 1815. The full reaction came at the end of the 19th century when the imaginative fabric of Nashe's account was shown up for what it was by Bapst in *Deux Gentilshommes-Poètes de la Cour de Henry VIII* (1891) and Court-hope in *History of English Poetry* (1897). According to this unromantic reading of the facts, Lady Elizabeth was a child of nine when Surrey wrote this sonnet for her; the sonnet being placed in 1537, the year in which Surrey was confined at Windsor for striking a courtier within the precincts of the Court. 'The truth probably is that Surrey whiled away an idle hour of confinement by composing a sonnet in compliment to a little girl of nine whose pretty face chanced to have caught his fancy' (Padelford, p. 219).

The most recent scholar to investigate the matter is Professor Ruth Hughey, who has edited *The Arundel Harington Manuscript of Tudor Poetry* (1960). In her notes to Surrey's poem *Gyrtt in my giltlesse gowne* she challenges the theory that *From Tuscan cam* was written for 'a little girl of nine or ten'. She suggests that the sonnet was written not in

1537 but in 1541, in which year ' "Geraldine" was thirteen or fourteen years old, of an age to command the chivalric admiration of a young courtier, who might profess to serve her in the courtly love tradition. . . . I suggest that Surrey wrote this particular sonnet during his visit to Windsor in May, 1541 (note line 12), for the Feast of the Garter, following his election as a Knight of the Garter the preceding April 23. . . . It was a compliment to a young girl who in a little more than a year would be married. To interpret Surrey's lines as written for a child of nine seems to me as wide of the mark as to incorporate the fantastic fiction of Nashe into the relationship.' Courthope's remarks concerning Surrey and 'Geraldine' (vol. ii. 78–79) should be borne in mind; he concludes 'with little doubt, that Surrey had professed himself her "man"', and that she had accepted his service after the manner prescribed by the laws of courtesy. . . . The tender age of the Lady Elizabeth is no objection to the literal interpretation of the expressions used by Surrey, as far as regards the ceremonious aspect of the matter, for we know from the code of André le Chapelain and numerous poetical examples, that twelve years was the age when the female sex became amenable to the service of love, fourteen being that prescribed for the male sex. . . .'

The question of the sonnet's date cannot be regarded as closed. Against Miss Hughey's otherwise persuasive hypothesis for a 1541 date may be urged the omission of any reference to Queen Catherine in whose service by this time Lady Elizabeth was.

1. *Tuscan*: a 16th-century form of *Tuscany*. Cf. Lord Morley's translation of Petrarch's *Trionfi* (1554; reprinted by Roxburghe Club, 1887, p. 9): 'And borne in Toscane where thou was borne perdye.'

2. *Florence*. The Fitzgeralds traced their descent from the Geraldi family of Florence.

her: possibly the older pronoun form of *their*. However, it may be the 3rd sg. poss. pron. and refer to 'my lady'. 'Her' would then be rhetorically parallel to *her* in l. 4.

6. *hir dame . . . bloud*. The mother of Lady Elizabeth Fitzgerald was Lady Elizabeth Grey, who was grand-daughter of Elizabeth Woodville, queen of Edward IV, and first cousin of Henry VIII.

9. *Honsdon*: '. . . in the period 1536–39 Mary and Elizabeth, i.e. the Princesses, had only one household and one cofferer. The accounts indicate that the household of the Princess Mary moved about frequently, including a good many stops both at Hunsdon and at Hampton, and that the Princess Elizabeth was often with her . . .' (Hughey, op. cit. ii. 80). On any one of these occasions Surrey could have met Lady Elizabeth in the suite of Princess Elizabeth.

12. *Windsor*. See introductory note to this poem.

10. *The fansy which that I have served long*

This sonnet was probably written some time between September 1545 and March 1546, during which period Surrey was lieutenant-general on the Continent and commander of Boulogne. No close source is known, but cf. Wyatt (ed. Muir, no. 59):

> Some tyme I fled the fyre that me brent,
>   By see, by land, by water and by wynd;
> And now I folow the coles that be quent
>   From Dovor to Calais against my mynde.
> Lo! how desire is boeth sprong and spent!
>   And he may se that whilome was so blynde;
> And all his labor now he laugh to scorne,
> Mashed in the breers that erst was all to torne.

With ll. 12–14 cf. Wyatt (ed. cit., no. 81. 6–8):

> So hangith in balaunce
> Off warr, my pees, reward of all my payne;
> At Mountzon thus I restles rest in Spayne.

9. *long*. For the repeated rhyme-words here and at l. 11, see note to 2. 14.

10. *my guyde*: i.e. 'Love'. *guyde* means 'leader'.

12. *base Bullayn*: the Lower Town of Boulogne, where Surrey was residing. However, the phrase *amiddes the hylles in base Bullayn* contributes verbally to the effect of paradox made by ll. 10–14.

11. *The sonne hath twyse brought forthe the tender grene*

Lines 19–20, wanting in the MS., are supplied from Tottel. The following MS. readings have been emended in the text, l. 22, *might*, and l. 52, *or me*. The metre is terza rima.

1–6. Cf. Chaucer, *Troilus and Criseyde*, v. 8–14.

10. *inflame*. Tottel has 'that mine in flame hath made', which may be the correct reading. *inflame* is otherwise not recorded.

16. *have . . . in skorne*: an Italian construction; ct. l. 30 below.

18. *At hand . . . to bourne*. Cf. Petrarch, *In Vita* ccxxiv. 12:

> S'arder da lunge et agghiacciar da presso.

This sonnet of Petrarch's was translated by Wyatt (ed. Muir, no. 12), who renders this line as 'Yf burning a farr of and fresing nere'. Cf. also 13. 40–41.

21–30. Surrey seems to have in mind the opening lines of Petrarch's sestina *In Vita* xxii. 1–6:

> A qualunque animale alberga in terra,
>   Se non alquanti c'hanno in odio il sole,
>   Tempo da travagliare è quanto è 'l giorno;
>   Ma, poi che 'l ciel accende le sue stelle,
>   Qual torna a casa e qual s'annida in selva,
>   Per aver posa al meno in fino a l'alba.

26. *cawser*: a common term in the courtly love poetry of the 15th and early 16th centuries; frequent in Wyatt. Cf. 41. 771.

30. *hath the light in haat*: cf. Petrarch's 'c'hanno in odio il sole'.

32–34. Cf. Petrarch, *In Vita* xxxv. 1–4:

> Solo e pensoso i piú deserti campi
>   Vo mesurando a passi tardi e lenti;
>   E gli occhi porto, per fuggire, intenti,
>   Ove vestigio uman l'arena stampi.

32. *And me withdrawe from everie haunted place* renders Petrarch's 'Ove vestigio uman l'arena stampi' (literally: 'where human footprint impresses the sand'). *haunted*: 'frequented'.

33. *to playne*: i.e. 'too plain', 'too obvious'. The difference in meaning between *to playne* here and in l. 31 permits the rhyme on identical words. In l. 31 *to playne* is the verbal infinitive. See note to 2. 14.

34. *And with my mynd I measure, paas by paas*. Petrarch's 'Vo mesurando a passi tardi e lenti' refers to an actual journeying; Surrey makes the journey a mental one. *with my mynd*: 'in my mind'.

35. *that place where I my self hadd lost*. Cf. Petrarch, *In Vita* clxxv. 1–4:

> Quando me vène innanzi il tempo e 'l loco
>   Ov'i' perdei me stesso, e 'l caro nodo
>   Ond'Amor di sua man m'avinse in modo
>   Che l'amar me fe' dolce e il pianger gioco. . . .

(i.e. 'When there come before me the time and the place where I lost myself. . . .')

36. *that laase*. Perhaps suggested by Petrarch's *caro nodo* ('sweet knot' —see previous note). But *laase* (or *las* or *lace*) is a common term in English medieval love poetry corresponding to *laccio* in Italian and *las* in French. It occurs several times in Petrarch, e.g. *In Vita* lix. 4–5:

> Tra le chiome de l'òr nascose il laccio,
>   Al qual mi strinse, Amore . . .

Cf. Chaucer, *C.T.* A. ll. 1815–18.

40. *that*: i.e. 'what'.

41–44. The metaphor of the ship for the despairing lover appears in Petrarch's sonnet *In Vita* clxxxix, which Wyatt translated (ed. Muir, no. 28: 'My galy charged with forgetfulnes'). The guiding stars, suggested by the eyes of the poet's lady, are also Petrarchan, e.g. *In Vita* lxxiii. 46–51:

> Come a forza di venti
> Stanco nocchier di notte alza la testa
> A' duo lumi c'ha sempre il nostro polo,
> Cosí ne la tempesta
> Ch'i' sostengo d'amor gli occhi lucenti
> Sono il mio segno e 'l mio conforto solo ...

Like the metaphor of love's noose or net, the guiding star is a common one in Renaissance love poetry. Shakespeare's 'It is the star to every wandring barke' (Sonnet 116) is probably the best-known example.

47–49: *And yf I flye . . . flight*. Cf. Petrarch, *In Vita* ccix. 9–11:

> E, qual cervo ferito di saetta
> Co 'l ferro avelenato dentr'al fianco
> Fugge, e piú duolsi quanto piú s'affretta ...

Petrarch's source is Virgil, *Aeneid* iv. 69–73.

51. *some percell of my will*: 'some part of my desires'. Nott finds the same phrase in Sir Thomas More's poem *To Them that Seke Fortune*, ll. 26–28:

> But for all that, she kepeth ever in store,
> From every manne some parcell of his wyll,
> That he may pray therfore and serve her styll.

13. *Suche waiwarde waies hath love*

Lines 31–32 are supplied from B.M. MS. Add. 28635. MS. reading in l. 45 *Which . . . seasoned* is emended in the text.

1–14. Cf. Ariosto, *Orlando Furioso*, ii. 1:

> Ingiustissimo Amor, perché sí raro
> Corrispondenti fai nostri desiri,
> Onde perfido avvien che t'è sí caro
> Il discorde voler ch'in duo cor miri?
> Gir non mi lasci al facil guado e chiaro,
> E nel piú cieco e maggior fondo tiri:
> Da chi disia il mio amor tu mi richiami,
> E chi m'ha in odio vuoi ch'adori et ami.

5–6. Cf. Ovid, *Metam.* i. 468–71; also Petrarch, *In Vita* ccvi. 10–11.

7. *easye*: 'slight', 'insignificant', i.e. as opposed to the strong 'gleames of burning fire'.

8. *by ame*: 'by hazard', 'by guess'.

9. *easye fourde*: cf. Ariosto's 'facil guado e chiaro' ('easy and clear ford').

15 ff. The rest of the poem draws on Petrarch, *Trionfo d'Amore* iii. 151–87:

> Or so come da sé 'l cor si disgiunge
>   e come sa far pace, guerra e tregua,
>   e coprir suo dolor, quand'altri il punge;
>
> e so come in un punto si dilegua
>   e poi si sparge per le guance il sangue,   155
>   se paura o vergogna avven che 'l segua;
>
> so come sta tra' fiori ascoso l'angue,
>   come sempre tra due si vegghia e dorme,
>   come senza languir si more e langue;
>
> so de la mia nemica cercar l'orme   160
>   e temer di trovarla, e so in qual guisa
>   l'amante ne l'amato si trasforme;
>
> so fra lunghi sospiri e brevi risa
>   stato, voglia, color cangiare spesso,
>   viver stando dal cor l'alma divisa;   165
>
> so mille volte il dì ingannar me stesso,
>   so, seguendo 'l mio foco ovunque e' fugge,
>   arder da lunge ed agghiacciar da presso.
>
> so com'Amor sovra la mente rugge
>   e com'ogni ragione indi discaccia;   170
>   e so in quante maniere il cor si strugge;
>
> so di che poco canape s'allaccia
>   un'anima gentil quand'ella è sola
>   e non v'è chi per lei difesa faccia;
>
> so com'Amor saetta e come vola   175
>   e so com'or minaccia ed or percote,
>   come ruba per forza e come invola,

e come sono instabili sue rote,
le mani armate, e gli occhi avvolti in fasce,
sue promesse di fé come son vote,   180

come nell'ossa il suo foco si pasce,
e ne le vene vive occulta piaga,
onde morte e palese incendio nesce.

In somma so che cosa è l'alma vaga,
rotto parlar con subito silenzio,   185
ché poco dolce molto amaro appaga,

di che s'ha il mel temprato con l'assenzio.

17. *I know ... lust*: 'I know how to form my will to the wishes of others' (Nott).

24. *The hamer of the restles forge*: the metaphor of the mind as a forge is common in 16th-century English poetry. An early example is Wyatt (ed. Muir, no. 137. 7–8):

> Suche hammers worke within my hed
> That sounde nought els unto my eris

Surrey uses it in his Epitaph on Wyatt (see 28. 6). Shakespeare makes frequent use of it, e.g. *Henry V*, Act V, Prol. l. 23: 'In the quick forge and working-house of thought.'

30. *resolving all hys fume*: i.e. 'for allaying his anguish'. For *fume* cf. Shakespeare, *Romeo*, I. i. 196: 'Love is a smoake made with the fume of sighes.'

36. *And live ... removed*. Cf. Petrarch, *In Vita* xv. 9–14:

> Tal or m'assale in mezzo a' tristi pianti
> Un dubbio: come posson queste membra
> Da lo spirito lor viver lontane?
> Ma rispondemi Amor: Non ti rimembra
> Che questo è privilegio de gli amanti,
> Sciolti da tutte qualitati umane?

37. *lawghters of the splene*: As well as being the seat of laughter or mirth, the spleen was regarded as the seat of melancholy; which must be its application here: 'forced, melancholy laughter'.

40. *how the lyon chastised is*. Rollins quotes Topsell's *Historie of Four-Footed Beastes* (1607): 'the best way to tame lyons is to bring up with them a little dogge, and often times to beate the same dogge in their presence, by which discipline, the lion is made more tractable to the will

of his keeper'. Cf. Chaucer, *C.T.* F. 491. Surrey is possibly making a personal allusion here: the lion was one of the heraldic supports of the Howards.

49–50. *slipper state . . . doubtfull hope . . . certayne woo.* Surrey may be remembering a passage in the *Trionfo d'Amore* (iv. 139–53) where similar phrases occur: 'lubrico sperar', 'certe doglie e d'allegrezze incerte'.

14. *Yf he that erst the fourme so lively drewe*

Nott points out that the source of this poem is a rondeau by Marot, *A La Fille D'un Painctre D'Orleans, Belle entre les Autres*:

> Au temps passé Apelles, Painctre sage,
> Feit seulement de Venus le visage,
> Par fiction: mais, pour plus haut attaindre,
> Ton pere ha fait de Venus, sans rien faindre,
> Entierement la face & le corsage.
>   Car il est Painctre, & tu es son ouvrage,
> Mieux ressemblant Venus, de forme, & d'aage,
> Que le tableau qu'Apelles voulut paindre
>   Au temps passé.
>   Vray est, qu'il feit si belle son image,
> Qu'elle eschauffoit en Amour maint courage:
> Mais celle là que ton pere ha sceu taindre,
> Y met le feu, & ha dequoy l'estaindre:
> L'autre n'eut pas un si gros avantage
>   Au temps passé.

1–2. *he that . . . faas*: Apelles, probably the greatest painter of antiquity. He lived from the time of Philip of Macedon till after the death of Alexander. One of his most famous paintings was of Aphrodite rising from the sea. This allusive and circuitous way of referring to Apelles without naming him directly is a rhetorical figure called *antonomasia*; it was much favoured by humanist poets. For other examples in Surrey cf. 31. 1 and 32. 1.

5. *Touchid with flame* should be construed with *some*, i.e. 'That image caused some men, enflamed with love, to come to grief'.

15. *When sommer toke in hand*

Tottel's *Unwillingly* in l. 34 has been emended to *Unwittingly*, which is the reading of the later editions. There is a certain general resemblance between this poem and the opening of Chaucer's *Troilus*. In both cases the season is spring; both Troilus and the poet are rebels against Love, and both are promptly subdued. With the ending of Surrey's poem, cf. *Troilus*, i. 232 ff.: 'Forthy ensample taketh of this man. . . .'

19. *Ver.* A common word for 'spring' in Chaucer and his imitators.

20. *the new betrothed birdes.* Birds were supposed to choose their mates on St. Valentine's Day. Cf. Chaucer, *Parliament of Fowls*, ll. 308–11. Surrey's word *ywrought*, oddly applied to the birds in l. 11, appears in the previous stanza of Chaucer's (l. 305).

25. *resolve.* Nott plausibly suggests that *revolve* is the correct reading.

28. *reject at nought*: 'set at nought', 'despised'. *reject* is past participle.

34. *to malice thy pretense*: 'to impugn thy claim to authority'.

16. *In winters just returne*

There are elements in this poem, as Padelford points out, of the French *pastourelle*, in which a shepherd complains to another of his mistress's hard usage, and of the *chanson à personnages*, in which the poet chances upon a man who is lamenting an unrequited love.

1–4. The wintry morning is chosen as a setting suitable for the woeful death of a shepherd. Cf. Spenser, *Shepheardes Calender; November*, ll. 9–20.

1. *Boreas*: the north wind.

3. *as*: for 'whenas'.

6. *palm*: a sallow or willow. See *O.E.D. palm* sb. 4 and *sallow* sb. 1. The willow was commonly associated with melancholy lovers. Cf. *As You Like It*, III. ii. 186: 'Look here what I found on a palm tree'— said by Rosalind of Orlando's love-verses. A modern example occurs in A. E. Housman's *March* (*A Shropshire Lad*):

> Afield for palms the girls repair,
> And sure enough the palms are there,
> And each will find by hedge or pond
> Her waving silver-tufted wand.

27. *rashly*: 'hastily'.

41. *His back against the tree.* The Man in Black, in Chaucer's *Boke of the Duchesse*, ll. 445–7, similarly sits against a tree.

44. *Such one . . . prove.* Cf. *Boke of the Duchesse*, ll. 908–11.

53. *beareth me in hand*: 'maintains against me'.

58. *Whose record, lo, I claime to have*: 'Whose testimony I wish to have.'

64. *an emperour.* The same comparison is made by Romeo: 'That I reviv'd and was an emperor' (*Rom. and Jul.* v. i. 9). [V. also p. 160].

67. *right*: 'immediately'.

69. *wonders*: the older and more correct form of 'wondrous'.

78. *Chreseids love ... Troilus.* Surrey was clearly well acquainted with Chaucer's poem.

80. *bleew.* The colour of constancy. Cf. Chaucer, *Troilus*, iii. 885, where Criseyde sends Troilus a 'blewe ring'.

81–82. *not so sone But*: 'no sooner than'.

17. *If care do cause men cry*

5–8. Cf. Petrarch, *In Vita* xxii. 1–6. Surrey has already used this Petrarchan passage in No. 11. See note to 11. 21–30.

8. *shyp boy.* In *2 Hen. IV*, III. i. 19, Shakespeare uses the same illustration to contrast with the king's sleeplessness.

13. For the cadence cf. 43. 1–8 and 19.

21. *the striken dere.* This notable phrase first makes its appearance here in English poetry. The source is probably Douglas, *Eneados*, IV. ii. 40, 'ane strykkyn hynd'; cf. Surrey's 'the striken hinde' at 42. 88.

35. *her servant*: i.e. *Servant d'Amour.*

48. *good hope.* In earlier love allegories *Good-hope* was a personification, sometimes opposed to *Wan-hope* (despair). Cf. *Romaunt of the Rose*, ll. 2760 ff., Lydgate, *Temple of Glas*, l. 1197, and James I, *Kingis Quair*, st. 113.

49. *to serve and suffer pacientlie.* This is the refrain of a song by Wyatt (ed. Muir, no. 187, beginning 'Synce love wyll nedes that I shall love').

55. *untill my brethe*: Nott suggests that 'untill my death' is the correct reading.

60. *I do bequeth my weried ghost.* Cf. Chaucer, *Troilus*, iv. 319–22 and *C.T.* A. ll. 2768–70.

18. *To dearely had I bought*

Like No. 27, this is essentially a poem of friendship. In *One Soul in Bodies Twain. Friendship in Tudor Literature and Stuart Drama*, 1937, p. 116, L. J. Mills quotes this poem for its reflexion of classical ideas of friendship. See Cicero, *De Amicitia*, for the notion that friends must give each other frank advice.

4. *colours dim*: 'dark colours', i.e. 'dark deceits'.

19. *in thy respect*: 'compared to thee'.

19. *O lothsome place, where I*

6–7. *As fortune it ne would*: 'As if fortune would not have it . . .'.

37–40. The rhymes *tought/aloft* and *furst/dust* were probably perfect in Surrey's day. *tought* would be pronounced 'toft' and *furst* 'fust'.

[20. See p. 160]

21. *Wrapt in my carelesse cloke*

1. *Wrapt in my careless cloke*: i.e. a garb suitable to the melancholy lover, 'demonstrating a careless desolation' (*As You Like It*, III. ii. 400). The phrase appears in Chapman's comedy *The Widdowes Teares* (1612), iii. 1: 'What wrapt in carelesse cloake, face hid in hat unbanded . . .'.

10. *liveth all to long*: 'wearies of his life'.

21. *wrasteth new her grace*: i.e. 'forces herself once more to bestow favour'.

27. *row*: 'company of lovers'.

30. *hory heares are powdred in her hedde*. Cf. Wyatt (ed. Muir, no. 35. 13): 'gray heres ben powdered in your sable'.

22. *Gyrtt in my giltlesse gowne*

A reply to the previous poem. The woman speaks for herself. In his first edition Tottel assigns the poem to an uncertain author; in the second it is placed among Surrey's poems, following *Wrapt in my carelesse cloke*. Tottel prints only the first twenty lines.

1. *Gyrtt in my giltye gowne*. This phrase and *wrapt in a craftye cloke* in l. 15 seem suggested by the opening of the previous poem ('the song now sung and past').

21. *storye*: i.e. Bible history. 'In early use the most frequent application [of 'story'] was to passages of Bible history and legends of saints' (*O.E.D.*).

22. The story of Susanna appears in the Vulgate, Daniel xiii—a chapter rejected by the Reformers, who assigned it to the Apocrypha.

28. *Childe*. 'In 13th and 14th c. "child" appears to have been applied to a young noble awaiting knighthood' (*O.E.D.*). Perhaps here: 'knight'.

23. *O happy dames, that may embrace*

This poem and No. 24 were probably written for the Countess of Surrey, from whom Surrey was separated while he was on military duty in France. 'In February, 1546, Surrey renewed his suit to the King for permission to bring his wife and family to Boulogne. Again his request was refused, the reason given being that the King "thinketh [it] not best now that time of service (which will bring some trouble and disquietness unmeet for women's imbecilities) approacheth, that your Lordship should send for my Lady your wife"' (E. Casady, *Henry Howard, Earl of Surrey*, 163). The poem owes something to *Epistola* 6 of Serafino de' Ciminelli dall'Aquila (*Rime*, ed. Menghini, 1894). Serafino's poem is in the manner of Ovid's *Heroides*.

7. *help to fill my moorning voyce*: i.e. 'join with me in my lamentations'.

8–14. For the ship image cf. Petrarch, *In Vita* clxxxix, beginning 'Passa la nave mia colma d'oblio'; it was translated by Wyatt (ed. Muir, no. 28: 'My galy charged with forgetfulnes').

22. *in armes acrosse*: i.e. embracing. Cf. 45. 19.

24–28. Cf. Serafino, *Epist.* 6. 37–40:

> Ah, quante volte quando el ciel se imbruna
> A mezzanotte uscío del freddo letto
> A sentir l'ore, a remirar la luna.
> Fatta son marinar per questo effetto.

Something may also be owing to Virgil, *Aeneid* iv. See 42. 730–1 and 782–3.

33. Cf. Serafino, ibid., ll. 79–81:

> E se affondato è alcun dal tempo rio
> Che 'l sappia, dico: ohimè, questo è summerso
> E uno altro mar de lacrime faccio io.

my swete fo. A conventional phrase; cf. Chaucer, *Troilus*, v. 228: 'O herte mine! Criseyde, my swete foe'.

24. *Good ladies, you that have*

Lines 15–16, wanting in the MS., are supplied from Tottel. In l. 37 MS. *the sower* has been emended, following Tottel. See note on No. 23. This is a poem on the same subject but written, as Nott observed, in a lower and more familiar style.

2. *Stepp in your foote*. The sense of *foote* meaning 'chorus or burden of a song' may be present.

11. *That . . . myndes*. Probably corrupt. Tottel reads: 'Whome I was wont tembrace with well contented minde', with the rhyme word 'winde'. Perhaps it should be emended to '. . . content in mynde, . . . wynde'.

21. *the same doth tell me*: i.e. 'The fearefull dreames' (l. 17).

22. *with T. his lytle sonne*: Surrey's eldest son, Thomas Howard, born in March 1516.

27. *saluith me agayne*: 'kisses me back'.

29–30. Cf. 26. 9–10 and Chaucer, *Troilus*, iv. 236–7:

> And in his brest the heped wo bygan
> Out breste . . .

34. *Some hydden wheare to steale the gryfe*. Possibly corrupt. It seems to mean: 'Some hidden place where I may beguile myself of my grief'. Tottel reads: 'Sum hidden place, wherein to slake the gnawing of my mind'.

41. *convart*: perhaps 'direct'. Tottel reads 'conjure'.

25. *Laid in my quyett bedd*

For the ages of man, cf. Horace, *Ars Poetica* 156 ff., and the 1st Satire for the theme that men are never satisfied with their lot. Horace divides human life into four ages; for a division into three, cf. Aristotle, *Rhetoric* ii. 12. We may compare with Surrey's handling of metre and subject the poem of Hardy's which begins:

> I look into my glass,
> And view my wasting skin,
> And say, 'Would God it came to pass
> My heart had shrunk so thin!'

17. *my right way*: 'my straight (direct) road', i.e. the way from the mouth to the belly. (This note and those to ll. 20 and 23 were supplied by Mr. J. B. Leishman.)

20. *lyke lynes of true belief*: i.e. 'like lines (or passages) of Scripture', such as 'All flesh is grass', &c.

22. *The whiche do wryte*: cf. Chaucer, *C.T.* A. 3869: 'This white top writeth myne olde yeris'.

23. *Hang upp . . . the bitt*: i.e. 'Hang up the bit and bridle of your young coltish time'—he is now an old horse fit only for the paddock. *bit* is probably to be understood as 'bit and bridle'.

26. *Trusse upp thie pack*: 'Apparently a proverbial expression; signifying, that it is time to remove, or change' (Nott). Cf. Thomas More's poem *To those that seke fortune*, l. 40: 'I counsayle you eche one, trusse up your packes'.

28. *to their tyme*: 'in their time'.

26. *When Windesor walles sustained my wearied arme*

In 1537 Surrey was confined to Windsor Castle for having struck a courtier in the precincts of the Court. See Biographical Note.

1–2. This attitude (chin resting on hand, elbow on knee) was conventionally expressive of melancholy thoughtfulness. Cf. Chapman, *Hero and Leander*, 3. 297–9:

> Her right hand leand on her hart-bowing knee, . . .
> Her knee stayd that, and that her falling face

5. See note to 15. 20.

7. *joily woes*: *joily* is a common 15th- and 16th-century form of *jolly*. *joily woes* is modelled on the conventional Italian phrase *dolci guai*. Chaucer has 'I have a joly wo, a lusty sorwe' (*Troilus*, ii. 1099).

the hateles shorte debate: i.e. 'friendly emulation in warlike sports and exercises' (Nott). Cf. 27. 17–20.

11. A Petrarchan hyperbole. Cf. *In Morte* cclxxxviii. 1:

> I'ho pien di sospir' quest' aere tutto

smoky may be a reminiscence of Chaucer's 'smoky reyn' (*Troilus*, iii. 628). But the immediate source is probably Wyatt, *Penitential Psalms* (ed. Muir, no. 206. 17–24):

> But who had bene withowt the Cavis mowth,
>   And herd the terys and syghes that he did strayne,
> He wold have sworne there had owt off the sowth
>   A lewk warme wynd browght forth a smoky rayne;
> But that so close the Cave was and unkowth
>   That none but god was record off his payne:
> Elles had the wynd blowne in all Israells erys
> The woffull plaint and off theire kyng the terys.

27. *So crewell prison howe could betyde, alas*

See introductory note to 26. The *Kinges soon* of l. 3 was Henry Fitzroy, Duke of Richmond, the natural son of Henry VIII. He married Surrey's sister, Lady Mary Howard, in 1533; he died of consumption in 1536, aged seventeen. The poem's structure, based on *parison* and *enumeratio*, is a development of 15th-century forms: cf. Lydgate, *Testament*, stanzas 6 and 7, and James I, *Kingis Quair*, stanza 121:

> Say on than, 'quhare is becummen, for schame!
>   The songis new, the fresch carolis and dance,
> The lusty lif, the mony change of game,
>   The fresche array,   the lusty contenance,
> The besy awayte, the hertly observance,
> That quhilum was amongis thame so ryf?
> Bid thaim repent in tyme, and mend thaire lyf.'

Surrey tacitly uses the *ubi sunt* convention, but without moralizing.

3. *my childish yeres*: *childish* here means 'youthful' and probably has a chivalric colouring. Cf. *childe* meaning 'youth of gentle birth awaiting knighthood' or 'knight' in 22. 28.

7. *maydens towre*: 'that part of the castle where the ladies of the court had their apartments' (Nott).

8. *easye sighes*: cf. Chaucer, *Troilus*, iii. 1361–4, and James I, *Kingis Quair*, stanza 96.

11. *tygers*: an allusion, half-humorous, to the extravagant language of love poetry. Tigers were types of unfeeling savagery; cf. 42. 480.

13. *The palme playe*: this was a game resembling tennis, in which the ball was struck with the palm of the hand instead of a racket. Erasmus commends it in one of his colloquies: 'Nulla res melius exercet omnes corporis partes, quam pila palmaria, sed aptior hiemi quam aestati' (*De Lusu*).

17. *The graveld ground*: the space enclosed within the lists and strewn with gravel for the tilting. *with sleeves tyed . . . helme*: the practice of knights of 'tying to their helmets a sleeve, or glove, or any favour received from their mistresses, which they wore not only in tilts and tournaments, but even in battle' (Nott).

19. Tottel reads: '. . . as though one should another whelme:'

32. *chace . . . a force*: '*Chasse à forcer* is the old hunting term for that game which is run down, in opposition to the *chasse à tirer*, that in which it is shot' (Nott).

43–44: *The which . . . Upsupped have*: cf. Wyatt, *Penitential Psalms* (ed. Muir, no. 206. 25): 'Off wych some part, when he upp suppyd hade', and see note on 26. 11. The word *upsupped* was clearly more acceptable in Surrey's day than it is now; *O.E.D.* cites examples from Wyclif and More ('As for al other sinnes whatsoever thei be, faith saith he . . . suppeth them al up in a moment', *Confutation of Tyndale*, 1532).

45. Nott compares Wyatt's 'The restfull place, renewer of my smart' (Muir prints a different version which reads 'Revyver of my smarte' (no. 115)). Cf. too Troilus's address to Criseyde's empty house (*Troilus*, v. 540–53).

49. *Eache stone, alas,*: the MS. reads 'eache alas'; Tottel has 'Eccho (alas)'. The 1574 edition of Tottel reads 'Eche stone, alas' which Nott prints. This is the reading adopted in the text.

51. *where all my fredome grew*: *fredome* here means 'nobility' or 'courtesy'. Cf. Chaucer, *C. T.* B.² ll. 2642: 'He was of knyghthod and of fredom flour'. However, Surrey exploits the other sense of *freedom* as well, as the next line shows. The poet had received his training in knighthood or courtesy at Windsor; the same place witnesses his loss of liberty.

53–54. *And with remembraunce . . . releif*: 'To banish the miseries of my present distress, I am forced on the wretched expedient of remembering a greater' (Warton). Surrey was grief-stricken when Richmond died. A year after his death the Duke of Norfolk wrote: '[My] son of Surrey is very weak, his nature running from him abundantly. He was in that case a great part of the last year, [which] . . . came to him for thought of my lord of Richmond' (*thought*: 'melancholy'); quoted by Casady, p. 57. For the general thought of the poem, that the greatest sorrow is remembering lost happiness, cf. Chaucer, *Troilus*, iii. 1625–8, where Chaucer is himself using Boethius, *Consolatio Philosophiae*, 2, pr. 4. 4–7.

28. *W. resteth here, that quick could never rest*

Sir Thomas Wyatt the poet died in October 1542. Surrey's admiration and affection for him are evidenced by this and the following two poems. Rollins remarks that this epitaph was probably Surrey's first appearance in print. It originally formed part of an eight-page booklet called *An excellent Epitaffe of syr Thomas Wyat, With two other compendious dytties, wherin are touchyd, and set forth the state of mannes lyfe*. It was probably printed shortly after Wyatt's death in 1542. Peter Betham was probably alluding to Surrey's poem when he wrote, in his dedication to *The preceptes of Warre* (1544): 'Wyate was a worthye floure of our tounge, as appereth by the mournefull ballet made of hys death in Englyshe, whyche is mooste wittye, fyne, and eloquent.' Surrey's tribute is notably laconic and elliptical, the style proper to epitaphs.

1. *W. resteth here . . . rest*: H. H. Hudson notes (*M.L.N.* xlv. 543) that this line is a translation of the epitaph which had been placed on the tomb in Milan of the Italian man of war, Jacopo Trivulzio (d. 1518). Camden (*Remaines*, 1614, p. 359) gives the epitaph as follows:

> HIC MORTVVS REQVIESCIT SEMEL,
> QVI VIVVS REQVIEVIT NVNQVAM.

2. *Whose . . . disdayn*: the meaning is clarified by l. 4, where *envy* means 'malice'. Rollins takes the *disdayn* to be Wyatt's: 'That is, increased by his own disdain of them: he did not boast of his own gifts.' But in view of ll. 4 and 30 and the prominence given to Wyatt's enemies in Surrey's two other tributes, it seems better to read: 'increased by the disdain, i.e. contempt of others'.

5. *misteries*. This seems to mean 'hidden meanings', hence 'profound or pregnant thoughts'. Cf. ll. 15–18 of the *Prologue* to Udall's *Ralph Roister Doister* (possibly written in 1540, printed in 1566):

> The wise Poets long time heretofore,
> Under merry Comedies secrets did declare,
> Wherein was contained very virtuous lore,
> With mysteries and forewarnings very rare

and Harington's *Preface* to *Orlando Furioso* (1591): 'The ancient Poets have . . . wrapped . . . in their writings divers . . . meanings, which they call the sences or mysteries thereof.'

6. *Whose hammers bet*: see note to 13. 24.

9. *where both did grow*: i.e. 'where both qualities (sternness and mildness) dwelt . . .'.

15. *unparfited for time*: 'unfinished for want of time'.

25–26. Surrey is using the *topos* of the good counsellor who, whatever the cost, speaks truth to the tyrant. Cf. Lydgate, *Fall of Princes*, bk. iv. 1331 ff.; this is the story of Callisthenes, the philosopher who dared to criticize his master Alexander for his drunkenness and violent habits:

> And to prolonge of his deth the payne,
>   Upon a boord he was leid along,
> His feet smet of & his hondes tweyne,
>   His eyen rent out: wer not his peynes strong?
>   Thus kan tiers tyrauntes, whan them list do wrong,
> Slen philosophres withoutyn any routhe,
> Which spared nat for to seyn hem trouthe.

27–28. Wyatt is the opposite of Surrey's Sardanapalus. See 32. 13.

30. Cf. 42. 876.

31. Cf. 42. 873. Both this and the preceding line are Virgilian in inspiration.

32. Cf. 12. 13–16.

34–35. An allusion to Wyatt's paraphrase of the seven Penitential Psalms. *that never shall be ded*: cf. the pseudo-Chaucerian *Flower and the Leaf*, ll. 479–81:

> And al they that of laurer chaplets bere
> Be such as hardy were and wan, indede,
> Victorious name which never may be bede.

29. *Dyvers thy death doo dyverslye bemone*

See introductory note to 28.

1. Cf. Chaucer, *C.T.* A. 3857: 'Diverse folk diversely they seyde.'

2–3. *Some . . . Lurked*: i.e. Edmund Bonner and Simon Heynes, who caused Wyatt to be impeached before the Privy Council and thus imprisoned.

that livelye hedd: Tottel reads 'thy livelyhed', i.e. 'thy living form', and for *sowne* 'swolne'; both readings may be correct.

4. *Cesars teres*: i.e. hypocritical. Cf. Petrarch, *In Vita* cii. 1–4:

Cesare, poi che 'l traditor d'Egitto
Li fece il don de l'onorata testa,
Celando l'allegrezza manifesta,
Pianse per gli occhi fuor, sí come è scritto. . . .

12. *kysse the ground*: cf. Chaucer, *Troilus*, v. 1791–2:

And kis the steppes, where as thow sees pace
Virgile, Ovide, Omer, Lucan, and Stace.

13–14. The allusion is unfortunately quite inapt.

30. *In the rude age when science was not so rife*

In this third tribute to Wyatt Surrey attempts an involved syntactical
scheme in the manner of Petrarch. The result is unfortunate; the sonnet
is a tangle, although good phrases occur. The text perhaps needs to be
emended, but the MS. has been printed without change.

1–2. Jove's birth-place was doubtful; hence pagan fable could be set
against Christian truth. Cf. Spenser, *Mutability Cantos*, vii. 53, where
Mutability questions Jove:

Where were ye borne? some say in *Crete* by name,
Others in *Thebes*, and others other where . . .

2. *other where*: 'elsewhere'. Tottel reads 'and other were that taught'.
The text as it stands is unsatisfactory, and it would be desirable to com-
bine the reading of the MS. with Tottel's so as to mean: 'if Jove in Crete
and elsewhere *and others* there were who taught . . .'. In the MS. text *their*
in l. 4 refers back to *Jove*, a difficulty which is removed by Tottel's reading; but he also spoils the sense by eliminating the allusion to Jove's
doubtful origin.

11–12. An allusion to Wyatt's paraphrase of the seven Penitential
Psalms.

13. *thy brest*: possibly Surrey is apostrophizing Bonner; see note to
29. 2–3. Tottel reads:

His lively face their brestes how did it freat,
Whose cindres yet with envye they do eate.

14. *cynders*. The word is used by Surrey in his translation of Virgil
(Lat. *cineres*). Cf. 41. 772, 42. 42, 560, and 835.
with envye doo the eate: 'consume thee with envy'.

31. *The greate Macedon that out of Perse chasyd*

1. *The great Macedon*: i.e. Alexander who, according to Plutarch, decided to use a rich coffer, which came into his possession after the defeat of Darius, to carry his copy of Homer in. The incident was commonly alluded to. The phrase is an example of *antonomasia* (see note to 14. 1–2). Elegance is here achieved by the contrast with the bluntly named and forcibly placed *Darius*.

Macedon is probably disyllabic; in early Tudor poetry it is two- or three-syllables according to the metre.

7. *the lyvely faythe and pure*: cf. *Paradise Lost*, i. 17: 'th'upright heart and pure'.

10. *myrrour*: 'pattern', 'example'.

12. Cf. 2 Samuel 11–12.

13–14. Possibly a covert allusion to Henry VIII.

32. *Th'Assyryans king, in peas with fowle desyre*

1. *Th'Assyryans king*: Sardanapalus. He was commonly cited as an example of degenerate kingship. Cf. especially Gower, *Confessio Amantis*, vii. 4313 ff. After a passage recommending chastity in princes Gower introduces Sardanapalus; historians tell that he

> Which hield al hol in his empire
> The grete kingdom of Assire,
> Was thurgh the slouthe of his corage
> Falle into thilke fyri rage
> Of love, which the men assoteth,

until he was defeated by the king of the Medes, who saw

> how this king in womanhede
> Was falle fro chivalerie . . .

The circumstances of Sardanapalus's suicide are related more fully by Lydgate, *Fall of Princes*, ii. 2311 ff. (ed. Bergen):

> And for his herte frowardli gan faile,
> Nat lik a knyht, but lik a losengour,
> His riche perre, his roial apparaile,
> His gold, his ieweles, uesseles & tresour
> Was brouht aforn hym doun [out] off a tour,
> Mid off his paleis, & gaff his men in charge
> Off cole and fagot to make a fir ful large.

> In which he caste his tresour and ieweles,
> Mor bestial than lik a manli man;
> And myd his riche stonys and uesseles,
> Into the fir furiousli he ran.
> This tryumphe Sardanapallus wan,
> With fir consumyd for his fynal meede,
> Brent al to asshes among the coles rede.

Surrey retains the chivalric element, but reverses Lydgate's point in making Sardanapalus's suicide his only 'manfull dede'. It is tempting, but not necessary, to see in this poem a covert allusion to Henry VIII.

33. *London, hast thow accused me*

In l. 22 MS. *Sceptures* has been emended.

Casady (p. 99) quotes a Privy Council record for 1 April 1543:

> Th'erle of Surrey, being sent for t'appere before the Counsell, was charged by the sayde presence, as well off eating off flesshe, as of a lewde and unsemely manner of walking in the night abowght the stretes and breaking wyth stone bowes off certayne wyndowes. And touching the eating of flesshe he alleged a license, albeitt he hadde nott so secretly used the same as apperteyned. And towching the stone bowes, he cowlde nott denye butt he hadde verye evyll done therein, submitting himselff therefore to soche ponishement as sholde to them be thowght good. Whereapon he was committed to the Fleete.

On the following day, two other members of Surrey's party, one of whom was Thomas Wyatt, the son of the poet, were committed to the Tower. Surrey seems to have been free by the end of May. See Casady for fuller details. The poem Surrey wrote about this incident has usually been interpreted as an amusing satire; but H. A. Mason (*Humanism and Poetry in the Early Tudor Period*, pp. 243–5) persuasively puts forward the view that it is the serious expression of Protestant sentiments. In this he agrees with Nott who had written: 'The conclusion of this poem affords a clear proof that Surrey was attached to the Reformed Religion, and that he regarded the Papal corruptions, in common with our Reformers, as the mystic Babylon of the Apocalypse.' In keeping with the nature of its subject, the poem is deliberately cryptic. It is written in *terza rima* except for ll. 29–40; l. 64 is inadvertently decasyllabic.

7. *convert*. The intransitive use of *convert* is well evidenced in Surrey's period. The *O.E.D.* quotes Rastell (1530): 'Many of them do never converte from those vyces.' Nott emends to *covet*.

8. *terrour*: 'fear of punishment'.

9–17. i.e. 'Mere words, as the preachers well know, are of small avail, and so I resorted to this novel method of voicing my protest. My punishment of the city, under cover of the night, accords with your secret sins, and should teach you that justice seeks out every fault, and that no one is secure from it' (Padelford).

20. Ruth Hughey points out that in Jer., l. 9, 14, 29, Surrey had scriptural authority for using the bow against the sinful city.

21. Cf. Isa. xlvii. 11.

28–41: the seven deadly sins.

32. *of eche*: 'for each'.

33. *The just shapp hyer*: 'The justly appointed punishment'. *shapp* is a past participle. For this sense of *shape*, see *O.E.D.*, shape (*v.*), 23.

49. *Thow hast . . . call*: an inversion characteristic of this poem, i.e. 'Thow hast my secret call to strief'. Perhaps *hast* should be emended to *hearst*.

51–55. Cf. Petrarch, *In Vita* cxxxviii. 1–11, a denunciation of the Avignon Papacy:

> Fontana di dolore, albergo d'ira,
> Scola d'errori e templo d'eresia,
> Già Roma, or Babilonia falsa e ria,
> Per cui tanto si piange e si sospira:
> O fucina d'inganni, o pregion dira
> Ove 'l ben more e 'l mal si nutro e cria,
> Di vivi inferno: un gran miracol fia,
> Se Cristo teco al fine non s'adira.
> Fondata in casta et umil povertate,
> Contra tuoi fondatori alzi le corna
> Putta sfacciata: e dov'hai posto spene?

56–64. Several scriptural allusions. Cf. Rev. xviii. 24 with ll. 56–58; Ezek. v. 12–17, vi. 11–14 with ll. 60–64. Cf. also Petrarch, *In Vita* cxxxvi. 1: 'Fiamma dal ciel su le tue trecce piova' with l. 59, and with ll. 62–64 cf. *In Vita* cxxxvii. 9–11:

> Gl'idoli suoi saranno in terra sparsi
> E le torri superbe al ciel nemiche,
> E' suoi torrier di for come dentro arsi....

34. *My Ratclif, when thy rechlesse youth offendes*

1. *Ratclif*: probably Thomas Radcliffe, third Earl of Sussex.

2. Nott cites Tibullus, III. 6. 43–44:

> Vos ego nunc moneo. Felix, quicunque dolore
> Alterius disces posse carere tuo

and Chaucer, *Troilus*, iii. 329: 'For wise ben by foles harm chastised'. Rollins adds the proverb 'Felix quem faciunt aliena pericula cautum'. Cf. also Terence, *Heauton Timorumenos*, l. 210: 'scitumst periclum ex aliis facere tibi quod ex usu siet'.

3. *callyng*: cf. 44. 36.

5. Probably Ecclesiasticus xxvii. 25 is alluded to.

6. Cf. Wyatt (ed. Muir, 168. 7–8):

> Sure I am, Brian, this wounde shall heale agayne,
> But yet, alas, the scarre shall styll remayne.

35. *Norfolk sprang thee, Lambeth holds thee dead*

Camden's text is emended in l. 2 *high* and l. 12 *seauen times seauen*. 'The subject of this poem is Thomas Clere (died April 14, 1545), Surrey's companion and squire, who, in saving the life of Surrey at the siege of Montreuil (September 19, 1544), received a wound from which he never recovered. Clere was buried at Lambeth, in the chapel assigned to the Howards, and the verses were inscribed on the tablet suspended near the tomb. . . . Clere was born at Ormesby, his father's seat in Norfolk. He was descended from the De Cleremont house. Nott emends line 2 to read: "Clere, of the County of Cleremont, thou'rt hight." But the emendation misses the meaning, for the whole point of the epitaph is to identify Clere with the Howard family. In effect, the thought is as follows: "Though of another house, the Howards claim you: you were born in Norfolk, your remains rest in our chapel, you had the blood of the Ormondes, a house united to ours by marriage (Clere's uncle, Thomas Boleyn, a grandson of the seventh Earl of Ormonde, having married Elizabeth Howard), your lady was Mary Shelton, daughter of another allied house (Mary being the cousin of Anne Boleyn) and you chose me as your lord, saving my life at the expense of your own." The epitaph demonstrates the propriety of burying Clere in the Howard chapel' (Padelford). The epitaph had been removed from Lambeth parish church by the time Horace Walpole wrote his account of Surrey (included in *Historical Anecdotes of some of the Howard Family* by the Honourable Charles Howard, 1769).

1. Surrey has adapted the epitaph which Virgil was believed to have composed for himself; it is quoted in the *Life* of Virgil by Donatus, which in Surrey's day was included in editions of Virgil:

> Mantua me genuit, Calabri rapuere, tenet nunc
> Parthenope; cecini pascua rura duces.

Cf. 28. 1, another epitaph, for a similar adaptation.

4. *thy cosine*: Anne Boleyn.

5. *Shelton*: Mary Shelton.

7. *Kelsall*: the Scottish town which was burned in the English expedition of 1542.

8–9. 'Surrey and Clere served under Sir John Wallop at the siege of Landrecy in October, 1543. Boulogne was taken by Henry in person, in September, 1544, a few days after the fall of Montreuil' (Padelford).

36. *When rechles youthe in an unquiet brest*

MS. *wher* (l. 1) has been emended. This and the following poem were almost certainly written during Surrey's last imprisonment while he was awaiting execution. In MS. Add. 36529 this poem precedes Surrey's version of Psalm lxxxviii for which it serves as prologue. 'I think that Surrey took over the form and spirit of his two psalm prologues (addressed to anti-Catholic friends) from Wyatt. Only one such prologue by Wyatt survives: it may have been addressed to Surrey' (H. A. Mason, *T.L.S.*, 6 Mar. 1953). The prologue by Wyatt (ed. Muir, p. 200) begins 'Somtyme the pryde of mye assured trothe'; it is addressed to 'Myne Earle' (l. 6).

5. *Deny*: Sir Anthony Denny. He was a member of the Privy Council and a secretary of state during the last years of Henry VIII's reign. Ruth Hughey remarks: 'It was his duty to affix the royal signature to official documents. For some time before the end of his life, Henry VIII was unable to sign his name, and a stamp was used. Surrey's enemies may have prevailed upon Denny to use the stamp upon the documents concerned with Surrey's execution.'

37. *The soudden stormes that heave me to and froo*

MS. *sondden* (l. 1) has been emended. See introductory note to No. 36. This poem is a prologue to Surrey's version of Psalm lxxiii.

11. *Blage*: Sir George Blage or Blagge. He was a follower of the 'New Religion'; in 1546 he was saved by the king's favour from being burned as a heretic.

38. *The stormes are past, these cloudes are overblowne*

There is a line missing after l. 7; Nott 'ventured to supply a verse': 'Who lives in privacy, is only blest.' Surrey's son, Henry Howard, Earl of Northampton, states in the Dedicatory Epistle to his *Dutiful Defence of the Royal Regimen of Women* that this poem was the last which his father wrote.

6. *The swete revenge*: the poet's philosophical deportment, which has converted his prison into a place of freedom.

7. *No company . . . owne*: probably an adaptation of Cicero's description of Scipio Africanus: 'Scipionem . . . dicere solitum scripsit Cato . . . numquam se minus otiosum esse quam cum otiosus, nec minus solum quam cum solus esset' (*De Officiis*, III. i).

9. Rollins (*Adams Memorial Studies*, p. 464) compares *Aeneid* i. 203: 'forsan et haec olim meminisse iuvabit'.

12. *glasse*: 'the reflective powers of the mind' (Nott). Cf. Chaucer, *Troilus*, i. 365: 'Thus gan he make a mirour of his minde.' Surrey's line was imitated by Sackville, *Induction*, ll. 163–5:

> And therwythall resortede to my minde
> My thought that late presented me the glas
> Of brittell state of cares that here we finde

presented: this is probably present tense; no emendation is necessary as the suffix *-ed* for *-eth* is well evidenced in this period.

14–17. The personal allusion has not been satisfactorily traced.

39. *Of thy lyfe, Thomas, this compasse well mark*

Surrey attempts to reproduce something of the concision and density of the Latin original (Horace, *Odes* ii. 10). Cf. Sidney's version of the same poem, which begins 'You better sure shall live, not evermore', and, for style, Milton's version of Horace's *Ode* i. 5: 'Rendred almost word for word without Rhyme according to the Latin Measure, as near as the Language will permit.'

1. *Thomas*: perhaps Surrey's elder son. *compasse*: see Glossary.

10. *falne*: the old 3rd pers. pl. indic. of *fall*.

15–20. These lines are scarcely comprehensible without the Latin:

> non, si male nunc, et olim
> sic erit: quondam cithara tacentem
> suscitat Musam neque semper arcum
>   tendit Apollo.
>
> rebus angustis animosus atque
> fortis appare: sapienter idem
> contrahes vento nimium secundo
>   turgida vela.

40. *Marshall, the thinges for to attayne*

This poem is a translation of Martial's epigram (x. xlvii):

> Vitam quae faciunt beatiorem,
> iucundissime Martialis, haec sunt:
> res non parta labore sed relicta;
> non ingratus ager, focus perennis;
> lis numquam, toga rara, mens quieta;
> vires ingenuae, salubre corpus;
> prudens simplicitas, pares amici,
> convictus facilis, sine arte mensa;
> nox non ebria sed soluta curis,
> non tristis torus et tamen pudicus;
> somnus qui faciat breves tenebras:
> quod sis esse velis nihilque malis;
> summum nec metuas diem nec optes.

8. *contynuance*: MS. *cotynuance*. It could mean either 'long duration, antiquity' or 'durability'. The former is more likely.

41. *They whisted all, with fixed face attent*

Surrey's translations of Books Two and Four of Virgil's *Aeneid* are the earliest blank verse poems in English. The textual problem is difficult. Book Two exists in one version only, Book Four in three. Book Four was the first to be published: this was in 1554, printed by John Day for William Owen and dedicated to Surrey's son, Thomas Howard, the fourth Duke of Norfolk. The full title is: 'The fourth boke of Virgill, intreating of the love betwene Aeneas & Dido, translated into English, and drawne into a straunge metre by Henrye late Earle of Surrey, worthy to be embraced.' In 1557 Tottel printed what he called 'Certain Bokes of Virgiles Aenaeis turned into English meter by the right honorable lorde, Henry Earle of Surrey'. These are Books Two and Four. The third version of Book Four exists in MS. Hargrave 205, which was probably written in the 1560's. The three versions of Book Four differ in numerous details. It is not known which, if any, should take priority or whether the different readings are due to Surrey himself or to some other 'improver' or 'improvers'. For a discussion of the problems and a collation of the texts, see Gladys D. Willcock's articles in *M.L.R.* xiv, xv, and xvii. Padelford printed Tottel and Hargrave on facing pages and lists variant readings in Day-Owen; the Day-Owen version has been edited by Herbert Hartman (1933). The texts of Books Two and Four printed in this volume are both Tottel's. In a large number of instances the readings peculiar to Tottel are preferable on literary grounds to Day-Owen and Hargrave; and, regarded as a translation, Tottel's version is the fullest and most accurate of the three. Considerations of uniformity also played their part in choosing the text of Book Four for this edition.

Blank Verse

Unrhyming heroic verse was a humanist ideal. Virgil wrote in unrhyming hexameters, and it was natural that in this, as in other respects, poets influenced by humanist teachers should have wished to imitate him. Experiments in unrhyming verse (*versi sciolti*) were made in Italy early in the 16th century, and it is possible that Surrey met the Florentine poet Luigi Alamanni while he was in Paris in 1532. In this same year Alamanni published his *Opere Toscane*, dedicated to Francis I, which contained a number of poems in *versi sciolti*. Surrey may also have known of the unrhyming Italian versions of Book Four of the *Aeneid* by Liburnio (1534), of Book Two by Cardinal Hippolito de Medici (1539), and of Book Four by Piccolomini (1539–40). But attempts to prove that Surrey was verbally indebted to these versions are unconvincing; they overlook possible common sources in Virgilian commentaries.

The line chosen by Surrey for his unrhyming verse was the 'pentameter' of more or less ten syllables. It should be noticed that he might have made the wrong choice of line: he might have tried (as others did later) to naturalize the hexameter. He did in fact translate one of the Psalms into unrhyming hexameters (see No. 50). But the ten-or-so syllable line was the line of the *Canterbury Tales*, the rhyme royal stanza, and the sonnets and satires of Wyatt (if the last indeed antedate Surrey's Virgil); and his instinct served him correctly in choosing it for his heroic verse. This is one of the reasons why, although strictly speaking a new metre, blank verse seems natural and 'inevitable' in English and why, despite his neo-classical motives, Surrey seems to be doing something which exploits the innate properties of the language. This may be better understood by glancing at French poetry in the same period. Unrhyming verse experiments failed in French for the reason that the French language (or so it seemed in this period) could support only a syllabic metrical system. The French language has a comparatively light stress accent, and without the bracing effect of rhyme French verse tends to lose its cohesiveness. Accordingly, until the 19th century French verse rhymes. English verse forms, on the other hand, remain persistently accentual, and rhyme in English is by no means essential. This is borne out by the use of the four-beat unrhyming alliterative line, which persisted from *Beowulf* to *Piers Plowman*. Structural alliteration, however, is no more essential than rhyme as a guard against formlessness. The recurring metrical beat within the line (always co-operating, it should be noted, with the forms of syntax and the direction of meaning) is capable itself of holding the line together as a satisfactory artistic unit: whether of four heavy stresses only, or four heavy stresses and one secondary, or five heavy stresses. In blank verse the poet has discarded both rhyme and structural alliteration. He may occasionally make use of alliteration for expressive purposes, but it is no longer needed to give shape to the line: it is no longer structural but rhetorical (e.g. the close of Surrey's Book Two, ll. 1061 *ad fin.*: 'prest to passe ... hasted to the hill'). By dropping structural alliteration the poet is free to develop a far wider range of subtle effect—for even so good a poet as the author of *Sir Gawain and the Green Knight* seems hampered by the obtrusiveness of his alliterative principle. Indeed, in such late alliterative poetry as *Piers Plowman* individual lines have already sometimes come close to the effect of blank verse:

> The most needy aren oure neighebores and we nyme good hede,
> As prisones in puttes and poure folke in cotes,
> Charged with children and chef lordes rente,
> That thei with spynnynge may spare spenen hit in hous-hyre,
> Bothe in mylk and in mele to make with papelotes,
> To a-glotye with here gurles that greden after fode.
> Al-so hem-selve suffren muche hunger,
> And wo in winter-tyme with wakynge a nyghtes ...
>
> (C Text, Passus x. 71–78)

(l. 77 is a good example of alliteration lightly used.)

For continental attempts at unrhyming verse see A. M. Clark, 'Milton and the Renaissance Revolt against Rhyme' (in his *Studies in Literary Modes*, 1946); for a brief account of Surrey's versification see O. F. Emerson, 'The Development of Blank Verse—A Study of Surrey', *M.L.N.* iv.

Surrey, Virgil, and Douglas

Surrey made extensive use of Gavin Douglas's translation of Virgil which, although not printed within Surrey's lifetime (it was first printed in 1553), was circulating in MSS. A line-by-line comparison shows that Surrey drew heavily on Douglas as a source for diction: a great number of individual words and phrases (in some cases whole lines) are taken over from him. However, they are not taken over uncritically, and the general effect of Surrey's version is very different. Surrey has different stylistic aims, which will be best understood by closely comparing Surrey with both Douglas and Virgil. A passage from Book Two will serve as an example: Surrey, ll. 29–53, see p. 36; Virgil, ll. 21–39; Douglas (ed. Coldwell), C. i, ll. 20–50. It is chosen as a middling example of Surrey's style. (The following analysis is selective: S = Surrey, Vg = Virgil, Dg = Douglas.)

Vg: Est in conspectu Tenedos, notissima fama
    insula, dives opum, Priami dum regna manebant,
    nunc tantum sinus et statio male fida carinis:
    huc se provecti deserto in litore condunt.
    nos abiisse rati et vento petiisse Mycenas.   25
    ergo omnis longo solvit se Teucria luctu.
    panduntur portae; iuvat ire et Dorica castra
    desertosque videre locos litusque relictum.
    hic Dolopum manus, hic saevus tendebat Achilles,
    classibus hic locus, hic acie certare solebant.   30
    pars stupet innuptae donum exitiale Minervae
    et molem mirantur equi; primusque Thymoetes
    duci intra muros hortatur et arce locari,
    sive dolo seu iam Troiae sic fata ferebant.
    at Capys, et quorum melior sententia menti,   35
    aut pelago Danaum insidias suspectasque dona
    praecipitare iubent subiectisque urere flammis,
    aut terebrare cavas uteri et temptare latebras.
    scinditur incertum studia in contraria volgus.

Dg: In desert costis of this iland thar   20
    The Grekis thame ful secretly withdrew,
    We wenyng thame hame passit and adew,
    And, with gude wynd, of Myce the realm had socht.
    Quharfor al thai of Troy, blyth as thai mocht,
    Thair langsum duyl and murnyng dyd away,   25
    Kest up the portis and yschit furth to play,
    The Grekis tentis desyrus forto se
    And voyd placis quhar thai war wont tobe,
    The cost and strandis left desert al cleyn.
    'Heir stude the army of Dolopeis,' sum wald meyn,   30
    'Cruel Achil heir stentit his pailʒeon;
    Quhar stude the navy, lo the place ʒonder down;
    Heir the ostis war wont to ioyn in feild.'
    And sum wondring the scaithful gyft beheld
    Suldbe offerit to the onweddit Pallas;   35
    Thai mervellit fast the horss samekill was.

Bot Tymetes exortis first of all
It forto leid and draw within the wall
And forto set it in the cheif palyce—
Quhidder for dissait I not, or for malyce,   40
Or destany of Troy wald sa suldbe.
Bot Capis than, with ane othir menȝe
Quhilk bettir avyss thar myndis set apon,
Bad cast or drown into the sey onone
That suspek presand of the Grekis dissait,   45
Or kyndill tharvndir flambe of fyris hait,
Or forto rype that holkit hug belly,
And the hyd hyrnys to serss and weil espy.
Quhat nedis mair? The onstabill common voce
Diuidit was in mony seir purpos . . .   50

(The passage, which forms a complete paragraph in Vg, breaks Dg off
in the middle of a sentence.) The Latin is characteristically firmly and
clearly articulated; it falls naturally into three parts:

    (1) ll. 21–24. A *topographia*: description of the shore.
    (2) ll. 25–30. The Trojans issue out and find the horse.
    (3) ll. 31–39. Diverse opinions.

    (1) S has used Dg as a base, but has simplified and pruned him so as
to bring out more clearly the form and movement of Vg. (For Vg's
4 lines, Dg has 7, S has 5.) Especially close is S's l. 31 to Vg's l. 23.
Vg's l. 24 is expanded by S, using elements of Dg, into two lines; they
have a confident rhythmic curve, marked by the alliterating 'Shrouding'
and 'shore' which 'frame' the second line:

    Hether them secretly the Grekes withdrew,
    Shrouding themselves under the desert shore.

There is also a symmetrical patterning which gives to the two lines
something of the self-contained chiastic effect of an Augustan couplet.
'Hether', placed first in l. 32, balances or complements 'under the desert
shore', placed last in l. 33. The balance is offset by the fact that the
four-word adverbial phrase is matched unequally by the single word
'Hether'. Moreover, the inversion in the normal word-order of l. 32
('them . . . withdrew') is countered by the normal word-order ('Shrouding themselves . . .') of l. 33.
    (2) S turns Vg's two sentences (ll. 25–26) into a single sentence of three
lines. Vg's sentences here are deliberately flat because they are merely
informative, in contrast to the more elaborately patterned writing of the

following lines, which expresses the people's feelings of wonder. S follows
the movement of Vg. In l. 34 S has 'wening we'; Dg 'We wenyng'.
Why the change of order? The reason is that S gains in point and shapeliness by juxtaposing 'we' and 'they': 'And wening we they had ben fled
and gone.' This is the sort of minute but telling effect which does not
seem to weigh with Dg. S's ll. 38–39 move confidently:

> The Grekish camp desirous to behold,
> The places void and the forsaken costes.

They may be analysed: l. 38: adj., noun, adj.+vbl. infinitive,
              l. 39: noun, adj.+adj., noun,

or figured simply in a series as: object, verb, object, object: that is, it
forms an aesthetically interesting shape (a broken series). The second line
is elegant in its variation of word-order: noun, adjective, adjective, noun;
it corresponds to Vg's l. 28 which has adjective, verb, noun, noun,
adjective. Thus Vg's line is framed by adjectives with nouns between,
S's by nouns with adjectives between. In S's ll. 40–41, the antitheses
'Here ... there' render Vg's 'hic ... hic'. In l. 40, S follows Vg in post-
poning the verb: 'pight' for 'tendebat'. In l. 41, S forms a different
pattern: two verbs, 'rode', 'joyne', the first preceding its subject, the
second following it.

(3) S's l. 42 reproduces the second half of Dg's line: 'the scathefull gift
beheld', but for Dg's 'And sum wondring' S substitutes 'Astonnied
some'. The change of word brings S closer to Vg's 'stupet'; but why the
change of order? The reason is again one of pointedness and emphasis:
S's line is both more energetic and mimetic than Dg's in that, syntactically,
his subject and object are juxtaposed; they are, so to speak, confronted.
S's l. 43 achieves an elegance of sound by means of its symmetrical
syllabic distribution. Thus:

> Behight by vow unto the chaste Minerve
>   2   1   1   2   1   1   2

The corresponding line in Dg is without any such aesthetic quality.
The collocated 'beheld, / Behight' contribute further shape to this three-
line sentence, which comes to an expressive climax with 'All wondring
at the hugenesse of the horse' (it takes over 'wondring' from Dg, l. 34).
S's line has a rhythmic exuberance which renders quite well 'et molem
mirantur equi', with its emphatic, primally placed 'et'. Vg's one and a
half lines 'primusque ... locari' are spun out by S to three; hence the
diffuseness and fill-in phrases ('the same', 'eke'). But the diffuseness is
countered by the concision of l. 48. S quite fails to capture Vg's elegant

word-order in l. 33, with its medially placed verb 'hortatur' framed by the infinitives 'duci' and 'locari'. But he makes some attempt at patterning: in l. 45 he keeps the verb till the end, unlike Dg, so that there is a gain in weightiness and sonority and in syntactical fluency: the verb 'advise' leads directly into the following two lines. In ll. 46 and 47, S sets up a chiastic pattern: in l. 46 the adverbial phrase is placed first and the verbs after, in l. 47 the verb is first and the adverbial phrase last. Despite the poor writing here, there is some artistry. In the corresponding place (ll. 38–39) Dg repeats his pattern; compared with S, the disposition is artless. Both poets have their otiose phrases: S has 'the same' and 'eke'; Dg his repeated 'forto'. And Dg does not much vary his prepositions: 'within', 'in'; S has 'Wythin', 'amidde'. The vigorous rhythm of S's ll. 50–51 is due to imbalance:

> Wild it to drown, or underset with flame
> The suspect present of the Grekes deceit.

The verb 'Wild' governs the whole sentence; the syntactical pattern is: object, infinitive verb, infinitive verb, object. However, the first object is 'it', the second object is 'The suspect present of the Grekes deceit'. Hence we experience an agreeable sense of tension or imbalance, which is due to the difference in syllabic weight between them. The syllabic difference between the verbs 'drown' and 'underset' ('with flame') also contributes to the mimetic striving of the two lines. Finally, S does away with Dg's 'That' ('That suspek presand'); it is too intimate for his rhetorical attitude, which demands a certain cool distance. Otherwise, the entire line is Dg's. S's l. 52 concludes the sentence; it has shape: two verbs followed by adj., noun, adj. S's l. 53 has the same function as Vg's l. 39. It arrests the movement, and sums up what has gone before.

With the appearance of Laocoon, there is a change from narrative style to oratorical:

Vg: 'o miseri, quae tanta insania, cives?
       creditis avectos hostis? aut ulla putatis
       dona carere dolis Danaum? sic notus Ulixes?
       aut hoc inclusi ligno occultantur Achivi,   45
       aut haec in nostros fabricata est machina muros,
       inspectura domos venturaque desuper urbi,
       aut aliquis latet error; equo ne credite, Teucri.
       quidquid id est, timeo Danaos et dona ferentis.'

Dg: On far, 'O wrachit pepil,' gan he cry,
       'Quhou gret wodness is this at ʒe now meyn,   55
       ʒour ennymyis away salit gif ʒe weyn,

138

Or gif ȝe traist ony Grekis gyftis be
Withowt dissait, falshed and subtelte.
Knaw ȝe na bettir the quent Vlixes slycht?
Owder in this tre ar Grekis closit ful rycht,   60
Or this engyne is byggit to our skaith,
To wach our wallis and our byggyngys bath,
Or to confound and ourquhelm our cite.
Thar lurkis sum falshed tharin, trastis me.
Lippyn nocht, Troianys, I pray ȝou in this horss;   65
Quhow ever it be, I dreid the Grekis forss,
And thame that sendis this gyft always I feir.'

The whole passage in S is quite successful; it is syntactically inventive
and conveys its meaning clearly. In this first speech, S works for sonorous
weight; he renders the movement of the Latin with some fidelity. To
Vg's 'o miseri . . . cives?', a characteristically compressed phrase,
S responds with

> O wretched citezens,
> What so great kind of frensie freteth you?

The alliterating verb helps to give the impression that 'freteth' is some-
how an extension of 'frensie'; it is as if S's sentence, like Vg's phrase, is
without a verb. S's l. 58 ('Deme ye the Grekes our enemies to be gone?')
makes a revealing contrast with Dg's l. 56. Dg's line is too tortuous for S;
its vowels sound half-swallowed. Beside it, S's line seems orotund; it
declaims well. S's ll. 59–60 are a good version, with the verb delayed till
the end of the line, as in Vg ('putatis').[1] And 'Is so Ulysses known?' is
excellent for 'sic notus Ulixes?' In S's ll. 61–63 the agitated movement
of Laocoon's speech is caught partly by the alternation of long and short
sentences. The Latin is closely followed. In l. 62 the natural word-order
is inverted: 'Or this an engin is.' S does it to set up a rhythmical opposition to 'Grekes are . . . hid' (l. 61). So there is an alternating pattern: in
l. 61 a noun followed by a passive verb, in l. 62 a noun followed by the
verb 'to be' (which is active in force). The effect is of a balance satisfyingly

---

[1] Cf. Dryden's remark on the blank versifiers of his time: 'Shakespeare . . . was
the first who, to shun the pains of continual rhyming invented that kind of writing
which we call blank verse, but the French, more properly, *prose mesurée*; into which
the English tongue so naturally slides, that, in writing prose, it is hardly to be
avoided. And therefore I admire some men should perpetually stumble in a way so
easy, and inverting the order of their words, constantly close their lines with verbs,
which though commended sometimes in writing Latin, yet we were whipt at
Westminster if we used it twice together. I know some, who, if they were to write
in blank verse, *Sir, I ask your pardon*, would think it sounded more heroically to
write, *Sir, I your pardon ask*' (*Epistle Dedicatory* of *The Rival Ladies*, 1664).

righted. In l. 63 the phrases are parallel ('To view our toures, and over-whelm our towne'). The line takes further shapeliness from alliteration and assonance (two of the commonest shaping devices) and from syllabic differentiation in the verbs and syllabic parity in the nouns. S's ll. 64–66: the expansive movement of ll. 61–63 is arrested by the brief and urgent 'Here lurkes some craft'. The whole speech is pointedly summed up with 'I dred the Grekes, yea, when they offer gyftes', which captures the force of 'et dona ferentis' ('even when bringing gifts') as Dg does not.

See Introduction for further comment on Surrey's translations of Virgil; see also F. H. Ridley's article 'Surrey's Debt to Gavin Douglas', *P.M.L.A.* lxxvi.

In the notes that follow S = Surrey, Vg = Virgil, and Dg = Douglas. The following readings in Tottel have been emended: l. 282, halter; l. 284, twine; l. 361, trauaiil of the; l. 481, where ye; l. 915, brand or; l. 924, Felow; l. 926, liue; l. 1015, table; l. 1026, mine *supplied*; l. 1061, flokke.

4. *a woe cannot be told*: Vg l. 3: *infandum . . . dolorem*. Cf. 42. 108.

10. *what Dolopes?*, i.e. 'what Dolopian?'

11. *What stern . . . soldiar?*, i.e. 'What mercenary soldier of fierce Ulysses?' *Ulysses* is possessive; cf. Vg l. 7: *duri miles Ulixi*.

15. *Troyes*. Here, as often elsewhere in Surrey's translation, a di-syllable.

21. *hye raised like a hill*. Vg ll. 15–16: *instar montis equum . . . aedificant*. S's *hye* is probably suggested by Dg's *in hy* (C. i. 4) which means 'in haste':

> Ane huge horss, lyke ane gret hil, in hy
> Craftely thai wrocht in wirschip of Pallas.

27. *enstuff*. See Glossary; cf. l. 299.

37. *cast up*: Dg has *Kest up the portis* (C. i. 26); Vg *panduntur portae*. Dg may imagine a portcullis.

45. *gan advise. gan* usually means 'did' and is often not much more than a 'filler'.

48. S's compressed line renders *sive dolo seu iam Troiae sic fata fere-bant* (l. 34).

51. Taken over from Dg: 'That suspek presand of the Grekis dissait' (C. i. 45).

52. For the phrasing cf. Wyatt, *Penitential Psalms* (ed. Muir, no. 206. 21): '. . . so close the Cave was and unkowth'; cf. note to 27. 43–44.

66. S accurately renders the force of Vg's *timeo Danaos et dona feren-tes* (l. 49), i.e. 'even when bringing gifts'.

71. *and for our blind forcast*. Vg's *si mens non laeva fuisset* (l. 54)

means considerably more than S's phrase; *laeva* means 'perverse' or 'infatuated'.

73. *had stand*. The past participle *stand* is not uncommon in S's day. It is probably chosen here for its sonority. *and Priams toures so hie*: S misses the dramatic force of Vg's apostrophe: *Priamique arx alta maneres* (l. 56).

85. S's unfinished line matches Vg's: *Disce omnes* (l. 66). Of Vg's nine other unfinished lines in Book Two, S imitates only one (l. 840 for Vg's l. 640). *all the rest*: 'all the other Greeks'.

85-92. On the use of assonance in this and other passages, see the article by Ants Oras, 'Surrey's Technique of Phonetic Echoes', in *J.E.G.P.* l.

101-8. This long tortuous sentence, eloquent of Sinon's wiles, closely follows the movement of the Latin (Vg ll. 81-87).

109. *by fate*: not in Vg.

110. *his realm . . . advise*: S is following a reading no longer accepted by modern editors of Vg: *regnumque vigebat / conciliis* (ll. 88-89). Modern editions read: *regumque*.

112. *Ulyssez*. This spelling with *z* is occasionally found with nouns ending in *s* in the possessive case. Cf. ll. 162 and 384.

122. *common*: 'of the community at large', for *in volgum* (l. 99).

123. *gylty*. Vg's *conscius* (l. 99) means rather 'aware of guilt', or perhaps 'as a conspirator'.

128. *It is enough ye here*: for *idque audire sat est* (l. 103).

141. *firre*. For *acernis* (l. 112), 'of maple'.

160. *But dayes twise five*: Vg: *bis quinos . . . dies* (l. 126). *But* here means 'neither more nor less than', 'fully', 'even'. See *O.E.D.*, *but*, 6 b.

164-6. *whereto . . . death*. For Vg ll. 130-1:

> adsensere omnes et, quae sibi quisque timebat,
> unius in miseri exitium conversa tulere.

Nott thought these lines corrupt; they certainly seem excessively compressed. S's *Returned* probably means 'converted', 'changed', and Vg's sense is recast to mean: 'what each man dreaded for himself all changed into my death'. The difficulty arises from S's failure to render Vg's *tulere*.

172-3. *while*: 'until'. S has changed Vg's meaning: *dum vela darent, si forte dedissent* (l. 136). Vg's Sinon is saying: 'I hid myself until they should set sail, if by chance they would.'

186. An effective recasting of *Quisquis es, amissos hinc iam obliviscere Graios* (l. 148).

190. *What holly vow?* Vg: *quae religio?* (l. 151). Dg clarifies by enlarging: 'Quhat is it—ane offerand of sum halynes' (C. iii. 13).

196. *hoste*: 'victim for sacrifice'; for *hostia* (l. 156).

211. *dame Pallas fatall forme*: for *fatale . . . Palladium* (ll. 165–6).

216. Probably corrupt. Nott suggests reading: '. . . their hope gan fail, and backward fall'. Vg has: *ex illo fluere ac retro sublapsa referri / spes Danaum . . .'* (ll. 169–70).

216–17. These lines vigorously conclude a long sentence with a pair of assonances: *faile/appeir; fall/withdraw*. The effect is analogous to that of a double rhyme; it emphatically arrests the movement.

217. *their goddesse grace withdraw*: for *aversa dea mens* (l. 170).

228. *had brought*. Vg's *avexere* (l. 179) is in the perfect tense, in order to indicate that this is Sinon's explanation; S takes it to be the conclusion, in *oratio obliqua*, of Calchas's prophecy.

232. *This order Calchas set*. For *ita digerit omina Calchas* (l. 182). Vg's words mean: 'Thus Calchas interprets the omens'; S's mean: 'These arrangements Calchas made', or perhaps: 'This form of service (*or* ceremony) Calchas prescribed.' As often in Dg and S, references to pagan religious practice are translated with a strong Christian colouring. S's choice of phrase has a Christian liturgical sound; see *O.E.D.*, *order* (sb), 17.

244. *offred warr*. An idiomatic term meaning 'war that was sought after'.

245. *in*: 'into'. See *O.E.D.*, *in* (prep.), 30.

248–9. *some / Trapt . . . teres*: Where modern editions of Virgil read *captique dolis lacrimisque coactis* (l. 196), S followed a reading found in some 16th-century editions: *captique dolis lacrimisque coacti'*.

252–3. For S's disturbed word-order, cf. the Virgilian model (ll. 199–200):

> Hic aliud maius miseris multoque tremendum
> obicitur magis atque improvida pectora turbat.

254–61. Vg's co-ordinate sentence is recast by S into a complex one. *sodenly*: not in Vg.

292–4. For Vg (ll. 232–3): *ducendum ad sedes simulacrum orandaque divae / numina conclamant*. S's l. 292 glosses Vg's *conclamant*. S gets the notion of speed (*blive*) from Dg (C. iv. 63): 'Onto that wark al sped thame bissely.'

299. *Stuft*: a military term. See Glossary. Cf. Dg (C. iv. 68): '. . . stuffit ful of armyt men'.

300. *Children and maides*: 'That is, boys and girls, *pueri innuptaeque puellae*. Anciently *child* (or *children*) was restrained to the young of the male sex. Thus [in S's Book Four, l. 201] we have, "the *Child* Iulus", in the original *puer* Ascanius. So the *children* of the chapel signifies the *boys* of the king's chapel. And in the royal kitchen, the *children*, i.e. the *boys*

of the Scullery. In the western counties, to this day, *maid* simply and distinctly means *girl*: as, "I have got a boy and a *maid*"—"My wife is brought to bed of a *maid*," &c. &c.' (Thomas Warton, *Hist. of Eng. Poetry*, section 37).

holly carolles: Vg: *sacra* (l. 239); Dg: *Syngand karrellis* (C. iv. 70).

303. *The subtil tree*: Dg not Vg (C. iv. 73): 'this suttell hors of tre'.

to Pallas temple ward: not in Vg.

316. For Vg (l. 250): *Vertitur interea caelum. gan whirle* probably has a pluperfect force: 'had whirled'.

320–1. A notable example of rhyme. Other examples of rhyme or possible rhyme in Book Two are the following: ll. 124–5; 206–7; 243, 245; 320–1; 386–7; 468, 470; 610–11; 929, 930, 932; 999, 1001. The same word is repeated in the final position in ll. 735, 740; and in ll. 880, 882, and 885. Some of these examples are probably accidental, but some (including ll. 320–1) seem deliberate.

324. Vg (l. 255): *tacitae per amica silentia lunae*; Dg (C. v. 11): 'Stil under frendly sylens of the moyn.' The Latin phrase refers to the first quarter of the moon, when it gives no light.

334. S has omitted *Pelidesque Neoptolemus*—unfortunately, in view of his later part in the action.

343. *With rufull chere* qualifies *Hector*.

345. *had be*. The past participle *be* is well attested in the 16th century.

352. *crisped*: not in Vg.

364. *alas so wide?* Not in Vg; suggested by Dg (C. v. 68): 'Or quhy se I tha feil woundis, allace?'

371. *Sufficeth that is done*: i.e. 'what is done'. Vg (l. 291): *sat patriae Priamoque datum*.

376–7. *Them joyne . . . for them*. For Vg (l. 294): *hos cape fatorum comites, his moenia quaere*.

378. *th'overwandred flood*: Vg (l. 295): *pererrato . . . ponto*.

388. *by drift of boisteous winde*: Vg (l. 304): *furentibus Austris*.

396. *all overspred with flash*: Vg (l. 311): *Volcano superante*. The odd word *flash* is probably due to a desire for variants on *afire* and *flame* in the following two lines.

399. Taken over from Dg (C. vi. 3i): 'Upsprang the cry of men and trumpys blist.'

404. *prickt*: an ingenious rendering of *praecipitant* (l. 317).

405. A good example of S's method of compressing Dg (C. vi. 39–40):

> So that we thocht maist semly in a feld
> To de feghtand, enarmyt under scheld.

415. The whole line glosses Vg's *ineluctabile* (l. 324).

428. *blind fight*: Vg (l. 335): *caeco Marte.*

429. *lightning of the gods*: Vg (l. 336): *numine divum.* S's expressive word *lightning* has a strong Christian colouring. See *O.E.D.*, *lightening* (vbl. sb²), which quotes *The Pilgrimage of Perfection* (1526): 'Grace is an illumynacyon or lyghtnynge of the soul.'

431. *As furie guided me*: Vg (l. 337): *quo tristis Erinys.*

436. *Mygdonius son.* 'It ought to have been the *Son of Mygdon*, not Mygdonius' (Nott). Vg has *Mygdonides* (l. 342).

443. *So desperatly.* Not in Vg or Dg. Vg has only (l. 347): *audere in proelia.* S probably takes the hint from a note of Donatus on Aeneas's speech below (ll. 445–54): 'Ergo iuvenes fortes estis, & prompti: sed auxilium vestrum incensae urbi quid proderit? sed una est salus victis, si salutem, quam tueri non possunt, desperando contemnant.'

445–54. S, following Dg, translates this speech in a different order from Vg. The rearrangement is probably due to the comment of Donatus, part of which has been quoted in the previous note. The first part runs: 'Ordo est: iuvenes fortissima pectora, Quae sit rebus fortuna videtis. Excessere omnes adytis, arisque relictis Dii, quibus imperium hoc steterat, frustra, succurritis urbi incensae. Si vobis audendi extrema Cupido, eamus & moriamur, & in media arma ruamus. Una salus victis nullam sperare salutem.'

471. *Manhod*: *virtus* (l. 367). Dg has *hardyment* (C. vii. 16).

472. *some victors Grekes*: S follows Dg (C. vii. 17): *sum Grekis victoris* for Vg (l. 368): *victoresque . . . Danai.*

486–9. For the diction cf. Wyatt (ed. Muir, no. 46. 1–3):

> The wandering gadlyng in the sommer tyde,
>   That fyndes the Adder with his recheles fote,
>   Startes not dismayd so soudenly a side . . .

488. *Rered . . . neck.* These phrases qualify, of course, *the adder* (l. 487).

493. *Striken . . . place*: i.e. Androgeus and his companions. As in l. 488, S's syntax is awkwardly compressed.

499. Vg (l. 390): *dolus an virtus, quis in hoste requirat?*

506. *for no good luck to us*: Vg (l. 396): *haud numine nostro.* S's reading is possible, but the primary sense is 'under a protection not our own'.

522. *through thickest of the swerdes.* Vg's *densis incurrimus armis* (l. 409) rather means 'we charge with serried (or linked) arms'.

533. *gladsom east proud of Auroraes horse*: Vg (ll. 417–18): *laetus Eois | Eurus equis.* Vg's single epithet gives rise to both of S's.

539. *appered first.* Modern editions of Vg read: *apparent; primi . . . adgnoscunt. . . .* But S's reading is found in some 16th-century editions of Vg: *apparent primi; . . .* (l. 422).

541. *our discording voice*: Vg (l. 423): *ora sono discordia*, i.e. 'our speech differing in sound'.

552. *Pitie, nor zele . . .* for *pietas* (l. 430). *Pitie* in the sense of 'piety' is well attested in this period.

554. *last flames of mine*: i.e. 'of my kin'. Vg (l. 431): *flamma extrema meorum*.

563. *crye*: i.e. 'the clamour'.

571. *Under the windowes*: Vg (l. 442): *postesque sub ipsos*. Modern editors translate *postes* as 'door-posts'. S's reading is perhaps prompted by Servius's note: 'Si circa portam, sub postibus: si circa fenestras, circa postes.'

577. *With such weapons*: i.e. 'with these (the *turrets hye* and the *palace roofe*) weapons'.

587. Vg (ll. 454–5): *postesque relicti / a tergo*. S's translation is misleading; the phrase rather means 'a doorway left (*or* abandoned) at the back'. Or possibly (as James Henry suggests) *a tergo* should be taken with *limen* (l. 453).

609. *all bolne*: 'swollen', i.e. *the adder*. As often in his rendering of Vg's similes, S's syntax buckles under the strain; in these places Vg's Latin is exceptionally difficult to turn into English with comparable elegance and compression.

610. *when she . . . had slong*. For phrasing cf. 2. 9. For the rhyme see note on ll. 320–1.

613. *With that*: Vg (l. 476): *una*, i.e. 'with him'.

620. For Vg (ll. 480–1): *postisque a cardine vellit / aeratos*. Cf. Dg (C. viii. 70–73):

> Bot first of al, ane stalwart ax hynt he,
> The stern Pyrrus, to hew and brek the зet,
> And furth of har the stapillis has he bet,
> And bandis all of brass yforgyt weill:

S's odd phrase *the staples out of brasse* combines *furth of har the stapillis* and *bandis all of brass*.

650–1. Vg (l. 504): *barbarico postes auro spoliisque superbi*. S takes *barbarico* not with *auro* but with *spoliis*: *the spoiles of other nations*.

655. *chaunce*: Vg (l. 507): *casum*, i.e. 'fall'.

687. *in hand*. The phrase means 'in the process of' doing something. Pyrrhus is in the act of striking Polites with his spear.

703–4. *tendring . . . faith*: an awkward rendering of Vg (ll. 541–2): *iura fidemque / supplicis erubuit*.

710. *Without sound*: on the contrary, it clanged: *rauco . . . aere* (l. 545).

714. *swarved out of kinde*: Vg (l. 549): *degeneremque*. Cf. 42. 18. For the phrase cf. Fisher (*Month's Mind Sermon of Margaret*, 1509): 'If oughte be good in the noblenes of bloode it is for that therby the noble men and women sholde be ashamed to go out of kynde from the vertuous maners of theyr auncetrye before.'

716. *At the altar*: i.e. 'to the altar'. Vg (l. 550): *altaria ad ipsa*. *At* is used for 'to' 'with certain verbs of motion' (*O.E.D.*).

721. *fatal fine*. Dg (C. ix. 79): *finale fait*.

757–8. Taken over from Dg (C. x. 32–33):

> Thocht I, sal scho pass to the realm of Spart
> Hailskarth, and se Mycene hir natyve land . . .'

770–1. Vg (ll. 586–7): *animumque explesse iuvabit* / *ultricis flammae*. Following Dg, S has recast Vg. The Latin means 'It will give me pleasure to have filled my soul with the fire of revenge'.

causer: see note to 11. 26.

808. Vg (l. 616): *nimbo effulgens et Gorgone saeva*. For *nimbo* there is an alternative reading *limbo* (meaning 'edge' or 'fringe' of a robe) which is followed by Dg (*weirlyke weid*, C. x. 99) and S.

840. Half-line in Vg (l. 640).

859. *yeld unto*: Vg (l. 653): *incumbere*. The Latin word means 'lean upon', 'add weight to'.

892. *as expert*: *expertus* (l. 676). S's transcription is too bald. The Latin word means 'experienced', hence 'from past trial'. It needs to be rendered by a clause: 'from what you have seen'.

894–5. Editors of Vg generally take this sentence as a question. It then runs: 'To whom is little Iulus, to whom is thy father, to whom am I, abandoned?'

898. S's line has an odd classical sound. It renders *namque manus inter maestorumque ora parentum* (l. 681).

899–900. Vg (ll. 682–3): *ecce levis summo de vertice visus Iuli* / *fundere lumen apex*. S's *butten* for *apex* is prompted by Servius's note: 'Proprie dicitur in summo flaminis pileo virga lanata; hoc est, in cuius extremitate modica lana est: quod primum constat apud Albam Ascanium statuisse. Modo autem summitatem pilei intelligimus.' Most modern editors translate *apex* as 'tongue of flame', so that it is unnecessary to suppose that Iulus is wearing a cap.

909–11. *beholde us then . . . thine ayd*: Vg (ll. 690–1): *aspice nos, hoc tantum, et, si pietate meremur*, / *da deinde augurium*. S has recast the Latin, taking *pietate* with *aspice* ('look on us with pity') and translating *hoc tantum* ('this only') as *at least*.

921. *beheld*: Vg (l. 699): *se tollit*.

924. *Folow*. Tottel: *Felow*. Vg (l. 701): *sequor et, qua ducitis, adsum*. S has combined Vg's two clauses: hence *at hand* for *adsum*.

965. Vg (l. 729): *pariter comitique onerique timentem*, i.e. 'fearful alike for my companion and my burden'.

971. Vg makes these words part of Anchises's speech; S mistakenly makes Aeneas see the glint of armour.

1007–8. Nott emends to *in blazing flame*.

1012–13. Vg (l. 762): *custodes lecti Phoenix et dirus Ulixes*. S omits *lecti* and substitutes *dirus* for it.

1025. *Th'unlucky figure*: *infelix simulacrum* (l. 772).

1046. *goddesse*. S here, as elsewhere, probably takes advantage of the pronunciation with the stress on the second syllable.

1055. *th'image*. Probably stressed on the second syllable.

1061. *prest*: i.e. 'ready'. The word is common in the 16th and 17th centuries; e.g. Fairfax, *Tasso's Jerusalem Delivered* (1600): 'I willing am, and prest / To follow where thou leadest . . .' (10. xiii).

1065. *lusty*. An emendation to *lofty* is tempting; Vg (l. 801): *summae . . . Idae*. S may well have written *lofty*, intending the literal sense 'extending to a great height in the air' which may have puzzled a copyist. The first example of *lofty* in this sense given by *O.E.D.* is from Spenser; before S the word is used only in figurative senses ('haughty, proud'). *Lusty*, on the other hand, is used in a wide variety of senses in this period ('pleasant, handsome', &c.), and to a copyist may have seemed the likelier word in this context.

42. *But now the wounded quene with hevy care*

See introductory note to 41. The following readings in Tottel have been emended: l. 10, dark; l. 80, debowled; l. 141, at; l. 194, in present countenaunce; l. 209, cotage; l. 232, decriue; l. 241, turrents; l. 326, bette; l. 327, thend; l. 334, the *supplied*; l. 337, flameed, eie; l. 347, he *supplied*; l. 353, Ascanus; l. 359, down; l. 362, by night; l. 398, bethrothed; l. 435, sielfe; l. 441, men; l. 443, haue haue; l. 447, thee; l. 458, darke; l. 475, silence; l. 505, thase; l. 587, her; l. 731, waite; l. 791, sone; l. 797, So; l. 798, goodes; l. 829, giltlesh; l. 834, Trians; l. 855, herforme; l. 884, damsell; l. 902, fosaken.

6. *pictures forme*: Vg (l. 4): *voltus*. *Picture* here seems to mean 'mental image'. In l. 107 *forme* is used to render *imagine*.

10. *dank*. Tottel: *dark*; Hargrave: *danke*. Vg (l. 7): *umentemque*; Dg (C. i. 13): *donk*. Cf. l. 458.

14. Hargrave's line is metrically smoother, if slightly tautologous: 'What newcome gest unto our realme is come!'

18. Vg (l. 13): *degeneres animos timor arguit.* Cf. 41. 714.

20. *atchived* has a chivalric colouring; cf. Chaucer, *Legend of Good Women* (l. 2111):

> So that I myghte liven and nat fayle
> To-morwe for t'acheve my batayle . . .

23. *dissevered.* Vg (l. 17): *fefellit;* Dg (C. i. 36): *By deth dissoverit.* S's reading seems prompted by Dg. It clearly should be *deceived;* cf. 41. 986 'deceiving us' for Vg's *fefellit.*

30. An alexandrine.

36. *enjoy it in his grave.* An over-concise rendering of Vg (l. 29): *ille habeat secum servetque sepulchro.* Hargrave reads: '. . . which still en-joye he in his grave'.

42. *Cinders* was no doubt felt to be closer to the feeling of *cinerem* (l. 34) than *ashes;* Day-Owen has *dust* at this point.

46–47. *the riche soile . . . triumphant.* Hyperbaton (unusual word-order) for 'the soil of Africa rich in triumphal honours'. Vg has: *quos Africa terra triumphis | dives alit* (ll. 37–38).

56. *What:* i.e. 'why'.

57. A half-line in Vg (l. 44).

63. *Cartages.* Presumably disyllabic with *g* hard.

67–68. The rendering is over-compressed. The last three phrases are governed by *Whiles,* with verbs 'to be' understood.

69. *the kindled mind with love:* a use of hyperbaton characteristic of S.

72. *hogreles of two yeares:* Vg (l. 57): *bidentis.* Servius comments: 'Dictae sunt, quasi *biennes:* quia neque minores, neque majores licebat hostias dare. Sunt etiam in ovibus duo eminentiores dentes inter octo, qui non nisi circa bimatum apparent: nec in omnibus, sed in his, quae sunt aptae sacrificiis, inveniuntur.'

73. *as ought:* Vg (l. 57): *de more.*

75. Taken over from Dg (C. ii. 15): 'Quhilk heth in cuyr the band of mariage.'

88. *the striken hinde:* Dg (C. ii. 40): *ane strykkyn hynd.*

96. Vg (l. 76): *incipit effari, mediaque in voce resistit.*

108. *cannot be told:* Vg (l. 87): *infandum.* Cf. 41. 4.

112. *Broken:* Vg (l. 88): *interrupta. workes:* 'fortification'. Cf. *Othello,* III. ii. 3–5.

118. *great gods of memory:* Vg (l. 94): *magnum et memorabile numen.*

120. *foreknew:* not in Vg.

128. *then.* Perhaps Hargrave's *them* is the right reading.

130. *Tirianes yeld:* i.e. 'yield Tyrians'. Vg (l. 104): *dotalisque tuae Tyrios permittere dextrae.*

156. *Th'assemble*: trisyllabic as in French. The whole sentence shows S's neo-classical compression at its most uncomfortably tight.

157-8. *Dido a cave . . . enter to*. This ingeniously catches the movement of the Latin (ll. 124-5):

> speluncam Dido dux et Troianus eandem
> deveniunt.

166-8. An unsatisfactory rendering. S is usually poor in passages describing vigorous or violent activity.

186. *The Candians*: Vg (l. 146): *Cretesque*. Candia was the name given to Crete by the Venetians when they acquired it in the 13th century. It remained the name commonly used by Europeans until about 1910.

196-200. Vg (ll. 152-5):

> ecce ferae saxi deiectae vertice caprae
> decurrere iugis; alia de parte patentis
> transmittunt cursu campos atque agmina cervi
> pulverulenta fuga glomerant montisque relinquunt.

This is garbled in Tottel: *roes (caprae)* becomes *rose*, a verb. Hargrave is the best text here:

> From the rockes toppe the wild savage rooes
> Availe the hill, & on the other side
> Over the laundes they gan to take ther course.
> The hartes likewise, in troopes taking ther flight,
> Raising the dust, the mountaynes fast forsoke.

Both Tottel and Hargrave follow a different punctuation from modern editors of Virgil, and take *alia de parte . . . campos* with *caprae* instead of with *cervi*.

201. *childe*: 'youth', possibly with a chivalric tinge—'youth of gentle birth awaiting knighthood'.

202. *them . . . thes*: 'those . . . these'.

215. Vg (ll. 167-8): *fulsere ignes et conscius Aether / conubiis*. But S has already translated *ignes* in 'burning gledes of fire'.

217. *mirth*. Some editions of Vg in S's day read *laeti* where modern editions read *leti*.

227. *Stayeth*. Vg (l. 177): *ingrediturque*. Day-Owen reads *Perecing*; Hargrave *Percing*. Perhaps S wrote *Pacing*.

218-19. *tempted by wrath / Of gods*: i.e. 'against the gods'. Vg (l. 178): *ira inritata deorum*. *tempted* means 'provoked'. S has in mind the phrase 'to tempt God'. Cf. 49. 19.

238. Vg (l. 184): *nocte volat caeli medio terraeque per umbram.* S misinterprets the Latin.

246. *to Tyrians court.* Not in Vg.

272. *citie:* Vg (ll. 211–12): *urbem / exiguam.* Day-Owen (*vyllage*) and Hargrave (*village*) catch the sarcasm of the original better than Tottel.

294. S, following Dg, is wrong here: *Dreedfull . . . charged . . . do not,* in Vg, qualify Aeneas but Italy:

> sed fore, qui gravidam imperiis belloque frementem
> Italiam regeret . . . (ll. 229–30)

304. *the land of Lavin:* Vg (l. 236): *Lavinia . . . arva.*

310. *With a light winde.* Vg's phrase *rapido pariter cum flamine* (l. 241) means 'swift as the rushing wind', not, as S takes it, literally 'with a wind'.

315. *closeth up.* Vg's *resignat* (l. 244) means 'unseal', 'open'.

334. *To fore the towers:* not in Vg.

341–4. Vg's order is reversed:

> tu nunc Karthaginis altae
> fundamenta locas pulchramque uxorius urbem
> extruis? heu! regni rerumque oblite tuarum! (ll. 265–7)

Hargrave, however, follows Vg, and departs considerably from Tottel:

> Thow, that of high Carthage
> Dost the fowndacouns laye to please thie wife,
> Raising on height a passing fayer citie!
> But oh, for woe, thine own thinges owt of minde!

347. *in hast* not in Vg; suggested by *celeris . . . per auras* (l. 270).

362. *by flight.* Tottel: *by night.* Vg (l. 281): *fuga.* Hargrave's reading has been adopted in the text.

371. *Cloanthus.* Modern editions read *Serestum* where some older ones have *Cloanthum.*

377. *when:* i.e. 'since', 'seeing that'.

389. *Bachus nunne:* cf. Dg (C. vi. 41): *thir nunnys of Bachus.*

390. S mistakenly takes over Vg's *Thyias* (l. 302), which means 'a Thyiad', 'a Bacchanal', as if it were the name of a person.

391. *third yeres sacrifice:* Vg (ll. 302–3): *trieterica . . . orgia.* The Latin means literally 'held every third year'; in modern terms 'every two years'. 'The ancient system of reckoning was inclusive, so that in a given group of years ABCD the festival would be held in the years A and C, the latter being the "third year" inclusive of A' (R. G. Austin, *Aeneidos, Liber Quartus,* 1955, p. 97).

393. *that:* i.e. 'when'.

394. This unsatisfactory line might be improved in sound, if not in sense, by inserting *her*, as Hargrave does: '. . . with noise of her dawnsing'.

407. *mariage*: trisyllabic, as in Chaucer and elsewhere in S.

420. Vg (l. 325): *quid moror?* S follows Dg (C. vi. 87): 'Bot quharto suld I my ded langar delay?' Dg in turn follows a note of Ascensius's: 'quid differo mortem'. Cf. l. 856 n. below.

423. *captive lead me away?*: Vg (l. 326): *captam ducat. captive* is stressed on the second syllable.

428. *to the gods advise*: i.e. 'by'. See *O.E.D.*, *to*, 20. a.

446. *scaped.* Not in Vg.

450. *advise*: i.e. 'command'. Vg (l. 346): *iussere.*

461. *advise*: i.e. 'bring to mind'. Vg (l. 353): *admonet.*

497. *As though*: Vg (l. 379): *scilicet.*

517. Vg (l. 392): *stratisque reponunt*: Ascensius: 'tapetibus instratis'.

528. S misses the stress of Vg's *migrantis cernas totaque ex urbe ruentis* (l. 401)—i.e. '. . . from all the city'.

536–9. S misses the force of Vg's apostrophe: *quis tibi tum, Dido, cernenti talia sensus* (l. 408). Dg follows Vg.

540. *O witlesse love*: Vg (l. 412): *improbe Amor*: Dg (C. viii. 9): *O wytles lufe!* Vg's *improbe* means rather 'merciless', 'relentless'. S follows Dg in turning the apostrophe into a rhyming couplet:

> O wytles lufe! quhat may be thocht or do,
> At thou constrenys nocht mortell myndis tharto?

544. *before her causelesse death*: i.e. 'and die needlessly'. It renders *frustra moritura* (l. 415).

550–1. Vg (ll. 419–20): *hunc ego si potui tantum sperare dolorem, / et perferre, soror, potero.* The meaning of the Latin is not what S takes it to be but rather: 'If I have had the strength to foresee this dreadful misery, I shall also, sister, have the strength to bear it now.'

553. *faithles* qualifies *He* (l. 554).

575. *if thou shalt vouchsafe.* Some older editions of Vg have *dederis* (l. 436) where modern ones have *dederit.*

581. Hargrave: 'Destenie withstandes, a god stoppes his meke eares.'

593. *in one*: 'in the same state'.

600. *holy water stocks*: Vg (l. 454): *latices . . . sacros* ('holy water'). S has added *stocks*, the word used for stoups in Christian churches.

615. *her thought*: 'it seemed to her'.

622–3. *In tragedies . . . Driven about*: Vg (l. 471): *scaenis agitatus.* S is probably drawing on Servius's note: 'Famosus, celebratus tragoediis. Qualiter a Graecis in scena inducitur. *Agitatus* autem, aut quia furiis agitatus, aut quia multae sunt de eo tragoediae: quasi frequenter actus.'

636. *wandring*. Not in Vg.

640. *should be*: i.e. 'is said to be'. See *O.E.D.*, *shall*, 15.

641-2. Vg (l. 484): *Hesperidum templi custos*. There is no mention of *garden* in Vg; S may be following Dg (C. ix. 24): 'Set in the gardyngis hecht Hesperida.' Or he may have used Servius's note: 'Hesperides Atlantis filiae Nymphae, secundum fabulam hortum habuerunt. . . .' Day-Owen and Hargrave use one line less in translating Vg's phrase and do not import a garden:

> Of the Hesperiane sisters temple old
> The garder, that gives the dragon foode

(Day-Owen omits *old*.)

670. *more grevous thing*: 'anything worse'; Vg (l. 502): *graviora*.

677. Vg (ll. 506-7): *fronde coronat | funerea*. S has mistaken the sense of the Latin: 'hangs it with funeral greenery'.

678-9. Vg (ll. 507-8): *super exuvias ensemque relictum | effigiemque toro locat*. S fails to see that *super* governs *toro* ('on the bed'); he invents *ther-upon* for *super* and adds *on a bed* for *toro*, and so suggests that there are two places in question rather than one.

682-3. i.e. the 'nunne' calls on 300 gods in a thunderous voice.

684. *the grisely*. Not in Vg; from Dg (C. ix. 76): *Herebus, the grysly*. *huge*. Not in Vg.

690. Dg (C. ix. 83): 'Spryngand herbys eftir the courss of the moyn.' Vg's *ad lunam* (l. 513) has been expanded by means of a note, perhaps Servius's ('Quia herbae aut secundum rationem Lunae tolluntur, aut in quas despumaverit Luna').

692-3. Vg (ll. 515-16): *quaeritur et nascentis equi de fronte revolsus | et matri praereptus amor*. The Latin means: 'she goes to fetch too a love-charm, ripped from the brow of a foal as it comes to birth, torn away before the mother can seize it' (R. G. Austin). S has gone astray in l. 693 by following Dg (C. ix. 88): 'And fra the moder byreft the lufe sa greyn', although he has altered Dg's diction.

694. *mole*: Vg (l. 517): *mola*, i.e. the sacrificial cake.

699. Hargrave improves the rhythm: 'And if that ther werr enie god had care.'

701. Vg (ll. 520-1): *si quod . . . numen habet iustumque memorque, pre-catur*. S has recast the Latin, which means 'she prays to whatever power, just and mindful . . .'.

702-3. Vg (ll. 522-3): *placidum carpebant fessa soporem | corpora per terras*. S reverses Vg's order by making *slepe* the subject of the verb. Vg's *carpebant* means 'were tasting', 'were enjoying'. S's line makes sense, though a different sense from Vg's.

704. Cf. 7. 5.

714. An alexandrine.

721. *vile commaundes*: Vg (ll. 537–8): *ultima . . . iussa*: Servius: 'Ultima, deterrima, an superba. . . .' *Deterrima* ('lowest', 'worst') prompts *vile*.

740–3. The Latin is subject to various interpretations. S has chosen to render as questions what are usually taken as statements.

754. Cf. Dg (C. x. 78): 'Nor harknys the fair wynd blawys of landis?'

759. i.e. 'the brands blazing . . .'. The phrase is the object of *shalt thou see*.

760. *And if*: 'If.'

795. *destenie*. Older editions of Vg have *fata* where modern ones have *facta* (l. 596).

818. *Withdraw*. Some older editions of Vg read *avertite* where they now read *advertite* (l. 611).

832. The curse is concluded with an alexandrine.

843. This line has no counterpart either in Vg or in Day-Owen and Hargrave.

850. *the body*: i.e. 'her body'.

856. *Troian statue*. Vg. (l. 640): *Dardaniique rogum capitis*; Dg. (C. xi. 112): *зon Troiane statw*. Dg is following either Servius who glosses *rogum* 'in quo ejus imago fuerat' or the 16th-century commentator Ascensius, who glosses it 'in quo est effigies aeneae'. D. F. C. Coldwell has demonstrated Dg's extensive use of Ascensius in his *Selections from Gavin Douglas* in the present series.

875. S omits, probably inadvertently, the line which in Vg follows this: *ulta virum poenas inimico a fratre recepi* (l. 656).

880. *thus and in this sort*: Vg (l. 660): *sic, sic*.

908. In Vg *cruel* applies to Anna: *sic te ut posita, crudelis, abessem?* (l. 681).

937. *On*: i.e. 'above'.

938. *to Pluto consecrate*: Vg (ll. 702–3): *Diti / sacrum*; Ascensius: *consecratum . . . Plutoni*. S follows Dg (C. xii. 117): *to Pluto consecrate*.

43. *I Salamon, Davids sonne*

Almost certainly Surrey's paraphrases of Ecclesiastes and the Psalms belong to the close of his life. 'The introductory verses to Psalms 88 and 73 [Nos. 36 and 37 in this edition] furnish unequivocal evidence, quite aside from internal evidence, that the Psalms were translated during Surrey's final imprisonment, and the like temper of the translations from Ecclesiastes is strong presumptive evidence that they were produced at the same time' (Padelford). H. A. Mason has shown that, like Wyatt, Surrey made use of the Latin paraphrases of the Psalms and Ecclesiastes by Joannes Campensis, a Hebrew scholar and disciple of the great German Hebraist, Reuchlin. These were first published in 1532 and enjoyed a great success; the title-page reads: *Psalmorum omnium iuxta Hebraicam veritatem paraphrastica interpretatio, authore Ioanne Campensi, publico, cum nasceretur & absolueretur, Louanii Hebraicarum literarum professore.* Below is added: *Paraphrasis in concionem Salomonis Ecclesiastae, quantum phrasis Hebraica permittit, ad literam proxime accedens per Ioannem Campensem.* For comment on Surrey's use of Campensis, see H. A. Mason's articles 'Wyatt and the Psalms' (*T.L.S.*, 27 Feb. 1953, 6 Mar. 1953) and his *Humanism and Poetry in the Early Tudor Period*, pp. 241–8.

1 ff. The extent to which Surrey departed from the Latin of the Vulgate with Campensis as his guide may be judged from the following extract from Campensis's paraphrase of *Eccles.* l.

Concio Filii David regis in Hierusalem.

Caput I.

1. Constanter affirmat concionator omnia omni tempore obnoxia esse vanissimae vanitati.

2. Quem enim stabilem fructum referet homo, ex iis quae sub Sole sunt: etiamsi multis modis se torqueat in hoc, ut fructum aliquem inveniat?

3. Qui nunc versantur in terra, assidue ad interitum properant, & alii in eorum locum succrescunt: terra interim immota manet, veluti theatrum, in quo haec fabula peragitur.

4. Orietur Sol, & occidet Sol: & ubi ad locum suum prae opere anhelans redierit, iterum ibi sine cessatione orietur.

5. Flat nunc versus Austrum ventus nunc versus Aquilonem: & versus alias deinde orbis partes, donec singula irrequiete lustrando revertatur eo, unde flare coeperat.

6. Omnia flumina influunt in mare & mare non exundat: remittit enim mare ea, ad loca unde fluere coeperant, ut rursus in mare influant.

7. Omnes res, dum absque ulla intermissione currunt, sic lassae fiunt, ut non possit homo apposite de eis quicquem proloqui: non enim substitunt donec oculis quantumvis diligenter contemplantis, vel auribus avidissime ausculantis fiat satis.

8. Quicquid olim fuit, nunc est, & simile est illi quod paulopost erit: quicquid factum est olim, nunc est, & aliquanto post simile illi fiet: In summa, nihil omnino est sub Sole novum, quod huic vicissitudine obnoxium non sit.

9. Inveniri ne poterit res ulla, de qua dicere liceat, haec res nova est? Non profecto: fuit enim saeculis superioribus, & interiit, sicut & haec interitura est.

10. Primorum nulla apud nos nunc extat memoria: funditus enim interierunt, neque horum quae nunc stulti miramur, ulla apud posteros memoria erit.

Details used by Surrey are the phrase *stabilem fructum* (2) in l. 4, the figure of the theatre (3) in l. 10, and the reference to the foolish (*quae nunc stulti miramur*, 10), which is rendered in the third person in l. 24.

2. The whole line renders the single word *Ecclesiastes* ('The Preacher').

9. *remove*: 'change place'. Cf. Coverdale, *Isa*. liv: 'The mountaynes shall remove, & the hilles shal fall downe.'

11–12. Cf. Wyatt's version of Petrarch's canzone *Sí è debile il filo* (ed. Muir, no. 96, 17–20):

Westward the sonne from owt th'est skant doth shew his lyght,
　When in the west he hyds hym straite within the darke of nyght;
And coms as fast where he began his path a wrye
　From est to west, from west to th'est so doth his jornei ly.

14. *Zephirus with his gentill breathe*. Cf. Chaucer, *Prologue*, l. 5: 'Whan Zephirus eek with his sweete breeth.'

29–30. Cf. Campensis: 'Hoc molestum cognoscendi studium, immisit Deus in animos hominum, ut eo se torqueant.'

41. *that doth applie his mynd*. Cf. Coverdale, *Eccles*. 1: 'Yee my hert had greate experience of wyszdome & knowlege, for there unto I applyed my mynde.'

43–44. Cf. Campensis: 'Qui enim conatur supra modum sapiens fieri, plurima valde ingrata: & quae ad priorem eruditionem aliquid addere volet, id sine magna molestia non perficiet.' Hence Surrey's departure from the Vulgate's 'in multa sapientia multa sit indignatio' ('in much wisdom is much grief').

44. *From pensif fanzies then*

See introductory note to 43. MS. readings *times* (l. 22), *lighsome* (l. 43), *rgarde* (l. 54) have been emended.

4. Cf. Campensis: 'Risui enim dixi, dementias: iocis vero, non pudet sic ineptire?'

5. Cf. Campensis: 'Statui itaque apud animum meum, longis conviviis & multo vino corpus meum molliter curare.'

12. Nothing corresponds either in the Vulgate or in Campensis.

13–16. Cf. Campensis: 'Paravi mihi hortos & paradisos, et in eis plantavi arbores fructiferas omnis generis. Aptavi mihi aquae ductus, quibus haec arborum fructiferarum sylva possit inrigari.' Surrey's l. 15 is amplified from the *aquae ductus* of Campensis.

19–20. Cf. Campensis: 'Congregavi mihi argentum & aurum, & ea quae proprie pertinent ad reges & provinciarum dominos.'

27–30. Cf. Campensis: 'Quicquid ex his oculis putavi fore gratum, illis obtuli, nihil ab eis abscondens: nec avocavi cor meum ab ullo laetitiae: quin potius animus meus explet se quantum potest oblectatione harum rerum, quae tanto studio conquisitae sunt: nec alium sensi fructum tam molesti conatus, quam ut oculos pascerem, & animus se nonnihil recrearet.'

33. *that abused fier*: i.e. feelings of pride or vainglory.

35–40. A free rendering of Campensis: 'Iterum me converti ad ea, ut saltem viderem quanta sapientia usus essem in omnibus illis: & deprehendi in vino insaniam multam, & in reliquis manifestam stultitiam: Quid enim est homo, ut imitatione regis Dei, aliquid magni conetur, cum nullam quantumvis parvam ex omnibus rebus quas ille innumeras fecit, aequare posset?' For the last sentence the Vulgate reads: 'quid est inquam homo ut sequi possit regem factorem suum?' Surrey follows Campensis in interpreting *regem* as God.

38. *the licor of the grape*. Nott points out Wyatt's use of the phrase in the second 'Satire' (ed. Muir, no. 197. 29): 'And when she list the licor of the grape / Doeth glad her hert. . . .'

76. *sumptius*: cf. Campensis: 'Quis enim me vixit sumptuosior & liberalior?' And cf. *Liberally* in l. 78.

77–82. A free rendering of Campensis: 'Certe homini cui bene volet Deus, dabit eam prudentiam, & eam sapientiam, ut audeat uti rebus suis: peccatori autem immittet solicitudinem augendi, et coacervandi in usus illius quem deus illa accipere volet: quare neque hoc insigni caret vanitate.'

45. *Like to the stereles boote*

See introductory note to 43. MS. reading *rioall* (l. 44) has been emended.

3–20. Surrey follows Campensis in abandoning the Vulgate's long series of anaphoras ('tempus nascendi et tempus moriendi, tempus plantandi et tempus evellendi quod plantatum est . . .'). Campensis reads as follows:

2. Qui nunc gignuntur, aliquando morientur: quae nunc plantantur, alio tempore evellentur.

3. Nunc amputamus quae olim ut adolescerent, curavimus: nunc destruimus quae olim extruximus.

4. Interdum flemus, interdum ridemus, interdum moesti lugemus, interdum pro laetitia subsilimus.

5. Nunc diruimus vetera aedificia, nunc ex eisdem lapidibus extruimus nova: nunc opera damus amplexibus, nunc ad amplexus nauseamus.

6. Nonnumquam magno studio quaerimus, quod paulopost perdamus: nonnumquam comparcimus quod postea dilapidemus.

7. Quandoque discerpimus, quod olim consuimus: quandoque velut muti tacemus, quandoque inepti garrimus.

8. Interdum amamus, & iterum odio prosequimur amatum: interdum inimicitias exercemus, quas iterum deponimus alio tempore, & pacem amplectimur.

5. *The grafted plants with payn.* A characteristic hyperbaton (or word involution); cf. l. 66.

19. *in folded armes*: i.e. clasped in an embrace.

33–34. Cf. Campensis: 'Si homini contigerit animus ut comedat ac bibat & fruatur suis, inter tam varias miserias, donum Dei manifestum esse putet.' Surrey's phrase *a secret gifte* may be understood to mean 'a gift of God'.

41–42. Nothing corresponds either in the Vulgate or in Campensis.

55–56. There is an emendation in the MS.: the first reading *hathe ether geuen to man* has been revised to *hathe geuen to ether man*. The revised reading has been adopted in the text. The meaning is: 'The perfect form which God has given whether to man or beast', i.e. to both man and beast.

61–62. Nothing corresponds either in the Vulgate or in Campensis.

66. *their gotton good with stryef.* See note on l. 5.

46. *When I be thought me well*

See introductory note to 43. MS. reading *the* (l. 22) has been emended.

15. *to them selves perswade.* This construction, with the dative of person, is occasionally found in the 16th century.

35–36. Cf. Vulgate, Eccles. iv. 13: 'Melior est puer pauper et sapiens rege sene et stulto qui nescit providere in posterum.' But Surrey is closer in the second part to Campensis: '. . . rege sene deliro, qui non sustinet amplius admoneri'.

37. *or this*: 'before now'.

39. *With such . . . mete*: 'Unexpected good fortune has fallen to such people at the moment when they were in deepest despair.'

40. *ware gives*: 'wore gyves', i.e. shackles.

43–50. Cf. Campensis: '15. Vidi maximo numero homines sequi adolescentem illum, qui seni in regno successurus est. 16. Non minor fuit numerus eorum qui senem hunc olim sequebantur, cum regno proficeretur, quam nunc est qui novum hunc ambiunt: & sicut gravis illis superioribus visa est potestas regia illius, qui nunc contemnitur ita & huius qui nunc tantopere placet gravis videbitur: quare & ambitus ille suam habet vanitatem, & anima taedia.'

43. *Other*: 'others'.
without respect: 'without discrimination'.

45. *strange*: 'diverse', 'various'. Cf. 42. 262.

49. *like great*: 'equally great'.

51–58. These lines render Vulgate, Eccles. iv. 17: 'custodi pedem tuum ingrediens domum Dei, multo enim melior est oboedientia quam stultorum victimae qui nesciunt quid faciant mali'. Surrey's amplification, which does not here follow Campensis, has a Protestant, or at least Reformist, bias.

54. *the yolden hoost*: 'the sacrificial victim that is completely submissive'. Cf. Vulgate, Ps. l. 19: 'Sacrificium Deo spiritus contribulatus: cor contritum et humiliatum Deus non spernet.'

47. *Thie name, O Lord, howe greate*

See introductory note to 43. This psalm stands apart from the other three translated by Surrey. It would seem not to have been written, as the other three almost certainly were, during Surrey's final imprisonment.

9–12. A free amplification of the Vulgate text. Perhaps *thy fygurde heaven so hye* owes something to Campensis's paraphrase: 'Quoties video coelos tuos, opera digitorum tuorum, lunam, & reliquas stellas, quas elegantissimo ordine in illis collocasti.' It is not impossible that Surrey wrote *fingerde* (or *fingurde*) for *opera digitorum tuorum*. But *fygurde heaven* is good, though unexpected. The thought is developed into something which anticipates the cloud fantasies of *Hamlet* (III. ii. 380–4) and *Antony and Cleopatra* (IV. xiv. 2–11).

14. *wondring*: i.e. 'wandering'.

19. *Adames sonne*. Cf. Campensis: *Adae nepos* (in this context).

40. *that goes*: 'that walks'.

42. *sea that fyndes the ayre his rayne*: 'the sea that supplies the air with water which descends in the form of rain'.

48. *Oh Lorde, uppon whose will*

See introductory note to 43. The order adopted for this and the following two psalms is that of the MS. 'Surrey's three Psalm versions (his paraphrase of Psalm 8 is a thing apart) have at least one feature in common with Wyatt's: they are strictly occasional poems, i.e. these particular Psalms were chosen for translation because of particular needs' (H. A. Mason, *T.L.S.*, 6 Mar. 1953).

1. Cf. Campensis: 'Domine Deus a quo pendet salus mea.'

9. *to please my fooe*. Nothing corresponds to this in the Vulgate. Here, as elsewhere in this and the following two poems, Surrey enlarges on the scriptural account to express his own situation.

22. *thy elect*. The Protestant colouring of the phrase is notable; cf. 49. 24.

49. *Thoughe, Lorde, to Israell*

See introductory note to 43. MS. readings *that* (for *doth*, l. 17) and *iniquititye* (l. 27) have been emended.

1–4. Cf. Campensis: 'Quamvis certissimum sit, nunquam non esse beneficum deum in Israelem, hoc est illos, qui candido sunt pectore. Mihi tamen hoc accidit absurdi ut quum mei pene oblitus essem, tantum non labi coeperint pedes mei, & quemadmodum accidere solet his, qui per lubrica ambulant, effuso gressu collapsus fuerim.'

8–10. Cf. Campensis: 'Tota enim vita non solum fortunata illis omnia fuerunt, sed & in morte illis accidere solet, ut aetate defecti sine longo cruciatu extinguantur, et palatia relinquant regia haeredibus suis. A molestiis, quibus ex ipsa conditione homo fragilis obnoxius est: liberi esse videntur, nec sicut reliqui homines flagellis a malo deterrentur.'

7. *appere*: i.e. 'appair': 'weaken', 'injure'.

27. *In terrour of the just*: i.e. 'in terror *to* the just'.

37. *dought*: 'a matter or point involved in difficulty' (*O.E.D.*). Here, a theological difficulty.

49. *And till that happye daye*. Nott remarks: 'The disjunctive instead of the connecting particle, is evidently here required'; he emends to *But*.

54. *in drede to drench*: 'in dread of being drowned', i.e. overwhelmed.

50. *Give eare to my suit, Lord*

See introductory note to 43. MS. reading *phalme* (l. 47) has been emended. This is the only one of Surrey's poems written in unrhyming hexameters. It is exceptionally rough, abrupt and obscure; it is probably unfinished.

22. *It was a frendly foo.* Although Surrey is here translating the Vulgate (Ps. liv. 13–14), he is possibly alluding to Sir Richard Southwell. This man had long been a friend of Surrey's, but it was he who brought before the Privy Council the charge which led to Surrey's execution. 'He testified that Surrey had placed in the first quarter of his heraldic shield the royal arms of England. Surrey's placing the royal arms of England in the first quarter, Southwell declared, signified that Surrey considered himself to have a direct right to the Crown of England. As there was not, however, the slightest discoverable evidence that Surrey had borne the arms of England so, the Privy Council had to drop this charge. Surrey had borne in his escutcheon the royal arms ascribed to Edward the Confessor. Although Surrey had a legal heraldic right to quarter these arms in his shield, Southwell professed to believe that this also was a treasonable act' (Casady, p. 191).

29. *hyde them in the see.* Obscure.

NOTES

33. *preloked.* O.E.D. quotes this and remarks: 'evidently some error'. It suggests *prikked*. But it may be a coinage; see Glossary.

38. *Butter fales not so soft.* Perhaps Surrey knew Coverdale's version of this psalm. Verse 21 is rendered: 'Their mouthes are softer then butter, & yet have they batell in their mynde: their wordes are smoother then oyle, and yet they be very swerdes.' Surrey departs altogether from the sense of the Vulgate.

42 ff. From here to the end of the poem Surrey drops all pretence of translating the psalm. The friar in question has not been identified.

47–48. It is not clear what the 'th'other Psalme' is. Padelford remarks: 'By "thother Psalm" I think that Surrey meant not another Psalm, but the untranslated verse (23) [of the Vulgate] of the present Psalm: *Jacta super Dominum curam tuam, et ipse te enutriet: non dabit in aeternum fluctua-tionem justo.*'

Additional Notes

16. 64: *an emperour.* Emperors were types of worldly happiness. Cf. the proverbial phrase 'happy as a king'. O.E.D. quotes *The Pilgrimage of Perfection* (1531): 'In heven, every man . . . shall be as an emperour.' Cf. also *Hamlet*, IV. iii. 22: 'Your worm is your only emperor for diet.' For a Petrarchan example, cf. *Trionfo della Morte*, cap. i. 79–80:

> Ivi eran quei che fur detti felici,
> Pontefici, regnanti e'mperatori . . .

20. 12: *frese*: i.e.' froze'. This form of the past tense is found in some 14th- and 15th-century texts.

GLOSSARY

abashed, confounded, dismayed.
abode, stayed, paused.
abye, pay.
accoll, embrace.
adders, serpents.
address, prepare, put in order.
adventurde, dared, ventured.
adventures, risks.
advertisement, warning.
advise, bid, warn; bring into view.
affect, passion; affection.
affray, frighten.
again, back.
agast, terrified.
agreved, annoyed, vexed.
alight, alighted, landed.
alightned, lit up, illumined.
aloft, on the top of; above.
alters, disturbs, affects (mentally).
alweried, utterly or quite worn out.
ame, guess, hazard.
and if, if.
anoy, molest, harm (militarily).
appaire, appere, decay, deteriorate.
appoint, ordain, prescribe.
arering, raising, erecting.
armour, military equipment.
assemble, (*n.*) assembly, company.
assigning, allotting, condemning.
asswage, diminish, fade.
astart, get away, escape.
astoined, stricken with consternation; confounded.
atchived, finished, brought to an end; performed.
atgaas, gazing.
at point, conveniently, suitably.
attaint, infect; affect.
attent, attentive.
aval(e), avail(e), (*n.*) profit, advantage; disembarkation, descent; (*v.*) be of use, help; descend, sail away on an ebb tide; **-d,** slackened (of reins); **~ing,** advantageous, favourable.

avaunce, make progress in.
avaunt, profess; boast.
awayted, waited upon.
ayer, wind, breeze.

bained, bathed.
bale, evil, harm.
bane, destroyer.
bare, destitute.
bayte, allure.
beare in hand, assert against, pretend; deceive.
beat, strive against contrary winds and currents at sea (nautical); **bet,** (*pp.*) beaten.
beck, nod.
behest, promise.
behight, (*n.*) promise; (*pp.*) promised.
bend, yield.
bereve, rob, snatch away.
besprent, besprinkled.
bested, helped, availed.
bestraught, distracted, distraught.
betoke, committed, gave in keeping.
betyde, happen, befall.
billettes, faggots, lengths of firewood.
bing, heap, pile.
blasing, proclaiming, publishing.
blasted, proclaimed.
blinde, secret, out of the way.
blive, quickly; at once.
boisteous, rough, violent; roughly massive, bulky.
boote, avail, help; **-lesse,** useless, unavailing.
bo(u)rde, burde, approach, accost; approach (a ship) hostilely; mock, deceive.
Borias, the North Wind.
bowlne, swollen.
brayde, break forth abruptly into speech.
bred, grew up.
brent, burnt.

broile, tumult, turmoil.

brondes, brands, torches.

brooke, enjoy.

brute, noise, clamour; rumour, report noised abroad; renown, reputation.

buckeled, prepared (as for battle), fully armed.

bulk, body, frame; belly.

bush, bushy head of hair.

bye .. dere, obtain at a great price; **bought,** (*pp.*) obtained (through sacrifice).

callyng, summoning.

car(e)full, sorrowful; grievous, causing sorrow.

carolles, holy songs; hymns of religious joy.

cart, chariot.

case, hazard.

castes, throws.

catif, 'poor wretch'.

caught, took hold, grasped.

caves, hollow places, cavities.

cendleing, kindling.

cense, incense.

chafed, fretted; aglow with work.

Chambares, Cambria's (i.e. Wales's).

chapps, jaws.

charge, (*n.*) burden, weight, responsibility; command, order; **-ed,** (*v.pp.*) burdened.

chase, drive; (*pa.t.*) chose.

chaunce, fortune.

chere, face, facial expression; aspect; mood, frame of mind.

chief, height (fig.).

child(e), son; youth of gentle birth awaiting knighthood; **-ren,** boys.

cinder(s), (funerary) ashes.

clame, climbed, was climbing.

clattring, rattling.

clepes, (*n.*) calls, shouts; **cleped,** (*pp.*) called; **cleping,** (*pres.p.*) calling.

clinched, firmly fastened.

close, secretly, covertly.

closures, confines, walls; fastenings.

clustred, matted, clotted.

coastes, bounds, borders.

coates, sheep-cotes.

common, public; of the community at large.

compace, circumference; globe.

compacted, joined, knit.

compas(s)e, (*n.*) measure, moderation; (*v.*) encircle, surround; obtain, acquire.

conjures, (*n.*) conspiracies; **conjured,** (*v.*) conspired; (*pp.*) sworn as a member of a traitorous association or conspiracy.

consecrate, consecrated.

consisted (in), resided in, was located in.

consume, waste away.

convenient, proportionate; proper, due.

convert, change.

corps, body.

cowardrie, cowardice.

craft, deceit.

creapes, goes on all fours.

crisped, closely curled.

croppes, top parts (of a tree).

cry, clamour, outcry.

cunning, skill.

curace, cuirass.

cure, care.

darts, spears, javelins.

debate, strife, contention; fight.

deboweled, disembowelled.

decay, downfall, destruction.

declare, manifest, show forth; proclaim.

decyphred, discovered, detected.

dedicate, dedicated.

defaute, misdeed, offence.

defende, hinder.

defensed, defended, protected.

defyne, describe.

degre, rank, estate; **degrees,** steps.

delay, allay, temper.

deme, think, imagine; declare, announce.

demeane, behave.

den, cavern.

depend, be dependants of.

dere, harm.

descrive, describe.

desert, barren, forlorn.

desired, longed for.

desperatly, recklessly.

determed, determined, resolute.

162

determinacion, fixed purpose.
devise, trick; contrivance; scheme.
devower, destroy.
disarme, render harmless.
disceace, unease, disquiet; disturbance.
discharged, relieved, disburdened.
disclosed, unclosed, opened.
discording, disagreeing; discordant.
discoursing, running over; turning over (in the mind).
discrete, prudent, circumspect.
discried, made known, revealed.
disdainfull, hateful.
dislodge, leave a place of encampment (military).
dispoiled, destroyed; undressed.
distained, stained, discoloured.
disturbed, unsettled, agitated.
do . . . on, put on (clothes, armour, &c.); **do,** (*pp.*) done.
do(o)le, grief, sorrow; mourning.
dome, judgement.
domm, dumb.
dought, a doubtful question, a difficulty.
dred, be anxious about, fear for.
drenche, drown.
drery, melancholy, doleful.
drive, be impelled; proceed.
drown, (of inanimate things) sink in the sea.
duraunce, imprisonment.
dured, lasted.

easye, easily kindled; (perh.) slight, insignificant.
eft, again; moreover, likewise; **-sithes,** often; **-sones,** forthwith; soon afterwards.
egre, keen, fierce; **-ly,** fiercely, impetuously.
embatel, battlement.
embradred, embroidered.
embrude, stained.
empressed, oppressed.
endite, indict, accuse; write, compose.
endlong, along.
endured, hardened, callous.
enstuff, furnish with soldiers, garrison.
enter, receive, admit.
envie, grudge.

erst, formerly, of old.
eschues, avoids, shuns.
estate, class, order, rank; fortune.
ever sithe, continuously; ever since that time.
excesse, violence of passion, immoderate grief.
excuse, obtain exemption or release for.
expert, experienced.

faint, faintness.
fansy, love; inclination, liking.
fatall, fateful.
fatte, rich, greasy.
favour, beauty, attractiveness.
feast, joy; rejoicing, festivity.
feelingly, by experience.
fell, fierce, cruel.
fere, friend, companion.
ferefull, timorous.
fet, arrive at, reach (nautical).
figure, image, effigy; shape; **figurde,** marked by figures or patterns.
finde, discover by experience; provide, furnish.
fine, end.
flash, burst of flame.
fleetes, floats; swims.
flitting, moving, going.
folowe, pursue.
fond, foolish; **-ed,** befooled, made mad.
foote, refrain or chorus of a song.
forbathed, bathed deeply, imbued.
forcast, forethought, prudence.
force, strength; **of ~,** of necessity, perforce.
fordoe, destroy, kill; **fordone,** (*pp.*) exhausted.
foregainst, directly opposite to; right against.
forespeaking, foretelling, predicting; **forespoke,** foretold.
forge, fashion, invent; **forged,** lying, false.
forgrown, overgrown.
forme, image.
frame, make; devise, contrive.
franckly, without constraint.
fraughted, stored, filled (with).
frayd, frightened, afraid.

fre(a)t, devour, consume, destroy; agitate.

fredome, nobility, generosity.

freight, fraught, laden.

frese, froze.

fromward, turned from.

froward, adverse, unfavourable.

frute, enjoyment; pleasurable possession.

further, promote; consign.

gainsay, contradict.

gainstand, withstand, resist.

gan, put (i.e. 'put on' armour).

gate, (*n.*) course, going; way; (*v.pa.t.*) reached.

geniall, nuptial.

gestes, deeds, exploits.

ghostes, spirits, souls.

gift, quality, power.

gin, machine, contrivance.

gives, fetters.

gladsom, cheerful, pleasant.

glaunces, sudden movements producing flashes or gleams.

gledes, fires; flashes; embers.

glome, frown.

glyns, glimpse; **glimsing,** glimmering, glittering.

goddish, godlike, divine.

goes, walks.

gostly, spiritual.

grace, attitude.

graft, grafted.

grave, engrave.

greeing, concordant.

grevous, heavy, severe.

grisly, horrible.

grove, small wood.

grow, dwell.

guyse, way, manner.

hainous, full of hate, malicious.

haled, dragged.

hallowed, shouted.

halseth, embraces.

hand, in, in the act, in the process; **~, at,** by hand.

hap, fortune.

harbroughe, harbour, haven.

harkning, herking, listening with attention.

harnesse, (*n.*) armour; (*v.*) put on armour.

hateles, void of hate; friendly.

haulture, height, altitude.

haunte, frequent.

hayes, nets.

headling, headlong.

health, safety.

heapes, with, accumulated, with interest.

heard, company of people.

hent, seized, affected.

herds, herdsmen.

hewe, form, appearance.

hier, hyre, payment, reward.

hight, called.

hogreles, young sheep (of the second year).

holte, wood, copse.

horishe, hoary.

hoste, victim for sacrifice.

hove, linger.

hoyse, hoist (nautical).

hye, hurry.

imagine, conjecture, guess.

imprest, imprinted.

infect, infected.

instruct with, schooled in.

invest, establish a person in the possession of; endow with.

irke, weary.

iron, iron weapon; sword.

judged, adjudged, condemned.

kind, nature; **kindly,** natural.

kindled, inflamed, excited.

knits, fastens, ties.

laase, net, noose, snare.

laied, bowed.

landes, glades.

large, wide, extensive.

lat(t)er, last.

launced, hurled, threw.

leaved, believed.

leche, physician.

leefe, lief, beloved, precious; **lever,** sooner, rather.

leful, lawful.

lemans, mistresses (lovers).
lettes, hinders, prevents.
levening, lightning.
lift, lifted.
light, lighten.
lightning, enlightenment, illumination (of mind).
linger, protract, delay.
listes, desires; **me listed,** I cared, I pleased.
livelie, living, animated, full of life; constantly flowing (of water).
lodges, small houses, dwelling-places.
loft, elevated, lofty; **loftye,** haughty, proud; upward looking (hence, suppliant).
loked for, expected.
longes, belongs.
lopen, leapt.
lorke, lurk.
lose, loosen, set free.
lothed, spurned.
lowre, look dark, scowl.
lustie, handsome; gay.
lyfsome, lively, full of life.

make, mate; husband.
malice, regard with malice, seek to injure.
manhod, courage, valour.
mansion place, dwelling-place.
manure, till, cultivate.
mark, observe, watch.
marrise, marsh.
mary, marrow.
mashe, enmesh.
mazde, bewildered, stupefied.
measure, travel over, traverse.
meete, suitable, proper.
meke, gentle, compassionate.
mercy, give thanks to.
mevings, motions (of heavenly bodies).
minding, intending.
minges, remembers.
miror, example.
mirth, joy; **-ful,** joyful.
mischiefe, 'a devil', 'a plague'.
misteries, hidden meanings; profound or pregnant thoughts.
mistrusted, suspected.
mitred, formed like a mitre.

mode, mind; (perh.) anger.
molde, (n.) model, pattern; (v.) lie unused.
mole, sacrificial cake.
mots, motes.

ne, nor.
nephew, grandson.
new, of, anew.
next, nearest.
nill, will not.
notes, distinguishes by a mark or brand.
nunne, priestess or votaress of a pagan deity.

offred, sought after (i.e. war).
offring, attempting, essaying.
often sithes, oftentimes.
one, in, in the same state.
opening, disclosing, declaring.
order, liturgical arrangements.
or that, before; **or this,** before now.
other, others; ~ **some,** some others.
outward, bodily, physical.
overlayd, overwhelmed.
overmore, moreover.
over passeth, surpasses.
overronne, overwhelm, crush.
overset, cover (with a net).
overthrewe, fell down, collapsed.
overthwartes, adverse experiences, 'crosses', rebuffs.
overtreate, prevail upon by entreaty.
overwandred, wandered over.
oynted, anointed.

paine, punishment, penalty; **paynes,** labour, toil.
pale, paleness, pallor.
parcase, perhaps, perchance.
parel, apparel, attire.
passe, surpass, excel.
patching, deceiving, knavish.
pease, appease, pacify.
pencell, paintbrush.
peping, emerging, appearing (of day).
percell, part, portion.
pere, appear.
performe, finish, complete.
perish, destroy, bring to ruin.

perswade, induce.

phrentik, frantic.

pick, assail, break up.

pight, pitched (of a camp).

pitie, piety.

plain(e), (*v.*) complain, lament; (*a.*) open, unobstructed; ~**esse,** honesty, frankness.

plaint, lamentation, grieving.

playe, wound.

pleasd, appeased, satisfied.

plied towards, made towards (nautical).

poale, sky.

pondereth, weighs.

port, carriage, bearing, mien.

post, post-rider, mounted dispatch- or letter-carrier.

powdred, sprinkled as with powder.

power, body of armed men; force.

practyse, machination, scheme, conspiracy.

preasse, (*n.*) crowd, throng; **in~,** in haste; with urgency; **presseth,** (*v.*) crushes, oppresses.

preloked, looked beforehand or with anticipation.

present, make present to mind; recall.

preserves, guards.

prest, (*n.*) priest; (*v.pp.*) prepared, ready; (*av.*) quickly.

pretense, claim.

price, estimate, value.

prickt, urged (as with a spur).

privie, previe, hidden; participating in the knowledge of; **privy gods,** household gods.

procure, endeavour, labour.

profe, experience.

prolong, delay.

proroged, prolonged, lengthened.

prosperous, auspicious, favourable.

prove, try; learn by experience.

purchase, obtain with effort; earn, win.

purveiance, providence.

pyne, labour, toil.

quench, be extinguished, go out (of fire).

quick, alive.

quiet, not shining (of the moon).

race, raze.

rage, violence (of wind).

rakhell, thoughtless, unconsidered.

rashed, dragged, torn.

rashly, hastily.

raught, seized.

raunge, traverse; search.

ravin, voracity, predatoriness.

reache, deal, strike; give (a wound).

rebell, rebellion.

re(t)chlesse, reckless, heedless.

record, (*n.*) testimony; (*v.*) remember; bear witness, put on record; **-ing,** recalling; repeating.

recover, reach, arrive at.

recuiled back, driven back.

recure, regain health; become whole.

redoub, remedy.

reduceth, brings back.

refrayne, refrein, restrain, check.

reft, bereft, robbed.

regrete, complaint, lament.

reherse, relate, utter, say.

reject, rejected.

rejoice, enjoy.

releve, lift again, support.

remorse, pity, compassion.

remove, change place; move (the feelings); **removed,** secluded.

render, give back, return; surrender.

reno(u)me, renown.

repaire, renew.

reportes, conveys; repeats.

reposed, settled, firmly fixed.

represented, appeared on the stage.

represt, checked, driven back; despondent.

reproche, shame, disgrace.

request, petition, prayer.

require, ask; beg, entreat, pray.

reserved, set apart, kept.

resolve, be dissipated, dissolved.

resort, return.

resouned, echoed, rang.

respect, without, without discrimination.

restes, remains, is left.

restore, take back; **restorde,** (*pa.t.*) revived.

returned, converted, changed.

reve, take; tear.

reverte, return; recall.

revested, clothed, attired.

rewe, rue, regret; have pity.

rift, reef (nautical).

rigged, equipped with rigging.

risting seat, resting place.

rives, splits, shatters.

rode, roadstead, harbour.

roll, roule, revolve (in the mind), meditate.

rond, round; on all sides.

roote, be, by rote.

rout, company, band; disorderly crowd.

row, company, assembly.

rude, ignorant, uneducated, unlearned.

rue, *see* **rewe.**

sad, serious, steadfast.

sales, halls, chambers.

saluith, salutes, greets, kisses.

savage, wild.

savegard, safety, protection.

scace, skace, scarce, scarcely.

scathe, harm; **-full,** hurtful, injurious.

sclaunder, slander.

scyence, knowledge, skill, art.

seat, residence, abode.

secret, hidden, secluded; **-ly,** tacitly.

seignorie, lordship, dominion.

semely, fair, beautiful; proper.

sentence, way of thinking, opinion.

sequell, descendants, posterity.

serche, look for, search out.

shapp, shapte, (*pp.* **shape**) destined, decreed, appointed (of punishment); **shope,** (*pa.t.*) prepared.

she(e)ne, (*v.*) shine; (*aj.*) bright, shining.

shopp, workshop.

shred, prune, lop.

shrouding, concealing.

sickles, free from sickness.

sight, sighed.

silly, simple, ignorant; rustic.

sit, suit, be fitting, proper; **it sat me on,** I was pressed, it was urgent.

sith, since.

skace, *see* **scace.**

skills, it ~ them not, it does not concern them.

sleping, sleep-inducing.

slide, glide; lapse (morally), err; **sliding,** flowing, gliding.

slipper, slippery, unsure.

slong, slung, cast.

small, slender.

somtime, once, at a certain time in the past.

sorte, group, band, company.

sory, vile, shameful; wretched.

sparcle, sparkle, (*v.*) scatter, disperse; **sparkled,** (*pp.*) dishevelled; filled with sparkles.

sparres, rafters, roof-beams.

spedde, succeeded.

spede, success.

spence, expense, expenditure.

spight, injury, harm.

spill, kill; waste.

splaid, spread out, displayed (of flags, sails, &c.).

spoild, plundered.

spreades, is diffused through.

spring, young plant growth, 'green'.

spritelesse, devoid of spirit, fainting.

stack, pile of faggots; pyre, burial pile.

staid, delayed.

stand, (*pp.*) stood.

state, power, prosperity.

statue, image, effigy.

stay, continuance.

steale, remove, take away.

stede, place.

stepe, high, lofty.

steppes, traces, vestiges.

stern, fierce, cruel.

sticks, is fastened (with its point embedded); is fixed (hanging).

stint, cease.

stirre, sturre, (*n.*) tumult, commotion; (*v.*) be roused, excited.

stithe, anvil.

stock, trunk (of a body); stoup, basin for holy water.

storye, narrative, historical relation.

strait, streight, tight; narrow.

strange, diverse, different; alien, foreign; **-ness,** coldness, aloofness.

streming, waving (of sails).

stripped, striped.

strond, coast-land.

stryef, striving, strong effort.

stuft, furnished (with soldiers); garrisoned.

subtle, artfully contrived.

suffraunce, forbearance, patient endurance.

suretie, in, for certain, surely.

surprised, supprised, (*pp.*) seized, overcome; (*aj.*) sudden, unexpected.

suspect, suspicion.

swage, assuage, mitigate.

swey, force, impetus.

tainted, tinged.

tale(s), words, utterance.

talowed, anointed with tallow, greased.

tapets, pieces of figured cloth, coverlets.

targe(tte), shield.

taried, delayed.

tast, perceive or recognize as by taste.

tayle, in ~ of, behind, after.

tell, count.

tempred, mixed, mingled.

tend, lead.

tendring, receiving favourably.

thankefull, pleasing, agreeable.

them, those.

thes, these.

thick, (*n.*) thicket; (*aj.*) rapid, frequent; **-en,** become dark or misty.

thinke (*pa.t.* **thought,** &c.), seem.

thirling, piercing.

tho, then.

thrall, bondage, captivity.

threpe, press, thrust.

throtal, throat.

throwing, struggling in death-agony; suffering the throes of death.

timely, betimes, early.

tirans, rulers, governors, princes.

tofore, before, in front of.

toke in hand, undertook.

tokens, signs.

to morne, tomorrow.

touch, stop; arrive and make a short stay (of a ship).

tracing, following, pursuing.

tract, trail, mark.

trade, way, path.

traile, crawling, creeping.

transposed, removed, transferred.

travell, labour, toil.

trayne, retinue, suite, followers.

tree, wooden structure (i.e. the Wooden Horse).

trusse, tie as in a bundle, pack.

tr(e)ye, experience, undergo; distinguish, ascertain; **tryed,** tested.

twine, 'twain', two.

uglie, horrible, frightful.

ugsome, horrible, loathsome.

unable, incompetent, ineffectual.

uncouth, strange, unfamiliar.

unfiled, undefiled.

unfold, unfolded, opened.

ungraved, unburied.

unloked for, unexpected.

unlucky, inauspicious, ill-omened.

unneth, with difficulty, scarcely.

unpind, unbolted.

unright, wrongdoing.

unsavereth, has no savour or agreeableness.

unsemely, inglorious.

unshave, not smoothed or planed.

unskilfull, ignorant.

unsound, diseased, in ill health.

unstock, remove (a ship) from the stocks.

untamed, wild, ungoverned.

unwist, unknown; unknowing; without its being known.

unwroken, unavenged.

upsupped, consumed, swallowed, absorbed.

ure, practice, effect, operation.

vaade, fade, disappear.

Ve(a)r(e), Spring.

vexe, afflict, harass.

viages, journeys.

violate, violated.

wades, goes.

waged, hired; mercenary (soldier).

wait on, attend (as a servant).

waiwarde, averted, askance.

waker, unsleeping, watchful.

waltring, wavering.

wan, contrived, managed (to do something).

wanderyd, wandred, bewildered, confused; **~ it,** was in circulation.

wanishe, wan, pale.

wanton, playful, waggish.

wards, courts.

warpe, tow, move along by hauling on a rope (nautical); **warped,** bent, curved.

wast, derelict.

watch, (*n.*) sentinel, guard; (*v.*) guard.

weale, well-being, happiness.

wealth, well-being, happiness.

wede, clothing, apparel.

welkin, sky.

wende, go.

wening, thinking.

werdes, the Fates.

what, why; ∼soe, whatever.

where as, where.

wherout, out of which, from which.

whisketh, rushes.

whist, be or become silent.

whiz, make a loud rustle, hiss.

wifebound, bound to a wife.

wight, man, person.

will, (*n.*) desire, inclination; self-will, wilfulness; (*v.pa.t.* **would**) wish; determine.

witlesse, foolish, unreasonable.

womb, belly.

wonders, wondrous.

wondring, wandering.

wonning place, dwelling-place.

wood, mad, wild.

workes, fortification.

worth, in ∼, in good part, patiently; **woe** ∼, may evil befall, a curse upon.

wreke, (*pa.t.* **wroke**), revenge; **wreaker,** avenger.

wreste, wraste, change, turn, divert.

wrethed, writhen, twisted, plaited.

writhed, turned aside.

writhen, *see* **wrethed.**

wroth, wrathful, angry.

wrought, exerted (oneself), worked; strove, raged.

wryte, designate.

ybatred, battered.

ybrethed, exercised.

ybroughte, brought.

yburied, buried.

yelden, yold(en), surrendered; submissive, exhausted.

yet, else.

yleft, left.

yprinted, impressed.

yshrowding, concealing.

yspred, spread.

ytired, tired.

ywrought, created, fashioned.

ywys, indeed, truly.

PRINTED IN GREAT BRITAIN
AT THE UNIVERSITY PRESS, OXFORD
BY VIVIAN RIDLER
PRINTER TO THE UNIVERSITY